Intellectuals in

Claus-Dieter Krohn

Intellectuals

Refugee Scholars and the

Translated by Rita and Robert Kimber
Foreword by Arthur J. Vidich

The University of Massachusetts Press   *Amherst*

in Exile

New School for Social Research

Original title: *Wissenschaft im Exil*
© 1987 by Campus-Verlag
Foreword and translation,
© 1993 by The University of Massachusetts Press
All rights reserved
Printed in the United States of America
LC 93-18625
ISBN 0-87023-864-7 (cloth); 874-4 (pbk.)
Designed by Milenda Nan Ok Lee
Set in Minion by Keystone Typesetting, Inc.
Printed and bound by Thomson-Shore, Inc.

Library of Congress Cataloging-in-Publication Data

Krohn, Claus-Dieter, 1941–
    [Wissenschaft im Exil. English]
    Intellectuals in exile : refugee scholars and the New School for Social Research /
Claus-Dieter Krohn ; translated by Rita and Robert Kimber ; foreword by Arthur J.
Vidich.
        p. cm.
    Includes bibliographical references (p.   ) and index.
    ISBN 0–87023–864–7 (alk. paper). — ISBN 0–87023–874–4 (pbk.: alk. paper)
    1. New School for Social Research (New York, N.Y.)—History.
    2. New School for Social Research (New York, N.Y.)—Faculty.
    3. Brain drain—Germany—History—20th century.   4. Social
    scientists—Germany—History—20th century.   5. Economists—
    Germany—History—20th century.   6. German Americans—History—
    20th century.   I. Title.
    LD3837.K7613   1993
    378.747′1—dc 20   93–18625
                                                                                  CIP

British Library Cataloguing in Publication data are available.

Contents

Contents

Foreword

Claus-Dieter Krohn's *Intellectuals in Exile: Refugee Scholars and the New School for Social Research* is the first in-depth intellectual history of a remarkable group of social and political scientists. Recruited from Europe by Alvin Johnson, then director of the New School, they were forged by him into the "University in Exile," later to be renamed the Graduate Faculty of Political and Social Science. Unlike any other, this book provides a comprehensive picture of that group's intellectual significance and of the impact of its seminal ideas on both European and American social science.

Looking back on these thinkers, we can now fully realize how critical their role was in preserving and enhancing what are now the key conceptions of contemporary social science. They drew inspiration and intellectual sustenance from their predecessors, who included Marx, Böhm-Bawerk, Weber, Simmel, Schmoller, Durkheim, Georg Jellinek, and other turn-of-the-century social and political analysts. However, these brilliant predecessors did not have to come to terms with the epoch-making events of the twentieth century—the rise and fall of national socialism, the Second World War, and the decolonization of the European seaborne empires. Thus they offered to their successors few cues for understanding them. Born to a world that took such unexpected turns, this new generation of thinkers also sought their own ways of analyzing the social, cultural, political, and economic problems of the twentieth century. Always mindful of the work of their predecessors, they charted new directions for the disciplines of economics, sociology, philosophy, psychology, and political science.

Escaping from Europe in the 1930s and 1940s, they brought to the United States a fully developed awareness of what would only later be recognized as the central problems of twentieth-century civilization. Almost immediately, they initiated a unique dialogue between continental and American thought. This dialogue remains unbroken as is substantiated by Krohn's list of the 184 emigré scholars who were originally affiliated with the New School and whose scholarship continues to be a vital part of American social science. This list includes Rudolf Arnheim, Paul Baran, Arnold Brecht, Gerhard Colm, Eduard Heimann, Erich Hula, Felix Kaufmann, Hans Kelsen, Alexandre Koyré, Emil Lederer, Claude Lévi-Strauss, Adolph Lowe, Bronislaw Malinowski, Jakob Marschak, Franco Modigliani, Kurt Riezler, Gaetano Salvemini, Alfred Schütz, Hans Speier, Leo Strauss, and Max Wertheimer. Their countries of origin included Germany, Poland, Italy, France, Russia, Austria, Algeria, Hungary, Czechoslovakia, Belgium, Spain, Switzerland, and Palestine. Without the single-minded and largely single-handed efforts of Alvin Johnson to provide them with a place at the New School, many of these intellectual figures would have lost their lives. In spite of Johnson's efforts, as Krohn observes, others did.

Readers of this book will learn that Alvin Johnson, more than any other American, quickly realized the need for action to prevent Hitler's destruction of the German intellectual tradition. Johnson had become aware of the immense importance of European scholarship while coediting the *Encyclopaedia of the Social Sciences*,[1] a monumental task he had undertaken in the mid 1920s in collaboration with his former teacher at Columbia University, Edwin R. A. Seligman. Designed as a comprehensive assessment of social scientific thought, comparable to the German *Handwörterbuch der Staatswissenchaften*, the *Encyclopaedia* was published in the midthirties. Although its contributors were recruited from many countries, the largest number from a single nation were German. Johnson's work as a coeditor brought him into close contact with many of the 600 contributors and consultants to the fifteen-volume *Encyclopaedia*. As a result, he became a leading expert on who was who in the world of social science. Even before the National Socialists took power in 1933, Johnson knew German scholars such as Gerhard Colm, Emil Lederer, Jakob Marschak, Fritz Lehmann, and Hans Speier, who would be invited to the New School that same year.

Johnson also understood the importance to scholars of being part of an intellectual community in which ideas are discussed and debated. It was for this reason, therefore, that when it was known that the Nazis would purge the universities Johnson acted to recruit an entire intellectual community.

Krohn's account of the creation by Johnson of this exiled community of scholars touches on a number of embarrassingly sensitive points. American universities and the State Department resisted and even opposed Johnson's efforts on the grounds that too many of the emigrés were Jews, radicals, or socialists. President Roosevelt sympathized with Johnson's efforts but was unable to break the xenophobic resistance of immigration authorities who doubted the Americanism of these foreigners or, worse, supposed that they might be Nazi agents. In the midst of the American depression and deep domestic problems, very few, other than Johnson, thought in terms of the consequences for civilization that would ensue should Europe's most educated and creative thinkers be eliminated.

Before the onset of the war (but more especially after Germany invaded France in 1940), an avalanche of refugees sought asylum in the United States. "From 1935–36 on," Krohn notes, "the New School was inundated with about 5,000 requests . . . annually [for support]." After the fall of France, this institution became a central clearinghouse for the rescue of intellectual and political refugees. In addition, refugee committees were created to help absorb into the United States these bearers of European culture. Doris Duke, the tobacco heiress, contributed $250,000 to the Graduate Faculty in order to supplement the support for faculty salaries provided by the Rockefeller Foundation. By the end of the war, thousands of European scholars had found their way to the United States and into its cultural institutions, leaving a permanent legacy for the intellectual life of the country.

For postwar Germany, the intellectual vacuum created by the expulsion of its major scholars, intellectuals, creators, and disturbers would never be filled. Krohn notes that the internal Nazi war against Weimar culture resulted in the diminution of about 12,000 intellectuals from the social and cultural life of Germany. Nothing like this had happened since the exodus of the "Greek leading class after the Osmanian conquest of the Byzantine Empire in the fifteenth century. . . . [T]he expulsion of German intellectuals after 1933 seemed like the transfer of an entire culture, primarily to the United States." The twelve-year gap in cultural continuity from 1933 to 1945 was sufficiently long to separate an entire generation from its own past. This break in Germany's intellectual and cultural life has been reconnected only slowly and in part.[2]

Not until the 1960s did another generation of German social scientists rediscover its roots in Weimar culture and in earlier German intellectual traditions. In spite of this rediscovery, the thread of intellectual culture that was broken in 1933 has not been fully repaired. The author of this book does not make this point directly, but it is implicit in the text. Indeed, in researching and writing this book, Professor Krohn has reconnected himself to his own cultural legacy. This monograph is in fact part of a larger German revival and rehabilitation of the works of that country's social scientific ancestors.

Krohn's discussion of the ideas of the social scientists who were the members of the Graduate Faculty of Political and Social Science is found in two chapters: "What the Exiled Social Scientists Brought to the United States: Trends in Economic Thought around 1933" and "Contributions of the Emigré Scholars at the New School." Krohn shows that the New School economists, primarily Emil Lederer, Gerhard Colm, Adolph Lowe, and Hans Neisser, while still in Germany had already addressed fundamental questions concerning unemployment in relation to market forces and technical change and had developed fiscal and monetary ideas about economic and social planning that anticipated much of what later became the foundation of Roosevelt's New Deal. Although Keynes provided some theoretical underpinnings for New Deal economic policies, these German "reform" economists not only thought, like Keynes, in short-range pragmatic terms but also hoped to resolve the long-range problems that beset Western capitalism. Their experience with the German economic crisis in the 1920s gave their work both theoretical and practical advantages over the ideas of Roosevelt's advisers.

Why do the innovative ideas of these economists receive so little attention now? According to Krohn this "is not solely the fault of scholarship on the exile but may be due even more to how the field of modern professional economics defines itself and regards its own history." The work of these politically and socially minded economists did not fit "the conventional models the discipline worked with." However, as Krohn shows, many of their ideas subsequently found their way into what is now conventional economic thought. These reform political economists were unique among twentieth-century economic thinkers because their conceptualization of theories was always derived from prevailing empirical realities, enabling them to provide a praxis grounded in a coherent framework of thought. Their work lacked the extreme specialization that is characteristic of economics, including and especially contemporary economics. They were learned beyond the conventional bounds of professional economics and thus, for example, did not adhere to a social psychology of human beings that restricted them to some computerlike *homo oeconomicus.* They understood the interconnections between economics and politics and worked on the assumption that the field of economics cannot be set apart from the broader social and cultural milieus of society. At no time since—including the contemporary period when the world so urgently needs a new economic theory—has there appeared such a theoretically and politically sophisticated group of economists. Their contemporary neglect speaks more to the impoverishment of modern economics than to the irrelevance of their ideas.

Now, in the aftermath of the collapse of European communism, the time may be ripe to reread the Graduate Faculty's reform economists. By focusing on the relationship between sociopolitical and economic institutions, their work transcended the rigid dichotomy between capitalism and communism. In this historic moment the market and monetarist approaches now employed by economists in both East and West would gain from the broader, more complex and refined approach to socioeconomic processes developed by these thinkers.

All the members of the Graduate Faculty—not only the economists, whose work is stressed in this book, but also the sociologists, political scientists, psychologists, and philosophers, whose ideas are also carefully evaluated—were obsessed with the emergence of national socialism and the problem of understanding it. The failure of democracy, to which they had been committed during the Weimar Republic, led them to study the relations among democratic politics, economics, and international relations. Krohn discusses the articles (appearing in the 1930s in *Social Research,* the journal of the Graduate Faculty) and books on these issues written by members of the faculty. Only after the war did this work on totalitarianism and democracy enter the mainstream of American academic thought through the publications of Hannah Arendt, not a member of the faculty until the 1960s but a collator and synthesizer of the work of the original generation. It is through her work that the German idea of a historically and philosophically informed approach to social research has reappeared in American academe, offering an alternative to quantitatively systematized American sociology.

I first learned about the Graduate Faculty as well as the Institute of Social Research, another emigré center located at Columbia University, from Hans Gerth when I was a student at the University of Wisconsin in the 1940s. Like the dramatis personae of this book, Gerth had brought with him the cultural and intellectual milieu of Weimarian Germany. Identifying with both the Graduate Faculty and the Institute, he transmitted part of that culture to his students, and he regarded the emigrés located at those centers as his intellectual community in the United States. For example, as soon as issues of *Social Research* and books by such emigré authors as Erich Fromm, Arnold Hauser, Karen Horney, Herbert Marcuse, Karl Mannheim, and Hans Speier were published, they appeared on Gerth's reading lists and were discussed in his classes. I mention this personal experience only to note that this aspect of my education led me to believe that these European authors were already in the mainstream of American social science. Later, much to my surprise, after I had become a member of the Graduate Faculty and thought of this appointment as an exceptional honor, I discovered that they had barely been remembered, let alone recognized for the influence they had on American social, economic, and political thought.

As Professor Krohn notes, similar misconceptions about the Graduate Faculty's impact continue to be held in both Germany and the United States. For example, he cites "[Rainer] Lepsius as an example of the general attitude in Germany. In this view, the Graduate Faculty had been an intellectual emigré center marked by originality but of no influence. [Lewis] Coser, by contrast, concluded in the United States that the group's outsider status was really an advantage because it allowed them to preserve unaltered the views they had formed in Germany." Both of these views, uninformed by Krohn's history, miss entirely the influence and the intellectual debt owed by both Germany and the United States to these emigré writers, intellectuals, scholars, and men and women of action.

When it became apparent that the United States would enter World War II, the members of the Graduate Faculty began to play a more substantial role in the practical affairs of the nation. The Graduate Faculty had not only the "largest staff of experts on international matters in America" but was also "the academic group most frequently consulted by U.S. government officials" on all aspects of Germany's leadership, military capabilities, economic conditions, propaganda capabilities, and future goals. Yet in spite of the heavy demands placed on them by government agencies even before America's entry into the war, members of the Graduate Faculty began to work on plans for organizing a democratic international order after the defeat of fascism. They were signers of a manifesto published in the spring of 1941 under the title *The City of Man: A Declaration of World Democracy*. This manifesto, utopian in its "vision of universal peace and a future world democracy," was a product of both Europeans and Americans and shows clearly that the Graduate Faculty had become an integral part of American intellectual life. Continuing its concern for shaping the postwar world order, immediately after the outbreak of the war the Graduate Faculty began a project entitled "Peace Research." The ideas articulated in this project remain largely unknown to the various peace researchers and peace institutes established during and after the cold war. The international orientation of the Graduate Faculty was a victim of the nationalism on which cold war policies depended. As a result it became marginal to cold war–oriented social sciences in the United States.[3]

Care should be taken not to idealize or mythologize the emigré epoch and its exemplars. In his chapter "Problems of Integration," Krohn describes their mundane conflicts, personal feuds, and polemics against those whose ideas differed from their own. However, it can be said that these men and women were committed to the life of the mind with a passion that is rarely found today. In spite of their emigré status, they had the strength to stand by their intellectual convictions. This fact is all the more remarkable when we consider that they were attacked by other Americans as "procommunist" or as a "near Bolshevist intelligentsia" and were investigated by the FBI, which on several occasions placed agents "in the guise of students" in classrooms to check on "complaints" about their ideas. As I saw at first hand, they fought, argued with, and in some cases disliked one another. But never did they resort to dissimulation in their mutual relations. Nor were their dislikes a product of petty personal considerations; at bottom they were always disagreements about ideas.

It is in this connection that Krohn corrects a number of misconceptions about the relations between members of the Graduate Faculty and the Frankfurt Institute of Social Research, due particularly to the work of Martin Jay. Although the ideological differences between some members of both groups were sharp and mutual criticism was open and unreserved, it is an egregious error to treat these disagreements as anything but passionate disagreements on principle.

Foreword

The academic milieu in most American universities tends to encourage the sublimation or even repression of intellectual disagreements in order to maintain an atmosphere of sociability among colleagues. I can attest that this was not the style of the emigrés described in this book. Krohn has come closer than anyone in elucidating the virtues of their intellectual honesty and candor.

Anyone interested in the origins, peregrinations, and destinations of ideas that have shaped the images of the world in the twentieth century will find this book an indispensable guide. Each reader will discover a part of his or her own intellectual ancestry of which he or she had been unaware.

Arthur J. Vidich

Intellectuals in Exile

1 / Introduction

Even though national socialism in Germany gave rise to one of the largest mass expulsions of population segments in a modern society, knowledge about this phenomenon is still relatively limited. The political circumstances of the exodus and the way stations of the refugees are known, and considerable information is available about the social structure of the expelled groups as well as about the cultural consequences of the expulsion, but this knowledge is rather general and superficial. This is true of research and public awareness in Germany as well as in the United States, even though the latter country has always been a haven for immigrants and absorbed the majority of refugees from Nazi Germany. The reasons for this shared phenomenon are, however, different for the two countries.

In the United States, the classical land of immigrants, historiographic and sociological research on immigration has always been very actively pursued, but for a long time it was dominated by the old melting-pot theory; that is, the research focused exclusively on the immigrants' assimilation to the standards of American society. Having developed from the study of earlier waves of immigration during the nineteenth century—when most immigrants were poor and only minimally educated and came from marginal and backward areas of Europe—this discipline was poorly equipped to understand fully the peculiar character of the refugees from Germany after 1933. Those who fled Germany—Jews and political opponents of national socialism—came primarily from the upper middle class and especially from intellectual milieus. Most of them arrived with well-defined world views, so that the criterion of assimilation was bound to

1

prove inadequate for understanding the problems of their integration into the new social world of the United States.

In the early 1950s the first isolated criticisms were voiced against this kind of analytically limited research that tended—in its quantitative and behavioristic form—to assess amorphous millions rather than individuals. The new intellectual immigrants themselves spoke up, too, rejecting emphatically the provincialism of the assimilation theory.[1] Nevertheless, the first studies after World War II were still completely within that tradition. Even a book on the "refugee intellectual" from Germany published in those years focused exclusively, as its subtitle indicates, on the Americanization of the post-1933 immigrants. It never asks whether or how the intellectual and political attitudes of the German immigrants might have changed, let alone what influence these immigrants might have had in America, but restricts itself entirely to examining their ability to adapt to everyday life.[2]

It was not until the 1960s that this traditional approach began to change. During the renaissance of so-called intellectual history, historians tried, against the background of the crisis in public consciousness brought about by the Vietnam War, to analyze the ideas and values of American society and politics, and this shift in perspective also changed the theoretical premises of immigration study. The American civil rights movement also played an obvious role here. The old melting-pot theories were replaced by a new, pluralistic understanding that was no longer based on the notion of powerless immigrant groups adapting passively but instead emphasized the active enrichment of American society provided by different ethnic, cultural, and social groups. Old one-way concepts like assimilation, adaptation, and adjustment gave way to the new term "acculturation," which pointed to a dynamic process of mutual enrichment and transformation.

This change brought with it a reassessment of the history of immigration between 1933 and 1945. Now there was increased interest in the details of the intellectual transfer from Europe to America during the 1930s and in its effects on and stimulation of American intellectual life. But American scholars quickly ran into difficulties. The author of an early study that tried for the first time to give a systematic overview of the integration of scholars who had fled from Germany to the United States had to confess that his work had certain limitations because he lacked knowledge about the European background, knowledge that was essential to an understanding of the intellectual ideas and traditions the refugees brought with them.[3]

The publications that have appeared since then were, with very few exceptions, written by the exiles themselves or by members of their immediate families. It was they who prepared the ground and, as H. Stuart Hughes put it, unveiled the secret. They themselves wanted to impress on Americans the magnitude of the intellectual emigration and its significance for American culture.[4] It is thus not surprising that collections of autobiographical writing by immigrants, edited by Americans, became the typical form of publication about the immigration history of European intellectuals.[5] An outstanding example of another sort is the extensive study, published in 1968, by Laura Fermi, who had fled fascist Italy with her husband, the physicist and Nobel Prize winner Enrico Fermi. Her ambition to present a comprehensive account of the emigration of European scholars, including its origins and effects, necessarily resulted in a rather general survey since one individual can hardly command specialized knowledge of the entire spectrum of scholarship.[6] In recent years existing gaps have been filled by Lewis Coser and Anthony Heilbut, the former having emigrated himself as a young man, the latter the son of parents who were driven from Berlin. But their excellent books, rich in material and details, show clearly what lacunae still exist in the study of the exodus of European scholars.[7]

Inadequate and rigid as conventional American scholarship on immigration was for many years after the war, this aspect of recent history never disappeared from American public awareness, thanks to the efforts of the emigrés themselves, who in many cases had come to occupy influential positions in various institutions. The situation was very different in Germany. The early years of the Federal Republic witnessed not only the continuation in power of those who had held it prior to 1945 but also a collective loss of memory, which made it possible to forget both past atrocities and the exodus of intellectuals after 1933. During the Adenauer era, anticommunism was elevated to a kind of state doctrine, and in this atmosphere the spokesmen for the earlier "other Germany," having mostly been on the left of the political and intellectual spectrum, were often associated in public and published opinion with traitorous behavior toward the fatherland or with cowardly personal escape from the fate of the nation.[8] In the former German Democratic Republic, on the other hand, where the numerically largest group of returning emigrants went after 1945, the exile was regarded as just another aspect of antifascism, so that here, too, there was no interest in detailed research about the phenomenon of the emigration as a whole, let alone about the many individuals who did not return.

Introduction

In the Federal Republic of Germany, as in the United States, the 1960s brought a change in public consciousness that spurred interest in research about the exile. A new generation at the universities now accomplished what should have happened during the rebuilding of democratic Germany. The cold war mentality and the desire to promote economic recovery gradually gave way to the question of what cultural, intellectual, and political traditions the Federal Republic could revitalize. In this search the emigration of the "other Germany" gradually came into closer focus. At first, exile literature and organized political groups were the major focus, whereas the emigration of scientists and scholars received only marginal attention, a fact deplored as late as the early 1980s.[9] This impression is justified in spite of isolated works, such as the early study by Helge Pross and some other later essays. These studies represented only a first taking of stock, and their suggestions for further exploration of this field were not taken up until much later.[10] The early writings of the Frankfurt Institute of Social Research, which emigrated in 1932–33, have, to be sure, received much fuller public discussion since the late 1960s, thanks to the commentaries of a younger generation of intellectuals at the universities. However, this exclusive focus has contributed to a truncated understanding of the exile as a whole, as though Max Horkheimer and his circle had been the sole representatives of the exodus of the social sciences.

The publication, begun in 1980, of the *International Biographical Dictionary of Central European Emigrés, 1933–1945*[11] represents a breakthrough; and a project to encourage studies of the exile set up by the German Research Association fifteen years ago is now producing its first results.[12] The present book, among others, was undertaken within the context of this project. How much uncertainty still exists in matters of both fact and interpretation is manifest in a recently published volume. Even though this volume was put together after the galleys of the second part of the *Biographical Dictionary*—which is devoted in part to the scholars in question—became available, it fails to include scholars who appear in the first volume of the *Dictionary* but who changed careers after emigrating.[13] Thus it is not surprising that as great an expert on the history of the social sciences as Rainer Lepsius still could state in the 1980s that the German economists who immigrated to the United States had hardly any impact on economic discussion there, whereas Coser arrived at very different conclusions.[14]

The present study of the emigré social scientists, chiefly economists, who taught at the New School for Social Research in New York deals with a

Introduction

limited number of the scholars who came from Germany to the United States after 1933 and takes into account both the conditions under which this transfer took place and the impact it had. There were several reasons for focusing on the New School and the group of emigrés gathered there.

First of all, the New School developed into a center of intellectual exile that after 1933 attracted the largest number of refugee scholars, and through the selective appointment of social scientists to its faculty it quickly acquired a very special character. Although the New School is frequently mentioned in literature on the exile, there is still no adequate historical account of this unique institution. Fairly large numbers of emigrated intellectuals found positions at other academic institutions, such as the Institute for Advanced Study at Princeton, Black Mountain College in North Carolina, and Roosevelt University in Chicago, where they gained considerable influence and lent these institutions a distinctive style. But nowhere did German scholars play such a major role in determining the academic structure, the teaching, the research, and the impact on the outside world as they did at the New School. Indeed, the New School acquired university status only through the "University in Exile," staffed entirely by immigrants, and through the Graduate Faculty that grew out of it. In terms both of institutional structure and of personnel, the New School more closely resembled the Institute of Social Research in Frankfurt, which found a home as a body at Columbia University; and there were many personal and intellectual connections between these two emigré centers. But where the Institute was autonomous because it had its own financial resources—a fact clearly reflected in its style as well as in its definition of scholarship and the research produced by its members—the Graduate Faculty of the New School was and always remained dependent on outside funding.

The financial problems that persisted after the initial and spontaneous rescue action point to a second aspect of the study of exiled scholars, an aspect most clearly evident in the example of the New School. Unlike Horkheimer's group, the New School depended on public support. The history of the University in Exile thus uniquely reflects the broader circumstances under which integration of the emigré scholars took place in the countries that took them in. Given the worldwide economic crisis of the time, the absorption of the German exiles into the United States and European countries was by no means always easy. Though a number of national and international aid committees were formed by concerned

5

colleagues and immediately set about raising the necessary funds to provide a financial incentive for universities to hire exiled scholars, this act of humanitarianism and solidarity would surely not have had any long-term success if the new arrivals had not brought with them something of interest.

The activities of these academic aid committees have been described in overall terms—mostly by the initiators themselves—and their success is to a large extent evident in the history of the immigrants' accomplishments.[15] However, the concrete and specific details—the financial commitments of the large American foundations and of other private donors and their motives for assisting individual scholars or entire groups for limited periods or for years at a time—are still largely unknown. The history of the New School after 1933 is intimately linked with the activities of the Rockefeller Foundation, for instance, whose worldwide program to promote scholarship included support as early as the 1920s for some academics who later emigrated from Germany. One of the questions this study will try to answer is whether the considerable funding this foundation granted to the New School after 1933 represented a continuation of earlier support for certain German scholars and their work or whether it reflected a new commitment to help refugees. An extensive monograph on the work of the Rockefeller Foundation, written by the organization's long-term president, does not touch on these questions at all,[16] even though the Rockefeller Archives, which have been open to public examination for some time, contain a huge amount of information on them.

There is still a third reason for concentrating on the New School. Although all the literature on exiled scholars mentions the New School, the focus is primarily on Alvin Johnson, the school's founder and head during the formation of the University in Exile, and on the institutional framework that made it possible for the displaced scholars to continue their work within the familiar context of academe. Considerably less attention has been given to the quality of the scholarly work produced, the specific theoretical perspectives the scholars brought with them from Germany, and the innovations they brought to the study of the social sciences at American universities.

A striking feature of the literature to date on the New School[17] is that the same picture of the institution is perpetuated from publication to publication. It is seen as an exceptional case, an interesting "social form" (Lepsius), or a "gilded ghetto" (Coser). Its significance is perceived to be primarily as a refuge and source of aid for hundreds of emigrants. Relatively negligible in this view are the stimuli the New School provided for the study of the social sciences in America. The prevailing atmosphere at the New School, traditional interpretation contends, favored the continuing cultivation of German academic traditions, and the scholars gathered there became more and more cut off from the developments in their disciplines in the rest of the country. In addition, the New School was supposedly inferior to the leading universities and was consequently able to train only a small number of future American scholars in the field.[18]

Clearly, this assessment cannot be dismissed entirely. A few of the many scholars who arrived at the New School never got over the shock of their expulsion; they remained uprooted and became increasingly isolated and ineffectual. But these individual cases hardly justify a negative picture of the New School as an institution.

It seems that this stereotypical impression can be traced back to a problem faced by any and all research on the exiles: the lack of a detailed, historical account that incorporates contemporary sources. When, in the 1960s, Charles Wetzel wrote his study of the integration of German scholars in the United States, he did not have access to the archives of foundations and aid organizations. In the meantime most of these sources, which contain a great many assessments of the scholars and their work as well as other documents useful for evaluating the refugee intellectuals and the general success of their acculturation, have become available. In investigating the University in Exile at the New School, however, the researcher finds that most of the documents bearing on its history have been lost over the years due to the negligence of the administrative staff. Consequently, the New School archives yield very little. However, a large number of private collections of materials and the posthumous papers of people who were active at the New School at various times more than make up for this lack, especially since these documents are often revealing of connections to other institutions.

It has also remained unclear just why the literature to date has produced such a static picture of the immigrants and their roles in American academic life. To be sure, scholarly influence is transmitted informally and does not lend itself to precise measurement. Still, there are external criteria that give some indication of how well or how badly the New School scholars fared in their acculturation in the United States. One can look at the establishment and intensity of the communications network with

7

American scholars, the gaining of an audience, the calls received to teach at other institutions of higher learning, the kind of publications and the audiences they reached, to mention just a few examples. None of these indicators confirms the notion that the New School occupied a marginal outsider position in the world of scholarship. On the contrary, many of the theoretical positions brought from Europe and the experience of having tested these theoretical insights in the real world soon gained these German scholars a reputation, and their advice and cooperation were frequently sought.

A single monograph cannot hope to encompass the entire phenomenon of the transfer of the social sciences from Germany. Such an undertaking is beyond the competence of one individual. That is why I have decided to focus on the most important group of scholars who, in terms of both numbers and outlook, were most influential in setting the agenda of the New School and also exerted the greatest influence beyond it.

Economists not only made up the greatest portion of exiled scholars in the social sciences but also accounted for the greatest number of immigrants at the New School. The German economists gathered at the New School had a special approach to their discipline that differed markedly from prevailing thought in the rest of the field. During the Weimar years the new questions raised by the core members of the group had enlivened the study of economics considerably, and their nontraditional perspective defined them even then as a relatively homogeneous group that stood apart from mainstream academic thinking.[19] It is not surprising, then, that when Johnson envisioned founding a university in exile he turned to these very scholars. Given the worldwide economic crisis, he hoped they would contribute important theoretical as well as practical and political suggestions during the initial phase of Roosevelt's New Deal. Their critical, reform-oriented approach, which departed radically from the deductive models of traditional economic thinking and incorporated new experiences and new ideas, may be seen as a first clue to the group's ability to become acculturated in the United States.

That the work of this circle and its ideas have received so little attention up to now is not solely the fault of scholarship on the exile but may be due even more to how the field of modern, professional economics defines itself and regards its own history. The history of economics, to the extent that it reflects on its dogmatic traditions at all, regards them merely as a linear, abstract accumulation of knowledge. Obviously, the approach of the

Introduction

New School economists did not readily fit the accepted "paradigms," that is, the conventional models the discipline worked with. But this outsider status does not necessarily detract from the significance of their work. An analysis of this work therefore not only fills a gap in the history of exile scholarship but may also cast some light on why this work has been essentially ignored in the history of economics. And, finally, a collective biography of this group can convey a picture of the intellectual milieu in Germany that came to such an abrupt end with the expulsion.

To suggest the extensive range of the group's work, we will briefly sketch the general economic debate of the time, including its underlying norms, preferences, and theoretical premises. Here the intent of our historical account is not to present an abstract summary of the developments in economics but to shed light on the discursive process of the discussion, including all the errors, false conclusions, and rigidities that resulted in fixed ideas. In applied disciplines like economics and the social sciences related to it, such a history has to take into account the context of concrete historical and social conditions. And against this background it becomes clear in what unique ways and with what sensitivity to inherent problems this group of economists incorporated actual experiences not only into their theories but also into their suggestions for progressive economic policy.

The group's history will therefore be viewed from two separate though related viewpoints. First, there are plenty of indications—contrary to the widely held assumptions of the literature to date—that the perspectives and suggestions the group offered through various channels during the New Deal era in the 1930s and 1940s had a striking effect on the discussion of American economics and that the group was able to translate some of its theoretical ideas into economic and political practice. Second, the group provided to its field an impetus whose import goes beyond a history of the exile. In the wake of the worldwide economic collapse of 1929, these economists formulated insights and ideas that not only were radically new at the time but remain of vital interest in view of today's worldwide economic problems. Indeed, it could be argued that the full importance of the work done by the so-called Kiel school on technical change, for example, has not been properly recognized until now.

What this study will focus on, then, are, first, the theories produced by this circle in the process of learning from historical experience in pre-1933 Germany and, second, the modifications and diffusion of these ideas in the new world encountered after emigration. The methodological procedures employed in this study are therefore derived from the categories of the sociology of knowledge. First presented in their classical form by Karl Mannheim, these categories established a connection between cognitive structures and their sociological substrates. In the methodology employed here, however, only those social structures that the scholars themselves considered essential to their cognitive experience are discussed. Compared to Mannheim's approach this represents a narrowing of focus, but it has an obvious advantage. The self-reflective type of scholar envisioned by Mannheim is a great exception among professional scholars, especially in a field as leery of ideology as economics. Economists generally think of themselves as absolute subjects and, as a profession, only rarely reflect on the social determinants of their work. It should be noted, by the way, that some individuals among the New School economists maintained close scholarly as well as personal contact with Mannheim.

Whether it be a sign of marginality or of the crisis in the dominant economic paradigms as defined by Thomas Kuhn, the fascinating thing about this group of economists is that they not only kept referring to actual historical and political conditions in their theoretical work but also subjected these conditions to constant critical reflection. Their scholarly work thus reveals a process of theoretical and political self-scrutiny in the historical context first of the Weimar Republic and then of the completely different social world of the United States.

2 / The Expulsion of German Scholars

It is difficult and will most likely remain difficult for some time to make precise statements about the extent of the emigration after 1933. This is true both for the total number of refugees, estimated by the League of Nations High Commissioner for Refugees to have approached 500,000 by the time the Nazi Reich collapsed, and for groups it would seem easier to survey, such as the exiled academics. According to information compiled by the various national and international aid committees formed in 1933 to rescue German intellectuals, about 1,200 academics lost their jobs in Germany during that year. This number was to grow by the end of the 1930s to about 1,700, to which another 400 university faculty were added after the annexation of Austria. If the various other academic professionals, doctors, lawyers, and so on, as well as students suspended from the universities are included, the total number comes to about 7,500. If we add writers, artists, and other free lancers, we may safely assume that—not counting family members—about 12,000 intellectuals lost their jobs and were eliminated from Germany's social and cultural life.[1]

The expulsion of Germany's intellectual elite was registered with surprise, indeed, with utter amazement, by the indigenous intellectuals in the countries that offered refuge. In several studies of this phenomenon a parallel is drawn to the exodus of the Greek leading class after the Osmanian conquest of the Byzantine Empire in the fifteenth century. This repeated comparison was not resorted to merely to convey the magnitude of the exodus but even more to illustrate the qualitative benefits gained by the countries taking in the exiled. If the westward flight of the Greeks could be regarded as the starting point of the Renaissance and of humanism,[2] the expulsion of German intellectuals after 1933 seemed like the transfer of an entire culture, primarily to the United States.

Even more telling than the total numbers are the figures indicating how strongly specific academic fields were affected. No sooner was the so-called "Law to Restore the Professional Civil Service" (*Gesetz zur Wiederherstellung des Berufsbeamtentums*) of April 1933 passed than over 16 percent of all university faculty were dismissed. During the following years, and especially after the Nuremberg "Race Laws," the dismissals rose to more than one-quarter of all university teachers.[3] In retrospect, the "loss" of university faculty through the end of 1938 has been assessed at 39 percent, with the percentage among economists and social scientists lying far above the average at 47 percent.[4] These figures are corroborated by contemporary statistics. According to what is probably the most comprehensive survey, the *List of Displaced German Scholars* compiled in the fall of 1936 by the Notgemeinschaft deutscher Wissenschaftler im Ausland (Emergency Association of German Scholars Abroad) together with the London Academic Assistance Council, the 1,639 scholars listed there who had been fired in Germany since 1933 belonged to the following disciplines.[5]

Natural sciences	497
Chemistry, 165	
Physics, 124	
Medicine	459
Social sciences	392
Economics, 148	
Law, 112	
History, 53	
Sociology, 40	
Psychology, 27	
Education, 12	
Humanities	291
Philology, 101	
Art history, 62	
Philosophy, 55	

If we take into account that many of the natural scientists and trained physicians had worked at research institutions outside the universities— such as the Kaiser Wilhelm Society—and that the total number of people

Table 1. *Dismissals for political or racial reasons between the 1932–33 and 1934–35 winter semesters* (%)

Universities (selected)	Total	Economists
Berlin	32.4	24
Frankfurt	32.3	40
Heidelberg	24.3	63
Breslau	21.9	14
Göttingen	18.9	20
Freiburg	18.8	9
Hamburg	18.5	33
Cologne	17.4	20
Kiel	12.1	50
Halle	10.0	38
Munich	8.3	0
Bonn	7.8	0
Rostock	4.2	0
Averages	16.6	24

Source: Evaluation of university catalogues; cf. "Changes in Teaching Corps in Economics in German Higher Institutions," a compilation of the Rockefeller Foundation, Feb. 18, 1936, RFA RG 2, 717/141/1050; Edward Y. Hartshorne, *The German Universities and National Socialism* (London, 1937), p. 94.

working in these fields was thus much larger, it becomes clear that the relative number of economists and social scientists driven from their jobs represents a far higher percentage in those fields than in other disciplines. Another striking fact revealed by the statistics is that the timing of the dismissals varied significantly from one discipline to another and that different universities were affected to varying degrees. Whereas the overall average of faculty dismissals in all academic fields until the winter semester of 1934–35 was 16 percent, as mentioned above, the quota among economists was already almost 24 percent, and at some universities, such as Heidelberg, Kiel, or Frankfurt, it stood at 63, 50, and 40 percent. A similar pattern can be discerned at many other universities (see Table 1).

The number of dismissed economists and social scientists includes not just individuals but also entire schools. Unlike dismissals in the fields of medicine or natural sciences, expulsion in these disciplines generally meant the elimination of an entire research tradition critical of the historicism and idealism long dominant in German thinking. The contributions of this relatively new, critical direction within the social sciences toward a realistic analysis of society and toward strategies for changes in actual practice—work imbued in the 1920s with hopes for more democratic social structures and for a more effective civil society—reflect the intellectual and social background from which most representatives of these disciplines came.

Perhaps the first element that should be mentioned is the special cultural milieu of the Jewish community in Central Europe. After the incomplete emancipation of the nineteenth century these Jews characteristically chose assimilation. However, this assimilation and the adoption by the Jewish minority of Enlightenment ideals, such as faith in reason, humanism, cosmopolitanism, and a belief in social progress, led not to integration into the society but rather to isolation. This was because the Enlightenment had adherents only within small circles of the educated middle class. It remained limited to urban centers, leaving the mass of society largely untouched. In this world of traditional values and prejudices it was impossible for the Jews to overcome their outsider status in spite of emancipation and assimilation. This situation sharpened the eyes of Jewish intellectuals for the developments that had failed to materialize in the historical process, and it encouraged critical thinking motivated by practical goals. This tendency was reinforced by modern racial anti-Semitism, latent ever since the great depression of the 1870s and threatening to break out in any crisis situation. This, too, contributed to the critical sociological attitude these Jewish intellectuals were practically born with. In view of all this it is not surprising that many of them joined forces both theoretically and practically with the workers' movement, which was also struggling to achieve equal opportunities for its members. At the same time the philosophical views of these intellectuals had been influenced by Marxist socialism with its macroanalysis of society and its promises rooted in the dialectic of history.[6]

This background explains the high number of instant dismissals in 1933 at the universities of Heidelberg, Kiel, and Frankfurt. The University of Frankfurt, for example, had been founded shortly before the outbreak of World War I with funds contributed by Jewish citizens. It was here that the first division of social sciences and economics was established at a German university. The very naming of the division, which suggested its program, set it apart from the customary institutes of *Staatswissenschaften* that existed at other universities, usually as part of the law school.

The double outsider status of many social scientists as Jews and socialists or liberals tended to make them exceptionally sensitive seismographs of political climate. The few personal accounts of their mood toward the end of the Weimar Republic show that these intellectuals expected their professional careers to end if or when national socialism triumphed. From this time on many of them, especially the younger ones, lived in tense uncertainty. Adolf Löwe, an economist who had left the University of Kiel to accept a position at Frankfurt one year earlier, always kept a few suitcases packed after 1932 in case of emergency. Similarly, Otto Kirchheimer and Franz Neumann, prominent lawyers and later to be members of the emigrated Institute of Social Research, began studying English intensively in 1932 to prepare for their anticipated emigration.[7] Some refugees— among them Henry Pachter, who later taught political science at Columbia University—have suggested in retrospect that the transition into exile had been psychologically prepared for and was relatively smooth for many intellectuals because they had already been outsiders in the Weimar Republic and had never felt in true sympathy with it.[8] However, this assessment holds true at most only for a small group of younger leftists. Neumann and Kirchheimer had long been active as judicial representatives of the unions, and for them as well as for Adolf Löwe and the Kiel school, it was, as we shall see later, precisely their practical but ultimately fruitless commitment to the Weimar Republic that moved them and other intellectuals of similar bent to take precautions as early as 1932. They were among the first to flee Hitler's state after March of 1933, correctly anticipating what was to come and often leaving before they were officially fired.

However, the number of academics who lost their jobs is not identical with that of the emigrants. Of the first wave of dismissed faculty, numbering about 1,200, only about 650 went into exile. This proportion did not change much during the following years. Of the approximately 1,800 scholars included in the *List of Displaced German Scholars* and its supplement, just over 1,000 left Germany. We can thus assume that during the 1930s about 60 percent of the fired scholars emigrated.

Although the United States was to absorb the greatest number of emigrated intellectuals in the period between 1933 and 1945, it was not the most popular immigration country immediately after 1933. Many scholars initially chose to remain in Europe—particularly Great Britain—or went to Palestine or to Turkey, where the modernization program imposed by Kemal Ataturk's dictatorship resulted in attractive offers to German scholars in all disciplines (see Table 2).

Table 2. *Placements up to February 1, 1935*

	Permanent positions	Temporary offers
Great Britain	49	172
France	3	40
Netherlands	1	24
Palestine	24	1
Turkey	37	1
United States	29	66

Source: Report of the Emergency Committee in Aid of Displaced German Scholars, Feb. 1, 1935, p. 9.

The number of permanent positions in the United States, compared to those in Great Britain, is obviously quite small. Even more striking is the fact that over half of these positions had been created at the New School for Social Research. It was only in the later 1930s and especially after the war broke out that the proportions began to shift. Of all the scholars who emigrated from Germany during the entire Nazi period, it is estimated that slightly less than half came to the United States. Of these, approximately one-quarter, about 180 individuals, were rescued by the New School.[9]

The reasons for the small initial numbers are to be found first of all in the United States, where isolationism prevailed and where the Great Depression also affected the universities. The picture was not to change until awareness spread in the United States of the caliber of scholars who had been expelled from Germany and until the large foundations dedicated to furthering scholarship, above all the Rockefeller Foundation, made available millions of dollars for bringing German scholars to American universities. Another reason is that the United States was not at first at the top of the list of where the exiled scholars wanted to go. Some still believed after 1933 that the Nazi regime was a passing aberration and that they would be able to return within the foreseeable future. Many thought of themselves not as emigrants who had permanently left Germany but as exiles who wanted to become only partially acculturated in their new environment and refused to relinquish hope of an eventual return. Distant America to them represented "a point of no return."[10]

Another, more deeply rooted motive that swayed many intellectuals against the United States and that suggests something of the traditional collective mentality of the German intellectual elite derives from the negative fascination that had always been part of the attitude the German educated class held toward America. On the one hand, educated Germans felt a deep skepticism about the suspected prevalence of materialism in American culture, which seemed to recognize no larger spiritual or intellectual needs. On the other hand, the critical intelligentsia in particular admired America's open society, its modernism, its freedom from class barriers, and the down-to-earth practicality and optimism of Americans that enabled them to play an active part in shaping their society. Also, living as exiles in European countries, the refugees found out that shedding one's status as an alien was difficult and sometimes impossible there, so that America, the classical immigration country with its less obvious ethnic barriers, now appeared even to former critics as the "the unsentimental child" in comparison to "hardhearted, superannuated Europe." Indeed, the refugees soon discovered, paradoxically, that one could be a better European in America than in Europe itself.[11]

Another obvious factor was the profound impression Franklin D. Roosevelt, the newly elected American president, and the euphoric optimism of the New Deal made on the immigrants. To their pleasant surprise, previously critical intellectuals realized that utopian experiments were possible in the United States despite the country's strong pragmatic traditions. Furthermore, the Roosevelt administration was proving—in sharp contrast to developments in Germany—that economic depression could be turned into an important vehicle for extending the democratization of society. Many intellectuals and scholars coming from Germany therefore thought they were seeing some ideas they had worked for unsuccessfully in the Weimar Republic becoming reality under the New Deal. Even as vehement a critic of capitalism as Max Horkheimer, whose Frankfurt Institute of Social Research is often identified with the harshest censures of America and its *Kulturindustrie* ("culture industry"), could hardly disguise his fascination on his first exploratory visits to New York. Not only did the whole atmosphere seem to him "extremely pleasant"; he also felt that the Americans' interest in furthering unorthodox research had led to uniquely "positive experiences."[12]

In her book about the immigration of European intellectuals to the United States, Laura Fermi attempted to put a dollar figure on the cost-free gain the displaced scholars and scientists represented for higher education in America.[13] According to her calculations, which set at about $45,000 the cost of educating someone in the United States up to the start of an academic career, the more than 700 foreign-born university teachers would have meant a saving to the United States of roughly $32 million. This estimate does not include the many other professions or the large number of younger academics who finished their studies in the United States and began their careers there.

To be sure, such attempts to quantify the value of education—attempts that have a deceptive appearance of exactness—are of questionable worth and, in any case, focus on only a minor aspect when compared to the nonmaterial new ideas the German and European scholars brought to their adopted countries in such fields as physics, the modern social sciences, the humanities, and architecture. In the United States these scholars became the founders of an entirely new tradition of scholarship. We need think here only of modern economic planning, which will be discussed more fully later, the field of international relations, or the kind of art history introduced by Erwin Panofsky. Nevertheless, Fermi's estimates do give some idea of the monetary gain the acceptance of expelled scholars represented for the United States, and they can serve as a yardstick against which to measure the funding provided by aid organizations and foundations. Conversely, the figures illustrate the losses Germany suffered as a result of the emigration.

Since we still lack detailed studies of the Nazi state's policies toward higher education, we often have to fall back on speculation. The expulsion of critically minded social scientists seems most in line with the ideological program of the Nazis, and it seems clear that the group of scholars this study focuses on were dismissed in April 1933 not just because many were of Jewish descent but also for political reasons. Matters are less clear in the fields of the natural sciences and of medicine. One important factor may have been the coincidence of the Great Depression with a cyclical glut of academics. Between 1929 and 1933 about half of those finishing their university studies were unable to find jobs for which they were qualified. Thus the Nazis may have wanted to win the support of unemployed academics and of the antidemocratic majority of university faculty by making room in the German universities and other arenas of academic life.[14] In this, as we know, they scored considerable success.

The embarrassing professions of support for Hitler issued by the faculties of the German universities immediately after the Nazi assumption of power are evidence of how readily the supposed representatives of the intellectual world abandoned all pretense of independent and critical thinking.[15] Nor has any sign of firm solidarity with dismissed and expelled colleagues come to light.

Still, it is doubtful that emotional proclamations like the one issued by Bernhard Rust was representative of the new policies as a whole. Rust, the new minister of education, asserted that in the future university teaching would no longer be devoted to intellectual goals but would have to be defined more intuitively. Nor should Joseph Goebbels's mean-spirited parting words to the exiled scholars necessarily be taken at face value, words to the effect that military weakness was a much graver danger to Germany than the loss of a few professors.[16] It is worth noting in this context that only a minute fraction of the emigrated academics was deprived of its German citizenship; and, as in the cases of Albert Einstein and Emil Julius Gumbel, the political prominence of the figures involved was the decisive reason. More striking than the number of exiles deprived of their citizenship is the vastly larger number that were not. Concerned for Germany's international reputation, the Foreign Office fought the revocation of Einstein's citizenship but did not prevail against the Reich Ministry of the Interior and the Gestapo.[17] In the sample of scholars discussed in this book, citizenship was revoked only in a few cases after the *Kristallnacht*. Also, immediately after 1933 and while they were still living in Germany, many scholars found positions at foreign universities with the aid of international committees. They were then able, with offers of what was usually temporary employment in hand, to obtain legal permission to leave the country for a given period.[18] Although we have no information about the rationale behind this practice, we may perhaps conclude that at least some of the bureaucracy of the Nazi state realized that the emigration of the intellectuals signified an irreparable loss and a provincialization of intellectual life at the German universities. At this stage of research it is still impossible to say whether there was any hope in some government circles in the 1930s that the exiled scholars might later be called back.

3 / The United States and the German Intellectuals

1. Xenophobia at the Universities

In the fall of 1933 the chairman of the American University Union, a professor of education at Columbia University, reported after a visit to Europe on the unique opportunity that the expulsion of university professors from Germany represented for higher education in America.[1] What is striking is the urgent tone of the report and the fear that the United States might be too late to compete for the highly qualified scholars. The Academic Assistance Council, founded in London in June 1933 to rescue German academics, had been very active and had been able to place a considerable number of them at British universities. An early survey of the time showed that 250 academics had already been placed internationally, of whom only 43 went to the United States—fourteen of them were at the New School—while the council had been able to find positions for 140 in England alone.[2] Another 800 persons were still available. In addition, the Notgemeinschaft deutscher Wissenschaftler im Ausland, a German self-help organization in exile founded in Zurich, had been able to find jobs for thirty colleagues at the University of Istanbul.

A few farsighted scholars in the United States had become active, too, and had founded the Emergency Committee in Aid of Displaced German Scholars, but at the time only Alvin Johnson, the director of the New School, had achieved any significant success, having hired for his newly founded University in Exile fourteen faculty members who in fact began teaching in the fall of 1933.

This apparent lag reflected the contradictory attitude of American academe toward the refugee problem. On the one hand, the German system of education and university structure had traditionally been held in high esteem in the United States. Many university professors had studied in Germany, and some universities, like Johns Hopkins, had been conceived on the German model. Indeed, American scholars educated in Germany would become the driving force in bringing German academics to the United States. In addition, the intellectual excitement generated by the New Deal accounted for the special interest in the modern social theories younger German scholars had begun to develop during the Weimar Republic.³ On the other hand, America's mood was isolationist in the wake of World War I, and that mood was not without effect in the world of academe. In the early 1920s the United States had introduced a strict quota system for immigrants. Even though scholars with several years of teaching experience were not subject to this system, it nevertheless set the stage for the restrictive immigration policies of the future. The Sacco–Vanzetti trial illustrates how powerful the sometimes hysterical fears were that had given rise to the quota system, and these fears of the subversive threat European immigrants supposedly represented had spread to the universities, too.

After 1933, scholars of German extraction, especially professors of German at small midwestern universities, formed an important lobby active against the university professors expelled by the National Socialists, denouncing them as a "fifth column" of socialists and as agitators against international understanding.⁴ This xenophobia was further aggravated by the Great Depression, when over 2,000 university faculty, almost 10 percent of all academics, lost their jobs. Even at universities that were able to avoid cutting academic positions and salaries, younger faculty members in particular saw the arrival of Germans competing for jobs as a threat to their own chances for promotion.⁵ In these circles, social fears, traditional isolationism with its various ideological justifications, and ignorance of events in Germany fueled vague resentments that often found expression in anti-Semitic sentiments. When Alvin Johnson first broached his plan of setting up a university in exile for displaced scholars, many of his colleagues thought he could not possibly succeed in placing Jews in an American university. Still others responded cynically that the expectation of finding "first-rate" scholars among the Germans was unrealistic since most of them were "only" Jews or Social Democrats.⁶ It is therefore not surprising that many universities deliberately sabotaged these efforts after

Hitler's invasion of Austria in 1938, when the emergency aid groups that had in the meantime become solidly organized were working feverishly to accommodate the second big wave of refugees. A questionnaire sent to institutions of higher education, asking which of the available scholars they might be interested in hiring, came back in a surprisingly large number of cases with a brief note to the effect that none of the scholars was known and that there was no need for them.[7]

The anti-Semitic tendencies that existed during the depression years not only in some sectors of public opinion but also at the universities were apparently so strong that they caused considerable insecurity among the newly arrived academics. The refugees quickly became aware of the "double handicap" of being stigmatized as both Jews and immigrants. In Europe they had been physically threatened with primitive vulgarity; in the United States they encountered subtler forms of rejection aimed at undermining self-confidence. The political scientist Franz Neumann even thought Germany was less anti-Semitic than the United States.[8] How strong anti-Semitic sentiments were is also indicated by the tactical considerations various aid organizations had to resort to. These organizations very quickly realized that "rising anti-Jewish feeling" was a greater obstacle to acceptance of these scholars than was inadequate funding, and they attempted to make up for this lack of commitment in the United States through international cooperation and through arrangements with similar organizations in other countries. Tactical considerations went so far that in the case of the jurist Arthur Nussbaum, for instance, it was felt necessary to mention cautiously Nussbaum's "very Jewish appearance" to institutions that might be interested in him.[9] The economist Joseph A. Schumpeter, who had been invited to teach at Harvard University one year earlier, attempted to create a temporary committee to aid colleagues in danger in Germany after January 30, 1933, but the prevailing anti-Semitic mood in the universities prompted him, too, to say that he wanted to attract "as few Jews as possible."[10]

The Rockefeller Foundation would become the largest financial donor to the numerous aid committees, but its example shows that the organizations committed to helping displaced intellectuals were not always immune to anti-Semitism themselves. Although the foundation's Paris office had been gathering detailed information on developments in higher education and on political conditions in Germany as well as in other European countries since the 1920s, some reports of its staff there during the first phase after 1933 conveyed no sense of alarm. It was true, the Paris representative declared in March and April of 1933, that the situation at the German universities appeared alarming, but it should not be forgotten "that during the past fifteen years the Jewish liberal element has been definitely favored in Germany" to a great degree. Many scholars had been fired, especially in the social sciences, but, the report pointed out, this could be explained by the fact that "the leaders in this field are Jews and Social Democrats, or worse." The foreign press was grossly exaggerating what was happening in Germany, and everyone could rest assured that the National Socialists would not go too far, if only because of the international repercussions that would follow. Their policies of repression were probably only a gesture that would be of short duration.[11]

It is often difficult to determine whether financial help was motivated by a true concern for the refugees or perhaps more by the pressure of international competition for the best scholars. In any case, the American aid organizations had to tread cautiously to avoid arousing xenophobic or anti-Semitic feelings at the universities. One consequently keeps encountering in the internal memos of the organizations the anxious question of whether the "saturation point" might not have been reached.[12]

The isolationist reservations at institutions of higher learning disappeared only gradually after word got around of how often the presence of German intellectuals on the faculty raised the academic level of a department and when it also became known that the aid committees were willing to pay half the salary of hired refugees. It was this phase that gave rise to numerous anecdotes and quotes by college and university presidents to the effect that a memorial should be dedicated to Hitler for his contribution to the advancement of American scholarship.[13]

2. Aid Committees for Exiled Scholars

Before World War II there existed no asylum procedure backed by international law, let alone an internationally codified right to asylum. Being granted asylum was not a right to which anyone persecuted for political, religious, racial, or other reasons was entitled. Instead, the offering of asylum was an act of grace handled differently by every state. Even the League of Nation's 1936 and 1938 conventions on refugees did not question the principle of national sovereignty in this matter, nor did international conferences on refugees, such as the one held at Evian in 1938. Nations that admitted persecuted aliens did not offer asylum but only allowed temporary residence or permanent immigration as provided for by the country's laws. We therefore cannot say with any accuracy how many refugees entered the United States after 1933 because American statistics reflect only "normal" immigration.

The refugees from Hitler's Germany were received nowhere with open arms except in a few countries such as Czechoslovakia and France, the traditional country of asylum—and even there their welcome was limited. The United States' response to the refugees is best described as one of "governmental apathy."[14] Given its low population density and its economic prosperity, the United States absorbed proportionately the fewest refugees as compared to European countries. Despite the massive efforts mounted by the president and his wife, Eleanor Roosevelt, who felt strongly about the refugee problem, there was relatively little the White House could do. Because of the pressure of isolationist public opinion—in opinion polls over two-thirds of those questioned consistently opposed relaxing immigration rules—and the influence of the southern wing of the president's own Democratic party, Roosevelt had few options. Another factor at work may have been the fear—evident in other countries as well—that a greater commitment to refugees from the Nazi state might encourage Hitler to adopt even harsher measures against Jews and those of different political persuasions or might motivate other countries to proceed along similar lines. Though these calculations may have been justifiable in the 1930s, it is a glaring fact that American quota regulations were not relaxed even after the defeat of France in June of 1940, when to thousands of refugees the United States appeared to be the only salvation from death.

The activities of the League of Nations further illustrate the precarious international conditions German refugees faced. Ten years earlier the League had been confronted with the numerically much greater problem of White Russian and Armenian refugees and had provided effective help through the organization founded by the polar explorer and Nobel Prize winner Fridtjof Nansen. Now, however, the refugee problem was handled in a dilatory manner at best. The High Commissioner for Refugees, who had been appointed in October 1933, was not, as a result of German pressure, legally or organizationally part of the League of Nations. His reports could not be presented to the League Council, and his office was set up in Lausanne rather than in Geneva to indicate by geographic location as well that his actions were completely autonomous. Without any backing he could exert little influence. The commissioner was never intended to provide direct help; instead, he was to encourage and support the initiatives of private organizations, coordinate their activities, and advocate the solution of the refugee problem through negotiations with the various governments. But invested with nothing but moral authority he could not accomplish much. The League members' unwillingness to cooperate with the commissioner undermined his efforts; he was treated like a "disowned child" and resigned, disillusioned, from his frustrating job after barely two years.[15]

Given the passivity and indifference at the governmental level, refugee aid was left up to private organizations in all countries. A fully developed relief system already existed for Jewish refugees. Some of the organizations of this system, such as the Joint Distribution Committee, the Hicem, and the Jewish Agency for Palestine, had been founded decades earlier to provide assistance for the endangered Jews of Eastern Europe. There were also numerous groups sponsored by Christian churches, the Quakers, and other organizations—groups that had a fairly long history of providing international help to various social strata. That the stream of refugees coming out of Germany now was qualitatively different is reflected in the founding—starting in the summer of 1933—of numerous aid committees aimed at assisting specific professional groups, such as physicians, lawyers, teachers, and writers. These committees focused on integrating specific professions into various countries, but the organizations for rescuing German scholars, though partially motivated by national interests, also worked together on an international level, sharing information and financial support.

Among the most important of these organizations were the Emergency Committee in Aid of Displaced German Scholars in the United States and the Academic Assistance Council in Great Britain, both of which were founded in the early summer of 1933 by concerned colleagues. In the United States there were also various individual initiatives. In addition to Alvin Johnson's experiment of setting up an entire University in Exile, the Institute for Advanced Study founded by Abraham Flexner at Princeton should be mentioned. By freeing prominent scientists like Albert Einstein from teaching duties, the Institute allowed eminent scientists and scholars to devote themselves entirely to research. Another such organization is the Notgemeinschaft deutscher Wissenschaftler im Ausland, founded in Zurich in April 1933 by university professors exiled from Germany.[16]

Close cooperation and a division of competencies soon developed among these three major self-help organizations. The Emergency Committee surveyed possibilities and arranged for jobs in the United States; the Academic Assistance Council did the same in England and the dominions of the British Empire; and the Notgemeinschaft, which had just scored a major success in placing German scholars in Turkey, acted as liaison for the Orient, the Soviet Union, and South America. The League of Nation's High Commissioner for Refugees tried to play a role, too, and the office he established specifically for dealing with academic refugees was intended as an umbrella organization for these committees. But these efforts once again reflected how little influence he actually had. There is something almost tragic in the vehemence with which he tried in his reports to create the impression that these organizations acted only as agencies dependent on him and that the successful placements were primarily due to his initiative.[17] The actual facts paint a different picture. The High Commissariat served not even as a clearinghouse for the national and international committees; instead, the Academic Assistance Council had taken over this function. It collected data on exiled scholars and passed them on to other organizations and to interested institutions of higher learning. From 1935 on, the council's quarters in London also housed the Notgemeinschaft, which, after the High Commissioner's resignation, was in theory the only international organization devoted to saving German scholars and finding new jobs for them. In reality, however, the Notgemeinschaft had no decision-making power because it was dependent financially on American sources and administratively on the council's office staff.

The different situations of the aid committees in England and the United States are reflected in their respective placement policies. The Academic Assistance Council saw itself as a kind of job clearinghouse; that is, it chose the scholars to be placed at the universities and paid part of the salaries of those actually hired. During the first phase the funding was raised largely through a kind of self-taxation of British scholars, who thus demonstrated a much greater commitment and solidarity than their American colleagues. The Emergency Committee's procedure was different from the outset. In view of the universities' financial problems during the depression and America's isolationist climate of opinion, the committee declared itself willing for a period of up to two years to pay half the salary—up to $2,000 annually—of scholars selected and hired by the institutions themselves. The founder and later secretary of the Emergency Committee was Stephen

Duggan of the Institute of International Education in New York, who already had helped many White Russian scholars during the 1920s. Because the intention was to place a large number of the available German scholars and because this was expected to cost a great deal, Duggan planned to dovetail the new organization's efforts closely with those of existing American philanthropic institutions[18] and to channel significant sums of money provided by several mostly Jewish foundations to the Emergency Committee. As a rule, responsibility for the other half of displaced scholars' salaries was assumed by foundations whose mission it had always been to support higher education. Thus the hiring of professors exiled from Germany did not cost the universities anything, at least for the first years.

In this way the following amounts were made available until 1945: $800,000 from the Emergency Committee for 335 scholars, of which $317,000 came from the New York Foundation alone; almost $1.4 million from the Rockefeller Foundation for 303 scholars; and $317,000 from the Oberlaender Trust for over 300 scholars. The Carnegie Foundation, another major supporter of higher education, chose to provide support indirectly through donations to other organizations totaling about $110,000.[19]

Although the universities' resistance to hiring German scholars soon melted away given such financial incentives—indeed, the waiting list of some universities had grown to remarkable length[20]—the Emergency Committee and the Rockefeller Foundation did everything they could to prevent misinterpretation of their refugee policy as motivated by philanthropy. The supreme guiding principle of all their efforts was "to save learning, not to provide personal help for individual scholars." For this reason, only first-rate scholars were to be supported, and an effort was made to spread them out widely among universities and colleges, so as to preclude concentrations in a few centers and the animosities that might result.

Younger scholars presented a special problem. Since it was considered important not to infringe on the professional chances of Americans in this age group, it was decided—despite grave doubts about the wisdom of the decision—to assist only immigrant scholars who were over thirty. The Oberlaender Trust did not adhere to this rule. An analysis of the funds it dispensed shows that it granted small fellowships to many young academics, supporting the same number of applicants as the Rockefeller Foundation. But the money paid out by the Oberlaender Trust amounted to barely 20 percent of the sums the Rockefeller Foundation made available. Starting in the early 1940s, a fund of the Rosenwald family, heirs to the Sears and Roebuck fortune, also helped by establishing a special fellowship program for younger scholars that was administered by the Emergency Committee.[21]

The founders of the Emergency Committee had hoped to finish their work in two years, assuming that the influx of displaced scholars would long have ceased by then and that the economic crisis in the United States would be over. These expectations proved to be an illusion. Despite increasing interest and contributions, the committee was less and less able to meet the needs of academics fleeing from Germany—and, after 1937–38, from Czechoslovakia, Austria, and Italy as well. In addition, there was the unforeseen problem that some of the successfully placed scholars lost their positions after their contracts ran out. Because of financial constraints the Emergency Committee was no longer able, beginning in 1937, to help finance scholars for two years and could offer only one-year commitments. In 1938 it adopted the rule that universities would receive support grants only if there was good reason to expect that the positions they were offering would become permanent. This change was introduced because only 55 of the 125 scholars placed with the aid of the Emergency Committee since 1933 had received permanent appointments.[22] The share of salary paid by the Emergency Committee had to be reduced drastically across the board. In 1933 the committee had contributed a maximum of $2,000. With payment of the other half of the salary assumed by other sources, a scholar obtaining an appointment received $4,000. At that time an American scholar at the top of his field could expect an annual salary of $12,000 to $15,000. But the share paid by the Emergency Committee gradually declined over the following years. By 1937–38 it was barely $1,400; a year later it amounted to only $1,000; and after the defeat of France, when scholars from all over Europe sought refuge, it sank to less than $650, though part of the loss could be recouped with increased contributions from other parties.[23]

3. The Rockefeller Foundation

By allocating $1.4 million for the rescue of displaced scholars, the Rockefeller Foundation by itself accounted for more than half the money raised in the United States for this cause. Its contributions far exceeded those of the other major sources of funding, the New York Foundation, the Carnegie Foundation, and the Oberlaender Trust, the latter of which had been

Table 3. *The Rockefeller Foundation Aid Program for Displaced Scholars, 1933–45*

303 scholars financed	$1,410,778

Academic field
- 113 in the social sciences (37%)
- 73 in the natural sciences (24%)
- 59 in the humanities (19%)
- 58 in medicine (19%)

Nationality
- 191 German
- 36 French
- 30 Austrian
- 12 Italian
- 11 Polish
- 6 Hungarian
- 6 Spanish
- 5 Czech
- 2 each, Scandinavian, Dutch, Belgian

Aid Programs

1. *Special Research Fund for Deposed Scholars, 1933–39*

192 scholars	$743,257

- 122 in the United States at 65 universities
- 70 in Europe

Academic field
- 74 in the social sciences
- 45 in the natural sciences
- 35 in the humanities
- 38 in medicine

2. *Aid for Deposed Scholars, 1940–45* (continuation of the existing program but no longer financed by the Special Research Fund for Refugees, funded instead through the regular program to promote research)

59 scholars	$229,862

19 in Great Britain and South America

Academic field
- 22 in the social sciences
- 16 in the natural sciences
- 10 in the humanities
- 11 in medicine

Table 3. *Continued*

3. *Emergency Program for European Scholars, 1940–45* (rescue action for European academics after the defeat of France, undertaken in cooperation with the New School for Social Research; of the 89 scholars invited only 52 reached the United States).

   52 scholars $437,659

   34 went to the New School

Academic field

   17 in the social sciences

   14 in the humanities

   12 in the natural sciences

    9 in medicine

Nationality

   24 French

   14 German

    4 Austrian

    4 Polish

    2 Spanish

    1 each, Italian, Hungarian, Belgian, Dutch

Note: Compilation based on the files of the Rockefeller Foundation, RG 1.1, Projects.

founded only in 1931. A summary of the amounts granted for salaries by the Rockefeller Foundation between 1933 and the end of World War II gives a clear picture of the several waves of refugees, their makeup, and the focus, both geographical and thematic, of the aid. About a third of the foundation money allocated to the aid programs went to scholars outside the United States, primarily in Great Britain and South America, and was routed through the Academic Assistance Council and the Notgemeinschaft. If we look at the fields represented among the 335 scholars aided by the Emergency Committee, the humanities predominated (137), followed by the social sciences (110), natural sciences (81), and medicine (7).[24] (There was also a special program for applicants in medicine.) The biggest share of aid from the Rockefeller Foundation, however, went to the social sciences (see Table 3).

The dollar amounts shown in the table were allocated just for salaries; beyond that, large sums were made available for other costs associated with research projects of the immigrant scholars. The following amounts, totaling $540,235, went to the University in Exile at the New School, the largest recipient of "refugee aid" from the Rockefeller funds: $301,486, salaries provided under the $1.4 million program; $173,210, research projects; $65,539, administrative costs.

The size of these amounts and how they were distributed suggest the crucial role the Rockefeller Foundation played in the integration of exiled scholars not just in the United States but in Europe as well, a point underscored by the striking contrast during the first years after 1933 between the huge sums expended and the relatively small number—compared to England—of placements in the United States. From the very beginning, representatives of the Emergency Committee had to concede that the foundation was in charge. It had in fact created its own program and authorized an initial $140,000 for it before the Emergency Committee was even formed. At the same time the foundation had defined the conditions for awarding grants in the United States, and there was nothing left for the Emergency Committee to do later on but adopt them. When someone from the committee finally went to Europe in the fall of 1933 to sound out which of the scholars might opt for the United States, he had to report back to New York with some embarrassment that he hardly knew what the purpose of his mission in Europe really was because the Paris office of the Rockefeller Foundation was firmly in charge of deciding "whether a grant should or should not be given."[25]

The foundation in fact started out with a situation very different from that of the Emergency Committee. Unlike the aid organizations that sprang up spontaneously in the early summer of 1933 and had to improvise in this unfamiliar territory, the activities of the Rockefeller Foundation were essentially continuations of existing programs that had been in place since the 1920s. The foundation thus not only had at its disposal detailed information about European and German scholarship, including awareness of individual scholars, but also had a functioning administrative presence in its Paris office. When it become known that William Beveridge, the director of the London School of Economics, was considering forming an aid committee for German scholars, which would become the Academic Assistance Council, the foundation was able to move on a similar plan within a few days.[26]

For many years after its formation at the beginning of the century, the Rockefeller Foundation had concentrated its support almost exclusively on medical research, especially tropical medicine. But in the mid 1920s it developed an interest in the modern social sciences as well. Rockefeller money helped found the Social Science Research Council in the United States, and it financed many research projects in Europe. For example, the proposed 1933 budget of $1.8 million for European research allocated funds as follows:

Medicine	$786,860
Social sciences	850,000
Humanities	74,000
Natural sciences	37,300
Administration, Paris office	92,300
Total	$1,840,460[27]

Included in the amount for the social sciences was a little under $75,000 for projects in Germany, most of them in economics at Kiel and at Heidelberg; in anthropology at Berlin; and in psychiatric research at Munich. Research in economics at the London School of Economics, in Rotterdam, and in Stockholm also received considerable support. The amounts granted, which seemed huge from a European perspective, were in fact minor from the foundation's point of view, given the almost $250 million worth of stock in the prospering Standard Oil Company owned by the Rockefeller dynasty, the interest of which alone allowed annual appropriations of $8 million and more.[28]

From the time the program was first set up in 1929 until 1933, a total of about $17.8 million was approved for the social sciences—the largest total assigned to any field except medical research. Of this money $830,650 went to Germany for the following purposes.

1. Financing of libraries in Berlin, Kiel, Heidelberg, and Munich: $137,500
2. Research grants to institutes, including $20,000 to the Institute for International Law in Hamburg; $60,000 to the Institute for Political Science in Heidelberg; $30,000 to the Institute of World Economics in Kiel; $110,000 to the *Hochschule für Politik* in Berlin: $239,000
3. Interuniversity research grants: $125,000 for anthropological research; $25,000 for studies on international relations
4. Grants: $4,150
5. Fellowships: 56 grants for two-year stays abroad, $300,000[29]

Compared with these sums, the support the Rockefeller Foundation provided for refugees after 1933 appears rather modest, but given the scarcity of other sources and because the foundation had a well-established infrastructure in place, it was able to supply funds and achieve results quickly and effectively. The foundation's newly created and expanding research program in the social sciences could absorb the exiled German social scientists, who constituted, relatively speaking, the largest group of exiled academics, and cushion for them the blow of having to start out for a new, uncertain future. This comparatively smooth transition was further eased by the fact that among the first expelled scholars were many whose research had been supported by the foundation before 1933, and many had already had contact with the Rockefeller people in Paris, who had carefully observed what was happening at the universities on their regular trips to Germany.[30]

The foundation's staff in Paris was well versed in a wide range of academic disciplines, and many of them had themselves studied in Germany or elsewhere in Europe. Their many reports not only give an excellent picture of the intellectual and political climate at the German universities during the rise of national socialism but also indicate what kind of projects the foundation and its representatives in Paris wanted to promote and what the criteria for their decisions were. The interuniversity anthropology project, for instance, had been financed to prove how absurd the race theory propagated by the National Socialists and legitimized by their intellectual accomplices was. Another striking aspect of the reports is their repeated criticism of the gerontocratic club of German professors who permitted advancement only to those younger faculty who had completely adopted the older generation's conservatism. In the social sciences, the reports pointed out, the senior tenured professors continued the tradition of intellectual history propounded by the Prussian mandarins. These professors, instead of producing concrete research, indulged in philosophical speculation or, in the case of economics where the historical school was still influential, mere description without any theoretical foundation.[31]

The questions raised and the new approaches to research practiced by younger outsiders were noted all the more positively. The Kiel Institute of World Economics, for example, was regarded as the "Mecca" of modern German economics because of its analyses of business cycles and its internationally oriented research. The work of Alfred Weber and Emil Lederer at Heidelberg was viewed in a similarly favorable light, as was the research conducted by Hans Kelsen and his assistant Erich Hula at the Cologne Institute for International Law. But the Rockefeller people were most impressed by the breadth of approach displayed at the University of Frankfurt, in particular by the sociologist Karl Mannheim, the economist Adolf Löwe, the specialist in labor law Hugo Sinzheimer and his assistant Hans Morgenthau, and the statistician of business cycles Eugen Altschul, all of whom left Germany in 1933. Frankfurt University with its open, international atmosphere was considered one of the "strongest" academic centers, and for this reason the Rockefeller Foundation would have liked to increase its financial support. But because so many Jews were at Frankfurt the Rockefeller people worried this might have a negative effect on public opinion in Germany.[32]

The foundation was faced with a dilemma. It considered the traditional and prestigious scholarship in the social sciences pursued in Germany too mediocre to deserve support, but at the same time it was afraid to finance the newer, innovative research more actively because of the political climate. Thus, though the sums awarded in Germany seemed quite large in the context of that country, they were in fact, compared to what was being paid out in other countries, "relatively modest," according to the foundation's Paris representative.[33]

This commitment to support the social sciences should not, however, be taken to mean that the Rockefeller administration financed critical research in Germany out of political conviction or to try to help the scholars involved overcome their outsider status. Rather, the research methods developed in Germany by the younger generation after World War I and under the extreme social and political conditions of the Weimar Republic happened to coincide with the particular national interests of the foundation. The Rockefeller Foundation initiated its program in the social sciences because in the United States knowledge about the development of modern societies and techniques for regulating dynamic industrial growth seemed to be lagging far behind advances being made in the natural sciences. The foundation's goal was, on the one hand, to advance the kind of knowledge that could be developed, in the hands of competent social technocrats, into tools for instituting "social controls" and, on the other, to find new, heuristic methods for the "simplification and solution of modern social problems."[34] It is no coincidence that after the New York stock market crash and the outbreak of the Great Depression the foundation placed a new emphasis on economic planning and control. Grants were given to economists working in this area. In Germany these economists were found primarily in Kiel and Heidelberg; in other countries they were gathered at the Stockholm School around Bertil Ohlin and Gunnar Myrdal and at the Dutch Institute of Economics in Rotterdam, where Verrijn Stuart and Jan Tinbergen were teaching. At the same time, however, the foundation supported work by the Austrian school of economic thought headed by Ludwig Mises in Vienna, which may be regarded as the center of neoclassical market theory in Europe.

After January 30, 1933, the Rockefeller Foundation was faced with the question of how it should react, if at all, to the new rulers in Germany and their terrorist measures against intellectuals. The foundation's policy up to that point had been pragmatic in practice and ambivalent in principle. There were considerable differences of opinion on this subject within the foundation. As the foundation's tactical statements made in response to the xenophobic atmosphere of the American universities have already shown, the people of the Paris office in particular, and especially those in the medical section, were not free of anti-Semitic prejudice themselves; and they were to display, in spite of having watched the German situation for years, the same failure to understand the developments in Germany that was evident in other areas of American political and public life.[35]

The Paris office soon sent home reassuring reports about the situation in Germany that occasionally expressed an undisguised sympathy for the National Socialist measures against Jewish scholars and intellectuals. For, the argument went, everybody had long since forgotten that it was the radicals—mostly Jews—who had come to power in Germany in 1918 and who had brought about social upheaval. Although the worst excesses had been eliminated, nothing had been done to change "the injustice of having such a large percentage of Jews" in many public institutions in Germany. No one had been able to eliminate this threat before the Nazi party came to power. The Nazis' expulsion of Jews, communists, and foreigners should be seen as a short-term measure. The best policy now was to wait and see and to continue supporting the programs in Germany undeterred.[36] Following this line of thought, some of the Rockefeller people suggested funding dismissed academics only if they remained in Germany. The Nazis could not, of course, reinstate the academics they had fired, but to avoid alienating world opinion they would not take further action against them and would in fact be quite pleased if these scholars could continue their work supported by funding from private sources. No matter what, the foundation should not discontinue the current funding of institutions or divert the money to refugees. Otherwise, it might give the impression to the public "that the Jewish scholar and the Weimar Republicans alone had our confidence."[37]

We will not attempt to decide here whether these recommendations represented the proponents' own convictions or whether they reflected what official National Socialist spokesmen and academics who had not been dismissed told the foundation people on their numerous visits to Germany. The Rockefeller reports as well as those from Emergency Committee representatives in Europe show with what indifference and sometimes satisfaction the dismissals were greeted at German universities. This attitude was obviously not without effect on the foundation's staff. Some of the German academics complained about the negative opinions of Hitler abroad, opinions that completely overlooked the fact that Hitler was primarily fighting communism.[38] The foundation's people also noted with amazement to what extent academics of opposing political convictions— such as Ernst Jaeckh, director of the Hochschule für Politik in Berlin and a "liberal", and Arthur Spiethoff, an economist at Bonn and "a rightist conservative"—agreed in their assessment of national socialism and its ability to restore order in Germany.[39]

Suggestions from the Paris office on how to continue supporting German research consequently remained ambivalent. Even after the key figures at the Kiel Institute of World Economics were dismissed, the Paris office recommended continuing support to it to protect it from state influence. Yet at the same time it was unclear whether any relevant research could still be carried on there. Funding for the Institute was revoked only after New York headquarters had asked the Swedish economist Gunnar Myrdal for a report, which contained a scathing condemnation of the personal integrity and the quality of research produced under the new administrative leadership.[40]

In late 1933 the Rockefeller Foundation's New York headquarters ordered a systematic withdrawal from German research in the social sciences. Research and library funding was not renewed, and the fellowships previously awarded in Germany were transferred to the program for exiled scholars. The Paris office continued to send reassuring reports about the situation in Germany, but by this time New York was receiving much more authentic information from the first expelled scholars arriving in the United States. The rosy picture that still came in from Paris was ignored more and more; the foundation had realized that further support awarded in Hitler's Germany "would be merely throwing away our money."[41]

From the $140 million budget approved for the refugee program in May 1933, salaries were paid out as early as that summer to the first seven scholars who had obtained academic appointments, most of them in England. Among them were the economists Adolf Löwe, former head of the Kiel Institute, and Jakob Marschak from Heidelberg; the sociologist Karl Mannheim; the statistician Eugen Altschul; and Hans Kelsen, an expert in political law from Cologne. Other contracts were in the making, and the Rockefeller Foundation had also received the first offers of positions and applications for support for them from France.[42] By the beginning of 1935, 135 exiled intellectuals were already receiving support, 67 of them in the United States, 34 in England, and 16 in France. By the time the war broke out, the number of scholars had risen to 192, 74 of whom were in the social sciences. These recipients represented only a small fraction of the scholars expelled from German universities, but their names read like a "who's who" of Germany's best critical thinkers. It should also be mentioned that the Rockefeller Foundation contributed several thousand dollars to finance the famous *List of Displaced German Scholars,* which was compiled by the Notgemeinschaft and mailed to interested universities to facilitate the placement process in the years 1935–36.[43]

4 / What the Exiled Social Scientists Brought to the United States:
Trends in Economic Thought around 1933

1. American Economics and the New Deal

The preferences established by the Rockefeller Foundation suggested which groups would have the greatest success—though to different degrees—in the United States after 1933. The two most important were the German reform economists, rooted in the classical tradition, and the neoclassical economists, who were essentially identical with the so-called Austrian school because market economics had hardly any followers in Germany. The few neoclassical economists who did come from Germany, like Georg Halm and Melchior Palyi, were not of the first rank. Almost all the economists who immigrated to the United States were associated more or less closely with one of these schools. Most of the reform economists found jobs at the New School. By contrast, the Austrians, whose careers add up to a remarkable success story documented recently by Coser,[1] obtained appointments at the most illustrious, usually conservative East Coast universities. With the exception of Friedrich A. Lutz, a student of Walter Eucken, the German neoclassical economists had to accept offers from less prestigious institutions.

Paradoxically, both schools owed their rapid and relatively smooth acceptance in the United States to Roosevelt's new economic program. The small group of New Deal economists hoped the German reform economists would have important new ideas to contribute to their cause. The majority of American academic economists, however, opposed innovations in economic policy, whether based on Keynes's ideas or on those of

America's "new economics"; and it was this opposition that counted on support from the neoclassical market theoreticians.

The adamancy with which American neoclassicists rejected the New Deal can be explained by that school's intellectual history, which bears many parallels to the same tradition in the German-speaking world and had been partially influenced by it. The early days of industrial and economic growth saw a rapid increase of jobs for economists at the many newly founded universities, and at the end of the nineteenth century the German historical school of economics exerted a profound influence on economics in the United States. The Humboldtian system of higher education had traditionally been held in high esteem in the United States, and many American economists had studied in Germany. A symbol of this high regard may perhaps be seen in Harvard's awarding of an honorary doctorate in 1906 to Friedrich Althoff, the director of the Prussian educational administration in charge of the university system.

After behaviorism swept through the social sciences in the United States early in this century, giving rise to the psychological school of economics, American economics became increasingly influenced by the Austrian theory of marginal utility. A reaction to this school of thinking set in a few years later in the form of institutionalism, which is associated primarily with Thorstein Veblen's name. This new approach went back methodologically to elements of the historical school. It examined both the institutional conditions affecting economic activity and the deviations these conditions caused in the market mechanism, which the proponents of the marginal utility theory had elevated to a dogma. Institutionalism also presented the economic system with new demands for social welfare. In the early 1930s the neoclassicists and the institutionalists formed two relatively isolated and irreconcilable camps. During the long period of prosperity in the 1920s the neoclassical theoreticians, led by John B. Clark and Frank A. Fetter among others, encountered little challenge and attracted a growing number of adherents to their deductive models. But after the Great Depression struck, these economists found themselves more and more at a loss and became increasingly rigid in their dogmatism. F. A. Fetter of Princeton could see in institutionalism nothing but destructiveness and "quasi-socialistic hostility toward all capitalistic institutions."[2] Yet, with the exception of Veblen, the proponents of institutionalism had never heard of Karl Marx and saw their work rooted instead in the traditional values of American society.

In the course of the 1920s the institutionalist school branched out in different directions. One group, exemplified by Berle and Means's standard work, concentrated on studying the monopolistic tendencies of industrial capitalism. Another group, led by Wesley C. Mitchell, a former student of Veblen, was made up of empiricists who attempted to describe business cycles statistically and without reference to any theoretical system. Finally, there was some affinity in philosophical outlook between the institutionalists and the theoreticians of social welfare, who were influenced by the works of Foster and Catchings on the theory of underconsumption.[3] Although these different groups all subscribed to the same intellectual tradition, they worked in relative isolation from each other. Wassily Leontief's impressions of American thinking on economics around 1930 seem very much to the point. Leontief, an emigré from Bolshevik Russia, was working at the Kiel Institute of World Economics at that time and would soon after be invited to the United States. What struck him when he familiarized himself with American literature on economics was how hard the authors apparently found it to combine theoretical analysis with solid empirical research. As Leontief put it, their work "always remained a kind of song with separate piano accompaniment." Other economists in Germany had a similar reaction. The empirical study of business cycles did not get underway in Germany until the mid 1920s, relatively late compared to the United States. But when the Germans did turn to this field, they found that research done at Harvard using so-called business barometers as activity indicators recently developed there had not progressed beyond the beginning level because, as the Germans felt, it failed to ask the "crucial question," namely, for what purpose and aims the statistics were being assembled.[4]

The New Deal brought a qualitative change that alleviated these shortcomings, although it remained unclear on what theoretical premises the New Deal's intellectual fathers based their pronouncements. The new sociopolitical paradigm of the New Dealers grew out of institutionalist research and underconsumption theories developed during the 1920s and was intended to bring about an upswing in the economy by instituting major structural reforms and boosting consumer demand through public spending. But the architects of the New Deal did not regard their efforts as merely a strategy to combat the present economic crisis. They also saw themselves as pioneers of a new culture that fundamentally challenged the norms of the existing social and political system. Liberals like the philoso-

41

pher and educator John Dewey and the historian Charles Beard had earlier, after World War I, propounded a new philosophy but without reference to any concrete problems that needed to be solved. This philosophy was aimed against the abstract liberal idealism formulated in the eighteenth century. The new philosophers attacked idealism because in the modern industrial, pecuniary culture it had long since deteriorated into mere ideology.

The empirical and experimental thrust of this new philosophy was summed up in Dewey's slogan "Learning by Doing," and its appeal was to the human ability to learn through social action. In Dewey's view America had to choose between the existing anarchic collectivism of a profit economy run by big business and a new, planned collectivism under public control. For the latter kind of collectivism to work, the public had to be educated to become aware, informed, and responsible; and only such a democratic collectivism, Dewey felt, could create the conditions necessary for building a new, authentic American society. Beard, writing as a historian, arrived at an even harsher assessment. According to him, American society had reached a point where only government control could correct the obvious abuses that had developed in it.[5]

Rexford Tugwell, an economist who, like most of the other authors mentioned above, taught at Columbia University, wrote about the defects of the market economy and of neoclassical theory. Whereas Adolf Berle and Gardiner Means had focused primarily on the contradictions between neoclassical economic theory and the reality of monopolistic market organizations with their system of fixed prices, Tugwell attacked the inherent shortcomings of neoclassical theory. It had, he claimed, become obvious during the current economic crisis, if not before, that the neoclassicists not only lacked the tools to deal with the crisis but were not even able to get beyond the "laissez-faire milieu" in their thinking. Academic economics was still stuck in the nineteenth century both in its premises and in its research methods. On the one hand, it regarded the institutional framework of economic activity as though it were eternal and immutable; on the other, it defined man as a *homo oeconomicus* whose behavior was determined by a supposed rationality principle operating in the market. This deductive "a priori system" had increasingly discredited economic theory as an empirical science, because the system had become less and less capable of analyzing the complex phenomena of real economic life. Tugwell therefore argued vehemently for an innovative science of economics that would not describe deductively a state that should exist but would instead formulate clear social goals and realistic measures to achieve these goals. In addition, it would check and be prepared to revise its assessments in an ongoing process of inductive testing.[6]

These liberal thinkers were among the intellectual leaders of the New Deal. Roosevelt invited Beard, Tugwell, and Berle to join his "brain trust," which was initially only to write his campaign speeches but which soon turned more and more into a planning committee for combating the depression.[7] Although this circle of advisers at first elaborated more on hopes for the future than devised programs that could be implemented, it still functioned as an important focus of the new intellectual fervor that characterized the beginning of Roosevelt's presidency. What attracted many younger intellectuals was the possibility of experimenting with new and unusual ideas. The rigid "country club conformity" into which Republican rule had settled since the end of World War I under its by now stale governing slogan of President Calvin Coolidge that the United States is a "business country" was no longer inviolable.[8] Under Roosevelt, government policy in fact moved from Wall Street to Washington and became deserving of that name only in the years that followed. Within a few years the Roosevelt administration would revamp the traditional American view of politics, putting a completely new and up to then unheard of emphasis on the public weal.[9]

To be sure, there was at first no consistent, unified New Deal ideology, nor was one soon formulated. Instead, the New Deal administrators, most of them young men and women, worked on a practical level with a heterogeneous mix deriving from populism, social reform, and war economy. The governing idea for them, however, seemed to be the theory of underconsumption presented by Tugwell and subscribed to by Roosevelt. This explanation of economic crises had formed the core of his presidential campaign of 1932. Again and again he stressed how much the consumer had been left out of the picture up to now and that one of the most urgent tasks of future policies would be to increase consumer demand.[10] Just how this was to be achieved remained unclear, for Roosevelt also promised to reduce government debt and to cut the budget by 25 percent. Hopes that the private sector might stimulate economic activity through wage increases, lowering of prices, or credit operations turned out to be illusory, however. A shift away from procyclical financial policy was undertaken hesitantly and only after a further worsening of the depression in 1937.

The economists exiled from Germany were able to sort out these contradictions and confusions. They arrived at a time when the new generation of social scientists and politically committed intellectuals were asking the same questions in America that had been asked earlier in Germany. The newly arrived academics and intellectuals were impressed to see that the economic crisis had not destroyed the political system as it had in Germany but had, on the contrary, released previously untapped democratic impulses. This explains the initial and abiding admiration German intellectuals, in particular those with leftist views, felt for Roosevelt.[11] The young, critically minded German economists found ready access to the debate on economic policy in America because they brought with them knowledge and experience that could help reduce the shortcomings of the New Deal.

The reform economists who found a place at the New School were especially qualified to contribute to the discussion of underconsumption theory, for in the wake of World War I theoretical debate in Germany had centered primarily on the defects of this influential theory. Socialists had been particularly receptive to this theory not only because it attributed individual social misery to meagerness of wages and therefore of purchasing power but also because it identified a solid cause for the sales slumps plaguing the entire economy and thus for the increasingly severe economic and political crises of the entire system. In real economic terms, however, the theory was hardly convincing, for it represented only the reverse side of neoclassical supply-side thinking. Both theories aimed only at changing the priorities in redistribution of income to balance production and demand. Because of this shortcoming, the reform debate in Germany during the 1920s had revived a second approach to crisis analysis, one that had also been previously formulated by the classical economists and by Marx and that focused primarily on the disproportionate development dynamics of the modern industrial system. Unlike underconsumption theory, this theory of disproportionality was interested not so much in the conditions of distribution and circulation within the economy as in analyzing the complex structure of production in industrial economies and their potential both for change and for crises generated by change.

Despite their fascination with the New Deal's optimistic fervor and their hopes of contributing to this reform effort, the European refugees often wondered if the new political activism in the United States would last and worried that it might soon—as they had just seen happen in Europe—provoke the conservative elites to reactionary responses.[12] Such counter-attacks were in fact quite obvious. As early as his first presidential campaign, Roosevelt was accused by Herbert Hoover, the incumbent Republican candidate, of having been poisoned by European ideas; and in the following years rightist organizations continued to assert that the new president was a secret communist or even a Soviet agent. In a similar vein and primarily because so many intellectuals who had fled from Europe were connected with it, the New Deal was disparagingly dubbed the "Jew Deal" and its emblem, the blue eagle, compared to the swastika or the hammer and sickle. Those who insinuated that the new economic program was merely a variant of socialistic totalitarianism often displayed, in a strange political dialectic, open sympathies for fascism, which they saw not only as a bulwark against bolshevism but also as an alternative to the new American social politics.[13]

Evidence of similar attitudes cropped up in the comparatively more serious academic environment. At Harvard University, for instance, a "Veritas Society" attempted to have the teaching of economic planning along the lines of the New Deal as well as of Keynesian economic policy removed from the curriculum. And as early as September 1931 the president of Columbia University, Nicholas M. Butler, himself a trained economist, had welcomed the new freshman class with the strange observation that authoritarian regimes brought forward "men of far greater intelligence, far stronger character, and far more courage than the system of elections."[14] It was these circles, their self-confidence obviously shaken, that turned to the solidly conservative neoclassicists of the Austrian school to formulate a counterprogram. And these same circles greeted with satisfaction a remark made by Joseph Schumpeter, an economist from the Austrian school who had been invited to teach at Harvard in 1932. Schumpeter had been heard to say at Harvard that he would rather have voted for Mussolini than for Roosevelt.[15]

2. Austrian Neoclassical Economics

The orthodoxy that is referred to in the history of economic theory as Austrian neoclassical economics gave rise to similar camps in Germany and in the United States. Given the dominant role the historical school had played in economics for several decades in Germany, economic theory was carried on primarily in Austria. Despite their opposing views of what economics should be, both the historical and the theoretical economists rejected British classical economics in the tradition of Adam Smith. The historical school had emerged in the middle of the nineteenth century with the express purpose of proving there were no timeless, supranational economic forces on which generalizations, let alone economic laws, could be based. The attempt to use precise historical and statistical research to free economics from "false abstractions"—a term used by Gustav Schmoller, the foremost representative of the younger historical school— had resulted in a great body of knowledge, which, however, was not so much economics as descriptive history of economic processes. Under the banner of the so-called *Staatswissenschaften*—a term that implied an entire political program—the historical school also wanted the authoritarian Prusso-German state to solve the social problems so dramatically aggravated by industrial growth.

Like the historical school, Austrian neoclassical economics, which may be regarded as the point of origin and center of the debate about market theory in the German-speaking world, had formed in reaction to British classical theory in the 1870s. The Austrian school proposed a theory of subjective utility (marginal utility) as an alternative to the theory of objective cost, which had been advanced by classical political economics and further amplified and systematized in Marxism's labor theory of value. The aim was clearly to find a scientific method to lay to rest socialistic theories. This explains why the Austrian school is associated above all with the defense of unrestrained laissez-faire capitalism, as reiterated untiringly in the 1920s by its major spokesman Ludwig Mises, among others.[16]

Another reason for the special dogmatism of the Austrians may have been that their theoretical premises had received only minimal attention from academic economists in Germany. Despite a partial reconciliation between the historical and neoclassical schools during the dispute in the *Methodenstreit* at the end of the nineteenth century, conditions at the universities in Germany had changed little for the neoclassical economists in the following years. In the 1920s most chairs in economics were still held by adherents of the historical school. To make matters worse, the neoclassicists were challenged to a debate of socialist theory by the labor movement, which had gained access to public power after 1918. It is therefore not surprising that most of the writing by neoclassical market theoreticians between 1918 and 1933 took on increasingly a tone of apologetics as they rallied their forces against "interventionism." Interventionism for them gradually came to include anything that did not conform to their own deductions based on market law and to the philosophy of individualism underlying them.

Neither of these two traditions of economic thought generated any significant ideas for dealing with the real economic problems at hand, such as hardship on an unprecedented scale resulting from the lost war, the profound structural transformations industry was undergoing in the mid 1920s (automation), and the global economic crisis. The top-ranking, gerontocratic circle of the historical school, of which Werner Sombart is an example, retreated to conservative intellectual and autarchic positions, defending a once great tradition in some rearguard skirmishes. The school was to have one brief revival under national socialism. Hardly any of its adherents emigrated. On the other side were the market theoreticians who, feeling more and more helpless in the face of the existing economic problems, raised increasingly shrill voices decrying the influence of the "masses," an influence supposedly grown to ominous proportions since 1918. After the economic crash of 1929 this attitude crystalized for a number of older representatives of this persuasion into authoritarian and anti-democratic concepts of order.

Clearly the masses' demands for participation in a modern industrial society and the need for collective regulation of potential social conflicts were perceived as threats. As early as 1927 Mises detected in Italian fascism a welcome bulwark against advancing collectivism, and it is unlikely that the enthusiasm of this arch-libertarian economist was sparked by Mussolini's corporative legislation. "It cannot be denied," Mises wrote, "that fascism and similar movements toward dictatorship are motivated by the best intentions and that their initiative has for the moment saved European civilization. The merits fascism has thereby earned will live on forever in history."[17]

To be sure, Mises was an extreme case. Nor did he and his comrades-in-arms from the older generation of neoclassicists have a significant part in the success of this school in the United States. Very few of them emigrated. Mises himself, who held only a lectureship at the University of Vienna and whose primary position was that of secretary of the Vienna Chamber of Commerce, did not immigrate to the United States directly. Starting in 1934 he taught for several years at the Institut des Hautes Etudes Internationales in Geneva. When his contract there ran out in 1940, he was not allowed, as a Jew, to return to Austria. He then immigrated to the United States, where he taught at New York University until 1969, but one can hardly speak of an academic career in his case, since he remained a visiting professor the whole time. One reason for this may have been his age; Mises was already fifty-nine years old in 1940. At least as decisive a factor may have been his acrimonious polemics against anything that did not conform to his Manchester-liberal vision. Even convinced anti–New Dealers were irritated by his tone and his argumentativeness, and the Yale University Press had good reason for rejecting the first draft of his book, originally titled "Nazi Challenge to Western Civilization," which subsumed everything from the Wilhelmine Reich to social democracy and on up to the modern welfare state under the rubric of national socialism. The manuscript was returned with the comment that it abounded in unwarranted exaggerations and was larded with claims and arguments that could hardly pass the test of objective scrutiny.[18] Not until the turn toward neoconservatism in the 1970s did Mises emerge as a cult figure of the new American "libertarians" and his old polemical writings as well as those of his disciple Hayek—for example, *Road to Serfdom* of 1944—become obligatory reading in this new orthodoxy.[19]

The story of the younger representatives of the Austrian school is quite different. Despite the verbal attacks on the existing economic order typical of all his writings after 1918, Mises was able to attract to his famous *Privatseminar* an audience that was to attain considerable fame later on. One would think that the seminar discussions with younger colleagues from other disciplines, among them sociologists, historians, and the "logical positivists" of the Vienna school of philosophy, should have resulted in an interdisciplinary approach, but there were practically no attempts to incorporate broader political perspectives into the sociological thinking of this group. Even Mises's closest associates had to admit in retrospect that his aversion to any kind of interventionism was so strong that everybody "instinctively avoided" the topic. Other important areas were similarly ignored. When, for instance, Oskar Morgenstern submitted for discussion his dissertation on "economic forecasting," which was published in 1928, nothing was said about the fruitfulness of exact mathematical methods in studying business cycles. The younger economists had to turn elsewhere for this kind of knowledge.[20]

In the late 1920s, these economists began to break away from the Austrian orthodoxy and made notable contributions to modern economic theory. But they did not make their mark until after immigration to Britain or to America. Among the names that come to mind are Friedrich

August Hayek, who with his theoretical analyses of business cycles became a major challenger of Keynes as early as 1931; Gottfried Haberler with his work on international trade; Oskar Morgenstern, who together with the mathematician John von Neumann developed game theory; and Fritz Machlup with his contributions to the "economics of the knowledge industry."

It was these younger economists the Rockefeller Foundation had been interested in since the 1920s, hoping that their input could benefit American economics. Their underlying conservatism together with their largely theoretical thinking in the tradition of Carl Menger and Eugen von Böhm-Bawerk—a tradition that will be discussed in later pages—promised effective support in countering the new "leftist" social theories. John van Sickle, the Paris representative of the Rockefeller Foundation's social science division, had himself studied under Mises and had become acquainted with the bright young economists in Mises's seminars, many of whom were subsequently given Rockefeller fellowships to spend several years in the United States.

Among these were Morgenstern (1925–28), Haberler (1927–29), Paul Rosenstein-Rodan (1930–33), Herbert Fürth (1931–32), and, a little later, Fritz Machlup (1933–36) and Gerhard Tintner (1934–36). The normative theoretical foundation these economists brought with them together with a network of personal ties and contacts established during their travels facilitated the rapid acceptance of these scholars at the most respected institutions. Most of them already felt quite at home in the United States by the mid 1930s, even before Germany's annexation of Austria in 1938 made refugees of them. Thus Haberler, who had been working since 1934 in the Secretariat of the League of Nations, was invited to teach at Harvard in 1936—the only immigrant, by the way, to be accepted into the faculty there. Oskar Morgenstern, who succeeded Hayek from 1929 to 1938 as director of the Austrian Institute for Business Cycles Research founded by the Vienna Chamber of Commerce, left in 1938 for Princeton. So did Friedrich A. Lutz from Freiburg. After his Rockefeller fellowship ran out in 1936, Fritz Machlup accepted a professorship at Buffalo and then went on to teach at Johns Hopkins before succeeding Jacob Viner at Princeton in 1960. Rosenstein-Rodan first worked for the World Bank and then taught at the Massachusetts Institute of Technology. Gerhard Tintner's career did not advance as rapidly or illustriously. Tintner was an important econometrist who also remained in the United States after his fellowship expired in 1936.

He spent the following decades working on a number of research and governmental committees and teaching in nontenured positions at various universities. Herbert Fürth, who had worked as a lawyer in Vienna, continued in this field and did not embark on an academic career in the United States.[21] Further signs of the high regard this group enjoyed in academe are the prestigious offices some of its members were elected to in the United States. Haberler and Machlup assumed presidency of the American Economic Association in 1962 and 1966, respectively. Machlup was also president of the International Economic Association from 1971 to 1974 and of the American Association of University Professors from 1962 to 1964.

In this context we should also mention Joseph A. Schumpeter, although he was not a refugee but had been recruited by Harvard from the University of Bonn in 1932. He was probably the most brilliant and stimulating teacher of all the older German-speaking economists of the 1920s. Although trained in the Austrian school, he by no means felt confined to its dogma. When he was invited to join the Harvard faculty he not only had behind him a distinguished academic career, a short term as minister of finance in the cabinet of the Austrian Marxist Otto Bauer after World War I, and the experience of operating a bank—which failed during the inflation—but had also produced a body of scholarly work that even then was of classical dimensions. We will mention only a few of his works here. *Das Wesen und der Hauptinhalt der theoretischen Nationalökonomie* [The Essence and main subject of theoretical economics] was written under the impact of the dispute over method and directed against all one-sided dogmatism. The essay "Das Sozialprodukt und die Rechenpfennige" [Money and the social product] of 1917 marked a significant breakthrough in the discussion of monetary theory in Germany. Just as important was Schumpeter's sociological study on the "Krise des Steuerstaats" [The Crisis of the tax state] written in 1918, which sought solutions to the structural problems accompanying the transition from a war economy to a peacetime economy. Finally, there was his *Theorie der wirtschaftlichen Entwicklung* [Theory of economic development], first published in 1912 and reissued in a revised edition in 1926, a book that contained probably the first dynamic theory of circular flow to appear in German.

In his plea for a plurality of methods Schumpeter had tried to combine historical interpretation with theoretical and quantitative analysis as well as with methodological considerations. Like no one else of his generation he had the ability to recognize burning economic issues and tackle them on broad and ambitious terms. One would expect such wide-ranging theoretical reflections to lead to some practical application, but nothing of the kind is to be found in Schumpeter. In this respect he was typical of the Austrian school. This abstinence was, however, in no way irreconcilable with his short forays, as minister and banker, into the area of practical economics immediately after World War I. Rather, this reveals another basic personality trait. In that period of his life, he picked quarrels with colleagues and co-workers and managed within a short time to alienate just about everyone with whom he came in contact. Schumpeter enjoyed the role of unconventional loner; he was quick to embrace various political and philosophical trends but dropped them just as quickly. That is why, even after his appointment at Harvard where he stayed until his death in 1950, he did not give rise to any school. Some of this theoretical and political ambivalence is evident in his *Theorie der wirtschaftlichen Entwicklung,* which introduced German economists to the important distinction between static and dynamic economics. In this work Schumpeter does not explain the causes of dynamic progress in a logical and empirical manner but attributes them to the psychological motives of a few daring "entrepreneurs of genius" who interrupt the static course of the economy with a series of spontaneous moves. That is why, when the second edition of Schumpeter's book came out, his theory of development had so little impact on the discussion of the problems of dynamic growth, even though this topic was of great interest to the younger generation of economists.

The same qualities are present in the two major works Schumpeter wrote in the United States, *Business Cycles* (1939) and *Capitalism, Socialism, and Democracy* (1942). Schumpeter set out to write an elegant theory of economic depressions, but since he was no empiricist and felt an understanding of underlying principles and ideas was more important than an analysis of the facts, he soon ran into difficulties and limitations in the actual writing and came to consider *Business Cycles* the weakest of his works. His last book demonstrates once more the philosophical ambivalence that was characteristic of his whole career. On the one hand he looked at socialist theory with scholarly objectivity, but on the other his methodological individualism, his admiration for monopolistic capitalism, and his glorification of the elite as the moving force behind social and cultural progress prevented him from drawing logical politicoeconomic conclusions. His fascination with the comprehensive nature of the Marxian system remained an intellectual abstraction.

Schumpeter was one of the most uncompromising opponents—first in Germany and later, even more so, in the United States—of economic and political interventionism of any kind, whether it took the form of the New Deal or of Keynesian economics. He held that intervention by the state would undermine the last pillars of bourgeois ideology and thus complete the destructive work, already far advanced, of Marxism. Thus he once again sang the praises of capitalism in his book of 1942, though in a more resigned mood this time, for he could already see the historical necessity with which socialism was rising from capitalism's "crumbling walls."[22]

3. The German Reform Economists

A glance at England and the great names in economics there—names like Marshall, Pigou, and Keynes—makes it clear that theory was much more practice-oriented there than in Germany or in the United States. In England economic theory tried to provide information about concrete social, political, and economic questions and to further the dynamic development of the existing economic system. This more practical approach precluded the dogmatic rigidities typical of neoclassical eco-nomics in the other two countries, where many adherents of neoclassicism isolated themselves from reality and the many new ideas that emerged during the 1920s. Dominated by a kind of camp mentality, these neoclassical economists lost sight of the task of science and scholarship, which is to recognize problems, analyze them, and propose solutions. Instead, battles were fought over slogans, and by the mid 1920s the discipline of economics was in a "chronic crisis."[23]

Like the institutionalists and future New Dealers in the United States, a young group in Germany at that time put an end to this stagnation. These German economists attacked not only the deductive model of neoclassicism but also Marxist theory, which they found analytically brilliant but of little practical value. Nor were they less critical of the practically oriented but theoretically unsophisticated economic thinking often encountered in the labor movement, which had gained some political power after 1918. Going back to the classical understanding of economics, which had included a general theory of society, these economists always saw economic theory in terms of practical application in economic and social policy. For them, no sharp line separated economic questions from sociological ones. The group's immediate aim during those years was to help build a more stable and functional economic and sociopolitical foundation for the German Republic, which was rocked by crises from its very beginning. At the same time the reform-oriented debate initiated by the group articulated problems that were not just important at the moment but also retained their urgency in the long run, were subjected to further analysis during the American exile, and remain pressing to this day.

What still appears revolutionary today is that this group revived classical thinking, which had been eclipsed by the victory of the marginalist school. Writing in the 1920s under the impact of the rapid automation taking place in industry, they produced works on technical change and gave center stage once again to the classical question of the relationship between capital accumulation, technical development, and employment. They were not preoccupied primarily with questions of social order, as were the neoclassicists and orthodox Marxists of their time, but were interested instead in a realistically oriented theory that would explain the instabilities they saw in short-term economic fluctuations, and these included unsolved postwar problems. But beyond that they also wanted to comprehend instabilities in long-term growth fueled by technical developments.

At the forefront of this work were members of the Kiel school, such as Adolf Löwe, Gerhard Colm, Hans Neisser, and Alfred Kähler, all of whom were among the first economists to be expelled by the Nazis. Löwe had made major contributions to the study of business cycles; he can in fact be considered the *spiritus rector* of realistic modern research on business cycles in Germany. To be sure, neoclassicists—especially Hayek—had worked in this field, too. The turbulent economic developments of the 1920s had made this one of the most crucial areas addressed by almost all economists and theoretical schools everywhere. But whereas Löwe and his associates included the problem of technical progress in their discussion, came up with qualitatively new approaches, and tried to develop tools for effective political and economic action, the neoclassicists hardly moved beyond their traditional, abstract models. The explanations of economic fluctuation they came up with left their old assumptions about market equilibrium largely intact; the only new element was that now some exogenous disruptive factors were added to the old crisis theory: For Mises and Hayek, the new element was monetary variables; for Schumpeter, the psychology of innovative entrepreneurs.

Building on Löwe's work, Gerhard Colm developed the study of public finance into an important theory of economic guidance and planning by assigning new functions to government expenditures. Alfred Kähler, a student of Löwe's, produced important preliminary work for such guidance and for a future theory of growth by constructing an early version of an input–output model. During this period Wassily Leontief, too, the Russian Menshevist who had come to Germany in the early 1920s, was still part of the Kiel circle. Although his interest in these years tended in other directions, he would later, in the United States, pick up and develop the ideas first formulated in Kiel by Kähler. For this work on the structural relationships of the economic system he received the Nobel Prize in 1973.[24] Hans Neisser, finally, published a fundamental study on the theory of the circular flow of money. This was, in effect, a new approach to the quantity theory of money, and it impressed even Keynes, who was not fluent in German and therefore registered research done in that language only very selectively. During the worldwide economic depression, this group of reformers—unique in the history of German economics—also offered a number of unorthodox suggestions for a realistic therapy, suggestions that differed considerably from the anticyclical, deficit-financed measures that would later be associated with the name of Keynes and that were designed to stimulate aggregate demand.

The work of the Kiel group was supplemented by Emil Lederer in Heidelberg, who explored, in addition to the problems inherent in technical progress, the economic effect of the growing concentration of economic power in the hands of large corporations. His former student, Jakob Marschak, who also spent some time working in Kiel, already belonged to the still small circle of econometricians during those years. In the United States he was later to become one of the pioneers of modern mathematical economics. Finally, in his book *Soziale Theorie des Kapitalismus* [Social theory of capitalism], published in 1929, Eduard Heimann of the University of Hamburg was the first to develop a consistent theory of social policy that was no longer based, as in the past, on the idea of protecting the socially weak and insuring their welfare in complete isolation from the economic system but instead saw this protection as a powerful vehicle for transforming society.

The intellectual outlook of this group seems to have been affected by the unusual paths by which most of them came to economics. With a few exceptions they were not trained economists and were therefore not captive to the established patterns of economic thinking. Almost all of them had gotten to know each other in 1918–19 while working as young officials in the demobilization bureaucracy after World War I or as members of the so-called Sozialisierungskommissionen (National Economic Councils). Except for Lederer and Heimann they first encountered economic questions in that context. Löwe and Neisser, for example, had law degrees; Colm came from sociology. He had written a dissertation in 1921 on the Ruhr uprising of 1920, a topic suggested by Max Weber, and later wrote articles on such subjects as "problems of disarmament" and "the masses" for the first large encyclopedia of sociology to be published in Germany.[25] Jakob Marschak, a Russian who came to Germany in 1919, had gained practical political experience at barely twenty years of age as minister of labor during the short rule of the Menshevik Republic in the northern Caucasus. He had a degree in engineering. Also part of this group was Hans Staudinger, who had studied under Alfred Weber and also had a degree in sociology. As a young official working for the Food Office he was first drawn to socialism in 1918 under the influence of Lederer and Rudolf Hilferding, the theoretician of the Social Democratic party, but was soon won over by the more skeptical Adolf Löwe to ideas of social planning. Unlike his friends, he did not enter academe in the 1920s but stayed in the administration and rose to the position of undersecretary in the Prussian Ministry of Commerce, where he became the leading practitioner and theoretician of the Gemeinwirtschaft ("commonweal economy"). He was the prime moving force behind the creation of the Preussag, a public association of all producers of energy in Prussia. He was not to resume closer contact with his old colleagues until he, too, was invited to teach political economy at the New School.

The experiences of the war, the "debacle of socialization" resulting from the Social Democrats' assumption of responsibilities during the revolution of 1918—responsibilities they were forced into taking but were unprepared to meet—and especially the demobilization problems that were of a hitherto unknown magnitude, all this determined the special outlook and frame of reference this group brought to its future work in economics. These influences are in marked contrast to those that formed the younger members of the Austrian school, men of about the same age v gathered practical economic experience before they produced arly work. But whereas the Austrians had been active in privat in associations of private businesses[26]—work that clearly s individualistic, market-theory-oriented position—the Germar oreticians' work in the economic administration and their enc with macroeconomic problems resulted in a supraindividualistic outlook focused on structural analysis. These influences soon led most of them, all from liberal bourgeois backgrounds, to become Social Democrats. In the days of the Kaiserreich the somewhat older Lederer had not joined the Social Democratic party because he thought political parties were unlikely to accomplish much against large economic units and consolidated interests, but even he joined the Independent Social Democratic party in the revolutionary situation of the winter of 1918–19. Similar is the biography of Eduard Heimann. His father, the publisher Hugo Heimann, had for many years been a Social Democratic representative to the Reichstag and a close friend of the party chief, August Bebel. Having been exposed to "fatalistic evolutionism" at home, the younger Heimann was the only one of the group who was skeptical about the political effectiveness of the Social Democratic party. He was therefore active for a long time only in organizations with philosophies somewhat different from that of the party, like the circles of young socialists who tried to counter the deterministic materialism of the party theory with a philosophy based more on the individual and his or her subjective needs. He finally joined the party in 1926 but continued to seek his true theoretical home elsewhere. He eventually joined the circle of religious socialists that had formed around the Protestant theologian Paul Tillich, and in New York in 1944, when Heimann was fifty-five, he asked Tillich to baptize him.[27]

The German university has typically produced autonomous individuals trained to develop self-contained intellectual structures in the German philosophical tradition. By contrast, the activities the members of the reform group engaged in fostered in them a more cooperative, interdisciplinary approach to research even before they embarked on their academic careers in the mid 1920s. Thus Löwe, together with Colm, had initiated the gathering of statistical data—both on a national and on a comparative international level—on economic fluctuations. This work was done by a staff of young specialists in the Reich Statistical Office. Both men were also among the expert advisers accompanying German delegates to the many big international conferences on economics and reparation held prior to the adoption of the Dawes Plan.

In 1926 and 1927, respectively, Bernhard Harms, the head of the Institute of World Economics in Kiel, offered the two men professorships. In Kiel, they developed a systematic science of economics with international applicability. The Institute had been established in 1914, and before Löwe and

Colm were hired it had consisted only of a library and a newspaper archive. The research now produced in Kiel, most of which appeared in the Institute's publication *Weltwirtschaftliches Archiv*, soon attracted attention beyond Germany. The Paris experts of the Rockefeller Foundation had good reason for considering the Kiel Institute the most significant research center in the field of international economics.[28]

From 1926 on, the Institute also published the official economic reports commissioned by the Reich government. These reports had grown to over sixty printed volumes by the early 1930s and for a long time constituted the largest body of detailed economic research in Germany. Hans Neisser had been hired as a secretary for this project, and the work he did was so impressive that after a few months Harms offered him a formal position at the Institute. The way this group transformed the reports is also characteristic. Originally, all that had been planned was a survey of expert opinion, but gradually the emphasis shifted toward research by the group itself, such as the studies published by Colm and Neisser on foreign trade and some studies on small-scale industry by Löwe and Marschak, the latter of whom the Institute hired for a time for this express purpose. The publication of other collections also demonstrates the group's cooperative method of working.[29] Because of this experience in processing information and their probably unequaled knowledge of the structure of the German economy, these scholars would later become a valuable resource for the American administration after the outbreak of World War II.

The practical work the members of the group did in the labor unions and the active role Eduard Heimann and Adolf Löwe took in the ecumenical circle of religious socialists also show that these men were by no means captive to narrow, academic scholarship. Marschak and Colm taught courses in economics for adults at the university, for workers' education clubs, and they even tutored union leaders like Fritz Tarnow in the theory of the circular flow of money. Something of the group's sense of mission can also be seen in its launching of the journal *Neue Blätter für den Sozialismus* in 1930. This venture grew out of the—illusory—hope of reaching the anticapitalistic element among the educated young and of rendering middle-class voters immune to the appeal of national socialism and winning them for the Republic.

All these social and political activities were motivated by the wish to present the workers with realizable goals, to bring about change in the status quo, and to overcome the rigid, deterministic doctrines that had dominated the thinking of the Social Democratic party since the mid 1920s, doctrines first encouraged by Bebel's hope for the inevitable collapse of capitalism and later by Hilferding's theory of "organized capitalism."[30] These reform economists were not intent on a grand analysis of the social and economic system, such as the one that had informed the attempt to create a socialistic society after 1918. Analysis of that kind, they thought, projected broadly defined goals that could be attained only through a long and painstaking transformation of society. What they sought instead was a way to move institutions—and with them the social center of the system— toward a more stable and just future less plagued by economic crises.

The circle expanded in 1931 when Löwe went to the University of Frankfurt to assume the chair of Carl Grünberg, the founder and head of the Institute of Social Research, who had just resigned. A close cooperation developed especially among Löwe, his friend the theologian Paul Tillich, and the sociologist Karl Mannheim, who had recently been called to Frankfurt, too, to assume Franz Oppenheimer's chair. This cooperation was to continue during the exile in spite of great geographic distances.[31] There were many connections, too, between this group and the circle around Max Horkheimer, a friend of Löwe's from his student days. Horkheimer had been appointed to succeed Grünberg, head of the Institute, and had been given a newly established chair in the philosophical faculty. But the contact between Horkheimer and Löwe was more of a personal nature because the Institute's increasing shift toward philosophy seemed to Löwe to lack political perspective. Nevertheless, Löwe looked after the Institute's affairs in Frankfurt after its leading members, anticipating a National Socialist victory, moved to Switzerland in the fall of 1932. He continued to do so until he himself emigrated on April 2, 1933. But after 1933 and in the new social context of the United States, the different conceptions the reform economists and the members of the Institute had of the practical mission of economics engendered considerable conflicts of opinion and limited cooperation between the two groups.

5 / The New School for Social Research

1. The Founding of the "University in Exile"

Almost every exiled scholar who can be counted among the reform economists found a haven at the New School for Social Research in New York.
The importance of this institution for German scholarship in exile lies not
just in its having accepted the largest group of expelled university faculty
but also in its offering a place where the German tradition in the social
sciences, having just been eradicated in its country of origin, could be
carried on. The school's division of social sciences, staffed by an international faculty unique among American institutions of higher learning,
would soon become the most significant center of its kind in the United
States.

Even before the various aid committees became active, Alvin Johnson,
the director of the New School, had worked with unparalleled personal
dedication to lay the groundwork, so that over a dozen scholars could be
invited to New York. His "protest in deeds" was directed both against Nazi
barbarism and lethargy in the United States. It was meant not just to show
solidarity but also to demonstrate to the isolationist public that such
actions did not turn America into a land of refugees but rather made it a
center of international scholarship of the highest order.[1] Of course, Johnson also had a personal agenda, for up to 1933 the New School had been
only a small experimental institution for adult education.

The rescue action the New School undertook in 1933 was fully in keeping
with the institution's origins. It was founded in early 1919 by a group

of liberals and radical democrats, among them Thorstein Veblen, John Dewey, Charles Beard, Wesley C. Mitchell, the English socialist Harold Laski, and the German-born anthropologist Franz Boas from Columbia University. Johnson, too, was among the founders. He had studied economics and had been teaching since the turn of the century at various American universities, including Columbia, Chicago, Stanford, and Cornell.

This circle started publishing the *New Republic* in 1914 as a forum for the many scattered progressive groups in America. The New School was established in a similar spirit. At a time of isolationism and red-baiting following World War I, international understanding and a critical analysis of society were to be the guiding principles of the curriculum. Another element in the New School's campaign for a "new social order" was its emphasis on adult and workers' education. At that time hardly any programs of this sort existed because expectations of upward mobility were still widespread in America, which had been an open, dynamic society until the beginning of the century. The New School thus became the pacesetter for a number of similar institutions, such as the Rand School and the Affiliated Workers School, both established in the 1920s in New York. In order to remain free and independent, the New School did not accept money from interested institutions but financed its operation solely with student fees. Contributions from the founders made up for any shortfalls at the end of the year.[2]

The first connections with Germany date back to these early years. The New School obviously took its orientation from the secondary schools for adults, the *Volkshochschulen*, that were founded there after 1918, largely adopting their pedagogical and political goals. Contacts with Germany on a different level developed in the mid 1920s when Johnson's former teacher, the Columbia economist Edwin R. A. Seligman, appointed him coeditor of a planned lexicon of the social sciences. Like many colleagues of his generation, Seligman had studied in Germany under Karl Knies and Gustav Schmoller at the end of the nineteenth century, and now he wanted to produce a reference work in English comparable to the German *Handwörterbuch der Staatswissenschaften*, which had just appeared in its fourth edition. Seligman's project, financed by the Rockefeller and Carnegie foundations to the tune of $1.25 million, resulted in the mid 1930s in the *Encyclopaedia of the Social Sciences*. It grew to fifteen volumes and was the largest compendium of its kind, one that has not been surpassed to this day, even in the entire field of international social studies. Over 600 scholars all over the world were consulted, and they, along with the many personal contacts Johnson established on his trips to Europe, provided detailed insight into the current work in the social sciences both in Germany and internationally. Interest in the work being done in Germany was obviously strong, and the number of articles German scholars were asked to submit soon became so large that a problem arose concerning international balance. The editors had originally considered grouping the authors by nationality in the index, but when all the work was in this idea was quickly abandoned in order not to draw attention to the disproportionate number of German contributions. Gerhard Colm, Emil Lederer, Jakob Marschak, Fritz Lehmann, and Hans Speier all authored substantial contributions to the *Encyclopaedia*[3]—some of them more than one—and were among the scholars Johnson was to invite to the New School in 1933.

In the course of this work Johnson became acquainted with the focal points of German research, so that he knew quite clearly in 1933 whom he wanted. He had also always admired the German university system with its academic freedom, its stress on methodology, and its ideal of education as exemplified in the humanities. The son of a Danish immigrant, he was fluent in German and, having been trained in the institutionalist vein, he was familiar with German accomplishments in the social sciences from the nineteenth century on. He also had personal contacts with the younger generation of reform economists dating from his visits to Germany during the 1920s—the latest in 1932. In the political, theoretical, and methodological outlook of these economists' work he saw an important tool for cracking open the pragmatism and empiricism that prevailed in American academe. One of his convictions was that only a teacher with a mission could be a good teacher.[4] Thus he wanted to bring not just individual scholars to the New School but a fairly large group in order to import the original character of the German university system and transplant it in American soil. This by no means implies that he accepted uncritically all the interests and peculiarities of German scholars. He repeatedly poked fun at the excesses of the German system and at the affectations and elitist attitude of the typical German professor, including the tendency to crown his life's work, no matter in what discipline, with a "Tractat der philosophie, seven volumes."[5] Having learned to appreciate the "privileges of Anglo-American simplicities," Johnson was contemptuous of such traits; instead, he looked for like-minded "practical idealists" who had tried to translate their academic insights into reality. This was the main reason why he placed his hopes on those social scientists who, as outsiders in the German academic community, had proved not just in their writings but also in their political attitudes that the traditions of German academe had not distorted their outlook.

A final criterion in Johnson's selection was the search for a realistic strategy to overcome the Great Depression. Johnson himself was actively involved in this issue, having, among other things, been appointed to the Commission on Economic Reconstruction organized by Columbia University's President Butler. Compared to the state of discussion in Europe, the American debate over the depression seemed to him limited. It was focused primarily on stimulating consumer demand through halfhearted, credit-financed monetary inducements without further supporting measures. And it reminded Johnson of the club wielding of the market "Neanderthalers" who still believed that security and stability could be regained by adhering to old-fashioned individualism. Such prehistoric tools, Johnson was convinced, were no longer sufficient; the only possible way was social action, "individual security" through "social means."[6]

Just as Johnson had given a push in the direction of a new social order with the founding of the New School in 1919, so he intended through his rescue action of 1933 to set an example that could not be ignored and so encourage revitalization of neglected branches of the social sciences in America. The University in Exile he planned was to be restricted to the social sciences, because the economic crisis had pushed these fields, now and for the foreseeable future, into the "center of the battle" of critical analyses.[7] Thus Adolf Löwe, Emil Lederer, Jakob Marschak, Hans Neisser, and Karl Mannheim were among the names at the top of Johnson's wish list.

This selection reflected not just Johnson's personal evaluations. These social scientists, though mostly quite young, had earned a considerable reputation in other academic circles as well. The University of Chicago also compiled a list of names—even before the activities at the New School became known—in whom it had a great interest, and here, too, the top names in the social sciences were those of Mannheim, Marschak, and—especially—Lederer, who was described as "one of the leading economists of the world." Alvin Hansen, a New Dealer and later a prominent interpreter of Keynes, hoped also that the "special approach" of these members of the Kiel circle would have a strong impact on New Deal policies.

Even Schumpeter pleaded the cause of these economists with American colleagues because he considered them the best and most innovative in Germany, though he made no secret of his own, differing political convictions.[8]

Johnson's plans stood in marked contrast to the actions initiated shortly afterward by the Emergency Committee and the Rockefeller Foundation. These organizations, misjudging the nature of the Nazi rise to power, thought aid would be needed for only a relatively short period. They also felt their only chance for success lay in distributing the German scholars as widely as possible among American institutions of higher learning. Johnson recognized from the beginning that the rescue would be a long-term process and might turn into permanent integration. In choosing the name "University in Exile" for his project he wanted to demonstrate publicly that the university tradition now suppressed in Germany was to be preserved for an indefinite period.

Before the project could become reality, however, the arduous task of procuring the necessary funding had to be taken care of. Immediately after the first boycott of Jews in Germany on April 1, 1933, Johnson began to ask for support for his program among academic circles. He wanted to raise $120,000 to insure the salaries of fifteen scholars for two years. Although he wrote endless appeals, contributions trickled in only slowly. By the end of May 1933 he had received barely $12,000, and it looked as though his idea, which seemed fantastic to start with, might have to be postponed into the distant future. For European concepts the entire project must have seemed unrealistic, and even more so the naive optimism with which Johnson held on to his conviction that "things would still somehow work out." And indeed, a few days after he had asked the *New York Times* to publish an article on the planned University in Exile, he received a call from Hiram Halle, a businessman in the oil industry, who offered to put up all the necessary money.[9]

This made it possible by early June to contact the German scholars, but the delegate sent to Europe returned shortly without having accomplished his mission. He had been too late to reach the people he had hoped to talk to, and Löwe, Marschak, and Mannheim had already decided in favor of Britain. It was not until July, after a telegram had been sent to Lederer, who had first fled to London but then immediately traveled to New York for a short visit, that concrete steps could be taken to hire exiled scholars.

By this time many of the social scientists who were to come to the New

School already had the most dramatic phase of the transition behind them. Even before the Nazi "Law to Restore the Professional Civil Service" was published on April 7, 1933, the first of these scholars had left Germany because they had long been on the blacklists of Nazi students. Löwe and his family fled to Switzerland the day after the boycott of Jews. Under the illusion that Nazi rule would be short-lived, he had decided to accept an appointment at the University of Manchester before the invitation to the New School reached him. The same was true in the case of Jakob Marschak. Marschak fled to Paris in April when the rector of Heidelberg University demanded that he present proof of "Aryan descent" even though Marschak was not even on the university's payroll but was an unsalaried lecturer supported by a Rockefeller fellowship. After teaching at the International University at Santander in May, he received an offer for a position, also financed by Rockefeller money, at Oxford. He had been recommended for this job by the Norwegian economist Ragnar Frisch. Shortly before this, Frisch had pushed through Marschak's nomination to the International Econometric Society despite the opposition of the largely conservative membership. It was to be several years before Löwe and Marschak joined the New School.

Johnson was also too late in the case of Karl Mannheim, probably the most important German sociologist after Max Weber's death. A Jew born in Hungary, Mannheim too had fled Germany precipitously in April 1933 and had found work at the University of London through the mediation of Harold Laski.

Emil Lederer left Germany in a comparatively "legal" manner. He had received an invitation in February 1933 from the director of the International Labor Office to take part in a conference in Paris in early April. He duly informed the Prussian minister of higher education of his planned trip and then chose not to return to Germany, especially since he had just taken part in an antifascist congress called "The Free Word" in February 1933 together with Albert Einstein and the novelist Heinrich Mann.[10]

It would be wrong, however, to assume from these biographical details that the transition was consciously planned or unproblematic for these scholars. Their correspondence between April and July reflects desperate helplessness and great uncertainty about the immediate future. Before they learned about the efforts of Alvin Johnson and of the aid organizations, their prospects looked very dim. Unlike their colleagues of the Austrian neoclassical school, they had practically no solid international contacts in the scholarly world, and they had no way of knowing that they had already come to the attention of the American New Dealers. This was true even of the older and more established Lederer, who had taught in Japan for some time in the mid 1920s. In this uncertain situation, several of them, along with many other colleagues in similar straits, pinned their hopes primarily on Schumpeter at Harvard, who was flooded during these dramatic weeks with inquiries about possible lecture tours, guest semesters, and so on, in America.[11]

Other colleagues among the reform economists were still living in Germany under almost unbearable conditions. In Kiel some co-workers at the Institute of World Economics who had joined the Brownshirts immediately after the Nazi takeover attacked Hans Neisser and Gerhard Colm with particular brutality—seriously injuring Colm—because these men's grandparents had been Jews.[12] Johnson's and Lederer's rescue efforts were aimed especially at this group. Lederer had rejected the offer from Manchester after his visit to New York and settled instead in London to help expedite the New School's hiring efforts from there.

Hans Speier functioned as a courier to Germany. He had earlier worked as Lederer's assistant and as editor of the *Archiv für Sozialwissenschaft und Sozialpolitik* published by Lederer. As a teacher at the Hochschule für Politik in Berlin, he too lost his job when the school was transformed into a Nazi elite school in 1933. His task was to deliver invitations to the scholars Lederer and Johnson had chosen. Equipped with a new preference list—enlarged by inquiries passed on by Schumpeter—Johnson himself went to London to see Lederer and to settle the final contracts. In the hectic and dramatic climate of these weeks, the task turned into a drawn-out and wearisome affair even for Johnson. A number of the desired candidates had already decided to go elsewhere; some could not make up their minds because they were negotiating elsewhere and did not know anything about the New School as an institution; others were simply afraid of faraway America. It was early August before he had assembled the group that would finally constitute the University in Exile. The core was made up of economists: the agricultural expert Karl Brandt from the Agricultural College in Berlin; the public finance expert Gerhard Colm from the Institute of World Economics in Kiel; the former editor of the financial section of the *Frankfurter Zeitung*, Arthur Feiler, who had just become a professor at the University of Königsberg; Eduard Heimann from the University of Hamburg; Emil Lederer, who had just been called to Berlin from the University of Heidelberg in 1931; and, finally, Frieda Wunderlich, an authority on labor theory and social policy, former professor of the Berufspädagogisches Institut in Berlin, and member of the Prussian Diet. To these were added representatives from related disciplines, like the jurist Hermann Kantorowicz; the sociologists Hans Speier, Albert Salomon, and Erich von Hornbostel; and the Gestalt psychologist Max Wertheimer. In early March, during the Nazi terror following the burning of the Reichstag, Wertheimer had left Germany in panicked flight and gone to Czechoslovakia, where Johnson's invitation caught up with him.

Löwe, Mannheim, and Marschak declined Johnson's invitation, as did the theologian Paul Tillich. Tillich, however, maintained old friendships among the religious socialists, stayed in close contact with the New School group after he joined Union Theological Seminary in New York, and was a regular guest at New School events. Others who did not come to the New School were the philosopher Ernst Cassirer and the jurists Gustav Radbruch and Hermann Heller. In the case of Hans Neisser, Johnson lost out to the Wharton School of Finance at the University of Pennsylvania, which, because of its links to the labor unions, also wanted a German reform economist of high standing. The decision as to where Lederer and Neisser would go was reached by drawing lots. Like Löwe and Marschak, Neisser eventually joined the New School after Arthur Feiler's death in 1943.

The only New School faculty that did not conform to the homogeneous profile of the group were the liberal economists Arthur Feiler and Karl Brandt, the latter being the only agricultural economist to have been fired in 1933 because of his opposition to the interests of the conservative landowner class. In exile he turned more and more into a German nationalist, however. After many conflicts within the New School group aggravated by the fact that Brandt, an authority on agricultural matters, was completely out of place in the metropolis of New York, he soon left the New School to join the Food Research Institute at Stanford. Nor was Feiler able to make much of a mark; he died quite soon, without having had any impact on the profile of the New School.

Others of that "Mayflower" group who stayed for only a short while were Kantorowicz, who moved on to the London School of Economics after just one year, and Hornbostel, who was forced to give up teaching in early 1934 because of illness. To fill their places came two former Prussian civil servants, the Social Democrat Hans Staudinger and the Democrat Arnold Brecht, both of whom had been put out of office as early as July 1932 after Chancellor Franz von Papen's coup d'état. Johnson hoped that their practical experience would add a useful perspective to the discussion of the economic crisis and generally strengthen the basis of New Deal policies.

The two men also had considerable scholarly work to their credit in their special fields, Staudinger as the theoretician of *Gemeinwirtschaft* and Arnold Brecht—the former director of the constitutional department of the Reich Ministry of the Interior and later Prussian representative in the Reichsrat—as an expert on constitutional and administrative matters as well as on public finance. Staudinger, who had joined the Reichstag after the November 1932 election as a Social Democrat, left Germany precipitously after an arrest by the Nazis. He was about to accept a job as an adviser in Turkey when Lederer approached him with an invitation from the New School. By contrast, Brecht, who had been permanently barred from the civil service on August 30, 1933, traveled to New York with an official permit from the German authorities to assume a temporary guest professorship. The biographical details of his case are interesting because they illustrate some of the opportunities and psychological inclinations of a German intellectual not directly threatened by national socialism because he was neither a Jew nor a socialist. But as an attorney of the Prussian government he had come under fire for his democratic stand before the Constitutional High Court (Staatsgerichtshof) after Papen's coup d'état in 1932 in Prussia. Brecht was initially reluctant to burn his bridges behind him in Germany, asking to be permitted to return to his home country at whatever time he chose and in fact regularly spending his summer vacations in Germany in the following years. This soon gave rise to major conflicts with other colleagues.[13]

Hans Simons, another high-ranking civil servant and the son of the former president of the Reich Supreme Court, joined the group in early 1935. He had been director of the Berlin Hochschule für Politik and then, until Papen's coup d'état, governor of the Prussian province of Lower Silesia. As a long-standing member of the Social Democratic party and a religious socialist he was one of those dismissed from the civil service in 1933 for "political unreliability." After working temporarily at the London School of Economics with a grant from the Rockefeller Foundation, he was invited in September 1934 to come to New York. There he did not distinguish himself particularly as a scholar but was active primarily as an administrator, first as dean of the Graduate Faculty and from 1950 until his retirement in 1960 as president of the New School.[14]

By the end of September 1933 most of the first group of scholars had arrived in New York, and in October the University in Exile opened its first fall semester, an event accompanied by considerable publicity.[15] Now that his institution was fully functioning, Johnson could start thinking about making use of the money offered by the Emergency Committee and the Rockefeller Foundation to finance more positions. This enabled him to bring the Italian political scientist Max Ascoli, a former student of Gaetano Salvemini, to the New School in the winter of 1933. Ascoli had lost his job teaching at the University of Cagliari in 1931 after the purge of the Italian universities in the late 1920s and after repeated arrests. He had been living in the United States supported by a fellowship from the Rockefeller Foundation. The foundation also paid his salary at the New School for the next few years. Until his fellow countryman Nino Levi joined the faculty as professor of sociology in the late 1930s Ascoli was the only Italian at the New School, a situation he found increasingly problematic because of the difficulty of asserting himself in a circle of exclusively German colleagues.[16] The social philosopher Horace M. Kallen from Columbia University, who had been among the founders of the New School, was the only American to be asked to teach in the Graduate Faculty during the winter of 1933–34, and even he was born in Germany, although his family immigrated to the United States when he was a small child.

Support from the Rockefeller Foundation, the Emergency Committee, and other organizations made it possible to hire several more scholars. One of them was Alfred Kähler from Kiel, who ran a secondary school for adults in Schleswig-Holstein after earning a diploma as a political economist. The school was turned into a Nazi work camp in 1933. Impressed by Kähler's dissertation, completed in 1932—a dissertation Löwe considered the equivalent of a habilitation (a paper that qualified its author to teach at a university)—A. C. Pigou tried to obtain a fellowship for him at Cambridge. He did not succeed because Keynes, when he heard that Kähler had earlier learned the trade of locksmithing, remarked that in that case the man would be able to make a living by other means. Löwe then put in a special word for Kähler with the Rockefeller people.

Other new arrivals at the New School were the sociologist Carl Mayer, who had taught at the Frankfurt Academy of Labor until it was shut down by the storm troopers, and the jurist and industrial manager Fritz Lehmann, who as assistant to Eugen Schmalenbach, founder of management science in Germany at the University of Cologne, also lost his job.[17] And,

University in Exile Opens First Semester in New York

Faculty of dismissed or furloughed German professors at the New School for Social Research. *Left to right, seated:* Emil Lederer, Alvin Johnson, director of the New School for Social Research; Frieda Wunderlich, and Karl Brandt. *Left to right, standing:* Hans Speier, Max Wertheimer, Arthur Feiler, Eduard Heimann, Gerhard Colm, and E. von Hornbostel. (*New York Times*, October 4, 1933) *Photo credit: Times Wide World Photo*

finally, a fellowship from the Littauer Fund made it possible to hire the young jurist of the same name, Rudolf Littauer, from the University of Leipzig in the winter of 1933–34. However, Littauer left the New School in 1938 to become secretary of the New York branch of the Notgemeinschaft deutscher Wissenschaftler im Ausland.[18]

The University in Exile was renamed when it opened on October 1, 1933, and was now officially the Graduate Faculty of Political and Social Science. This was done, first of all, because the German scholars objected to the original name, which implied a provisional state and emphasized their outsider status within the American system of higher education. Second, the use of the term "university" for a single department of social sciences was misleading. Although the Graduate Faculty started operating under the aegis of the New School, it became an autonomous institution that had its own independent administration, its own dean, a separate budget, and separate course offerings. This made sense, among other reasons, because it would not have been possible otherwise to obtain the necessary funds from the various dispensers of refugee aid. Before a new constitution was adopted at the beginning of 1935 that gave legal status to the new arrangements, the school's affairs were conducted by a provisional advisory committee. Johnson had enlisted John Dewey, Edwin R. A. Seligman, Felix Frankfurter, and Robert M. Hutchins, president of the University of Chicago—all of them illustrious and influential New Dealers—to serve on the committee.

Johnson had made clear when he first started planning his project that the primary goal of the new Graduate Faculty was to internationalize the American social sciences by importing first-rate European scholars. The school's constitution reflected the same mission. It stated explicitly that the institution's policies were to be determined not by criteria of race, religion, or political conviction but solely by standards of scholarship and the competence and integrity of the members.[19] The tactical considerations exhibited by the major aid organizations in their placement policies give a sense of how little these elementary principles could be taken for granted in academe in the United States at that point in history. Thus, at the time when the Graduate Faculty was formulating its constitution, prestigious Bryn Mawr College, which was also deeply committed to helping the immigrants, inquired "in all confidentiality" whether Eduard Heimann, who had recommended a number of colleagues, was Jewish.[20] It therefore hardly appears as an exaggeration if the New School claimed during those years that it was the only institution of higher learning in America completely free of racial discrimination.[21]

Unlike the refugee scholars who were hired individually by other universities and colleges, the group at the New School had the good fortune not only of remaining together but also of continuing to teach in their accustomed mode. Given the traditional division between undergraduate and graduate education in the United States, many other immigrated scholars were generally able to or allowed to teach only undergraduate courses, which accounts for their shock, so often expressed, at the educational level of American students. By contrast, the New School scholars of the Graduate Faculty were able to work with advanced students. Johnson required that everyone teach one course in the adult education program, too, but this was nothing new for them, since most of them had already worked with similar groups in Germany.

It would be several years before the Graduate Faculty received full accreditation as an institution authorized to award graduate degrees, and even then it remained an anomaly in academe because it did not include an undergraduate college with a bachelor of arts program. The lack of infrastructure, including such things as an adequate library and a legally required pension program for faculty members, resulted in New York State's Board of Education granting only partial accreditation in 1934. The school was permitted to train students, but master's and doctoral examinations had to be taken at New York University. In spite of this anomalous state, American students who had finished college elsewhere were drawn to the school, for there was a fivefold increase in students within just a few years. The fall semester of 1933 had opened with 92 students, and by the fall of 1940 the number had already risen to 520. At this point the Graduate Faculty received the long-awaited "permanency," which included the right to administer all examinations.[22]

The school still was in a provisional state, however, because its financial position was precarious from the beginning—and was always to remain so. The administrative records that are still extant show over a period of decades how the school had to learn to live hand-to-mouth. Again and again Alvin Johnson, utterly convinced of his mission and equipped with an astonishing optimism and the necessary self-confidence, succeeded in finding donors at the last minute to fill the financial gaps. He was later ably assisted in this task by Hans Staudinger, who in his many years as dean exhibited great talent and stamina in locating new sources of money. In the first decades the salaries of the group, which soon numbered over thirty, were never assured for more than one or two years ahead. The many fundraising dinners and membership drives brought in only modest sums when measured against the expenditures. Even the practice, begun in 1935, of nominating influential and affluent persons to the Board of Trustees did not spell economic security. Without the financial support of foundations and philanthropists, who sometimes gave several hundred thousand dollars at a time, the Graduate Faculty could hardly have survived and could not have embarked on its major research projects, especially during and after World War II. We have already mentioned the grants of the Rockefeller Foundation, which by 1945 totaled over $540,000 and were earmarked for salaries and projects. During this period the school also received about $100,000 from the Rosenwald family—into which Max Ascoli had married—an amount that was to rise to almost $400,000 by the 1960s. Doris Duke, heiress to a tobacco empire and a donor to Duke University in North Carolina as well, gave $250,000; roughly $100,000 came from the Lucius D. Littauer Fund, and over $23,000 from the New York Foundation—to mention some of the most generous donations.[23]

A letter written by Johnson to the Rockefeller Foundation in March 1935, when the funds provided since 1933 had run out, may serve to illustrate the powers of persuasion he employed in his quest for funding. With great urgency Johnson tried to convince the foundation that it should contribute about $50,000 of the necessary $375,000 needed to enable the Graduate Faculty to continue its work for the next five years. This longer perspective was necessary, he explained, first of all to be able to attract students but also to plan for the eventuality that the Graduate Faculty might not work out as a permanent institution after all and the faculty just hired would have to look for other jobs. If this were to happen, they would be competing for funds with the clients of the other aid committees. A financial commitment on the part of the Rockefeller Foundation would not only serve a bellwether function for other potential sponsors, Johnson went on, but would above all contradict the suggestion voiced in public with increasing frequency that the New School was employing persons who were perhaps fired for good reason by the Nazis. A refusal by the foundation, Johnson argued dramatically, would be taken as support for this unfounded suspicion. Also, up to this point the Graduate Faculty had been financed mostly by Jewish contributions and it would have to continue to rely on them, which was bound to give rise to further misunderstandings in the public mind. Quite apart from the fact—irrelevant from the school's point of view—that only half of its eighteen members belonged to the Jewish faith, there was no good reason why Jewish organizations should continue to shoulder the burden of financing the school by themselves since academic freedom was not just a Jewish concern.[24]

The budgets for the first two years in fact show that even in the future it would be impossible for the school to pay its bills without massive outside help. Of the yearly totals spent, which amounted to $72,000 and $79,000 for 1933 and 1934, respectively, over 80 percent were covered by contributions from Hiram Halle alone; student fees made up barely 7 percent. The distribution of the expenditures is also significant: $55,000 and $62,750, or almost 80 percent of the budget, were spent on academic salaries; about $4,000 per year went to subsidize the newly founded publication *Social Research;* and $3,000 were spent annually for secretaries. That left a meager $37 and $500 for building up the library.[25] The figures show that the faculty had to make do with almost no secretarial help and without a library. They also show that the average annual salary was less than $3,500. To be sure, salaries were graduated, but even top earners like Lederer and Brecht did not make more than $5,000, which was not even half of what most of the major universities paid for comparable positions. A man like Schumpeter at that time earned about $12,000.

In spite of Johnson's eloquence, the Rockefeller Foundation rejected his request for $50,000, citing its principle of not awarding general grants to institutions.[26] However, in the next few years Johnson managed to receive most of the sum he had originally asked for in the form of specific grants for salaries. Although the foundation reiterated every year during the annual negotiations that its assumption of half the cost of salary was definitely for one year only and that afterward the institution had to rely on its own means to pay the person in question, it kept making exceptions for the financially strapped New School. Thus Ascoli, Simons, and Kähler from the first group and, after 1938, several refugees from Austria received continuing financial assistance until the 1940s, when the foundation, in response to the defeat of France and the new wave of European scholars arriving in the United States, formulated a new policy with the New School and changed the guidelines of its funding.

2. Center for Refugee Problems

In spite of the permanent financial straits in which the Graduate School found itself, it accepted a number of other German and European refugees throughout the 1930s and not just at times of extreme emergency, as when the "annexation" of Austria sent a new wave of scholars to the United States. By the time war broke out, the number of faculty members had almost doubled—from eighteen in the spring of 1934 to thirty-three in the summer of 1939. This was before 1940–41, when the New School became the last refuge for over 170 scholars in the wake of France's defeat. Contrary to its practice in the days of the University in Exile, when the "Mayflower" group presented a relatively uniform profile, the school from the mid 1930s on also accepted as emergency cases refugees of quite different political and philosophical backgrounds. The criterion of selection now was how original and substantial a contribution the scholars might make to American scholarship and not a reform-oriented outlook. This was less true in economics than in areas peripheral to the social sciences. The conservative philosopher Leo Strauss may be the most famous example. Strauss, a scholar at the Akademie für die Wissenschaft des Judentums in Berlin, had left Germany in 1932 with a Rockefeller fellowship to go to England and France. He joined the Graduate Faculty in early 1938, where he was to remain for ten years but had no notable impact beyond the school. It was not until he moved to the University of Chicago in 1948 that he became the celebrated guru of American conservatives because of his antimodern philosophy of history, which rejected all Enlightenment traditions, regarding them as modern destructionism, and instead aimed to reach only a small elite of the like-minded. In Chicago he conveyed to a growing number of students his antiegalitarian message that a just society was an impossibility.[27]

The sociologist and social philosopher Ernst Karl Winter was also a conservative. A representative of romantic, Catholic socialism from Austria, his career as a university teacher had been blocked at the end of the 1920s because the faculty at the University of Vienna was by and large German-national in outlook. After the workers' unrest of 1934, Chancellor Dollfuss asked Winter, as vice-mayor of Vienna, to draw up plans for the integration of labor into the Austrian corporate government, and Winter continued to advocate corporate monarchy in Austria as a bulwark against national socialism until 1938. He was recommended to the Graduate Faculty by the Emergency Committee—as Strauss was by the Rockefeller Foundation—and the two organizations paid these scholars' salaries. But because of his dubious political stance, which hardly fit in with the antifascist atmosphere of the Graduate Faculty, Winter was let go very shortly.

The situation was quite different in the case of Kurt Riezler, a former German diplomat and later administrator and philosophy professor at the University of Frankfurt. Riezler had been dismissed from his post by the National Socialists in 1933 because he was primarily responsible for the university's hiring policies, that is, the appointment of progressive social scientists. Riezler was offered a position in the Graduate Faculty in early

1938 because of his experience at the University of Frankfurt as well as in government, having served for a time as chief of staff for Reich president Friedrich Ebert. He, too, did not distinguish himself particularly in his academic field, philosophy, while at the New School. His overly metaphysical thinking ran counter to the basic position of most of his colleagues in the Graduate Faculty, and because of his speculative approach he also failed to have much impact on the broader field of American scholarship. He had never thought of himself as a pure scholar; his abilities lay more in the direction of academic management, in stimulating and influencing ideas and making things happen. Riezler's importance for the Graduate Faculty therefore lay mostly in the lasting influence he had on internal discussions as an experienced and broadly educated man of letters. He was good at voicing provocative questions that guided his colleagues' debates on social theory—debates often in danger of becoming narrowly one-dimensional— back into the broader channels of fundamental philosophical reflection.[28]

Other arrivals from Austria included Erich Hula, former assistant to the constitutional lawyer Hans Kelsen, and Felix Kaufmann, an epistemologist and Husserl student who had started out as a jurist of the Kelsen school. In this same period the Italian sociologist Nino Levi and the Spanish political scientist Fernando de los Rios, ambassador to Washington during the brief existence of the Spanish Republic, were also appointed, to give a few more examples suggesting the variety this university of exiles included toward the end of the 1930s. Unlike Strauss and Winter and with the exception of Levi, who died after a few months, all these scholars were to stay at the New School permanently and have an important impact there. Hula had originally been invited to the New School by Johnson in the winter of 1933–34 after he had been fired at Cologne together with his teacher, but he first chose to return to Austria, where he became secretary of the Labor Office in Graz. (Hans Simons was invited in Hula's place at that time.) Together with John Herz and Hans Morgenthau, Hula was among the German jurists who introduced questions of international law and comparative government into American academe. Kaufmann was to do important, groundbreaking work in methodology. He continued working on the epistemological theory he had started to develop in Vienna as a member of the circle of logical positivists there, and he also contributed studies on the tautological nature of logic and mathematics. Building on this work, Alfred Schütz was later to introduce phenomenology into American thinking. The Spaniard de los Rios, being intimately acquainted with Latin American

75

developments, added some perspectives to the global economic analyses begun by the German group during World War II. These analyses culminated after 1945 in many studies on underdevelopment in the Third World.

As word spread about Alvin Johnson's commitment to the cause of refugee scholars and about the special status of the Graduate Faculty as an emigré university, the New School received a flood of requests for help. Interestingly enough, these inquiries came less from the exiled scholars themselves than from American institutions and university faculties. Although the large foundations and the Emergency Committee could not award any aid unless a university or college had decided to hire a particular scholar, the Graduate Faculty enabled it, as the cases of Strauss and Winter show, to act independently and without delay. In addition, the New School became the central place to which American university faculty and other interested parties who wanted to help a German colleague could turn if they were unable or reluctant to invite the scholar to their own institutions.

Quite clearly, too, the New School served as an alibi for the inaction at a number of universities. This is especially true of Harvard University, whose faculty recommended many of the most highly qualified scholars to the New School but did not itself accept any immigrants.[29] Indeed, it seemed as though Schumpeter and Haberler in particular had an interest in "keeping other German gentlemen away," as the Harvard political scientist Carl J. Friedrich put it. Immediately after 1933, when Schumpeter became an important figure to whom exiled scholars turned for help and advice and when Johnson, too, had asked him to participate in his planned rescue action, Schumpeter clearly stated his refusal to be involved in any actions not directly related to his professional duties and competencies as an economist. He insisted that efforts on behalf of the refugees might be taken as an affront by the Nazis, and he even stated explicitly that he had nothing against the Hitler regime because he knew what conditions had been like in Germany before. This remark presumably grew out of his deep-seated resentment toward the Social Democratic government of Prussia, which he blamed among other things for conspiring against his appointment to the University of Berlin in 1931. In reality, it was the Berlin faculty, dominated by conservative adherents of the historical school, that was opposed to hiring him. Schumpeter not only expressed this unfounded suspicion repeatedly among American colleagues but also criticized the Weimar governments in his *History of Economic Analysis,* written in the 1940s and published posthumously. There he asserted that from 1918 on there had been a widespread tendency in German universities to favor candidates with leftist political leanings and that, given this situation, the National Socialist practice did not represent "such a great change and did not [cause] as much harm as a foreign observer might expect." Johnson's protests against such a distortion of the truth were of no avail. With his typical ambivalence Schumpeter remained noncommittal toward the future development of Nazi Germany. "Recent events" there, he wrote, "may mean a catastrophe, but they also may mean salvation."[30]

The antirefugee attitude of the great American universities as expressed by Isaiah Bowman, president of Johns Hopkins University, assumed a different guise. Bowman argued that since the capacity of American institutions of higher learning to absorb emigré scholars was limited, the New School was the only place where the refugee problem could be solved to everyone's satisfaction.[31] The New School had to respond—and did so with no little indignation—to requests even from Britain, since attempts were made there, too, to pass some emigrés on to the New School. An example was the historian Veit Valentin, who had been at London University for years and had long since acquired British citizenship but was strongly "recommended" to the New School in response to growing anti-German sentiments on the eve of World War II.[32]

Another wave of applications to help friends in danger came from various emigré intellectuals. Among these were Thomas Mann, who pleaded for the writer Max Brod, and the former Prussian minister of the interior Grzesinski, who hoped to find a place in the Graduate Faculty for the journalist Georg Bernhard. From 1935–36 on, the New School was inundated with about 5,000 requests of this sort annually, all of which had to be answered and for all of which contacts to other organizations had to be sought. In addition, the aid committees considered the members of the Graduate Faculty an important source of information, and—particularly since Colm, Lederer, and Wertheimer were the American representatives of the Notgemeinschaft deutscher Wissenschaftler im Ausland—responding to these inquiries was something else they had to do on top of their regular schedules of teaching and doing research.[33]

The New School people had to deal not only with vexing placement policies but also with the indifference of many German scholars who had found teaching jobs and showed little interest in helping their less privileged colleagues. One gets a glimpse of this side of emigré psychology from the constant complaints in the newsletters of the Notgemeinschaft to the effect that only a small group of colleagues was taking seriously the social responsibility of helping others who were going through difficult times. The majority of those not in acute need were becoming more and more indifferent.[34] The lack of commitment made itself felt not only in the crucial area of fundraising but also in the reluctance to set up new support centers that could pick up some of the work load and pass on recommendations.

Thus most of the actions initiated by German emigré scholars in the United States originated with the small group at the New School. The same pattern is evident in the relatively unimpressive contributions to the Notgemeinschaft. Although the average salary at the Graduate Faculty was only about a third of what someone like Schumpeter earned, the Graduate Faculty members made the largest annual per capita contributions.[35] In addition, they followed the lead of faculty at Oxford and committed themselves to donating 3 percent of their salaries (the members of the Institute for Advanced Study in Princeton soon followed their example). The sum raised this way was large enough to provide twenty scholarships for young scholars. This generosity was intended not just to relieve the most urgent material needs but also to serve as a moral example, and in some cases it proved effective. The large foundations had been reluctant to support young emigré scholars because they represented competition for jobs that young American academics would otherwise fill. But some foundations did come around to funding positions for a few individuals.[36]

A similar action was aimed less at helping scholars in need. Together with some other German intellectuals primarily in New York—among them the journalist Toni Stolper, the theologian Paul Tillich, and the economist Friedrich Pollock from the Institute of Social Research—a number of members of the New School founded the so-called Selfhelp for German Emigrés in the fall of 1936. The plan of this group was to ask emigrés from all circles and camps to impose a tax on themselves and thus to accumulate a fund that could then be used for prompt one-time assistance in situations of extreme emergency. The idea was to work closely with existing organizations and to offer help in the many cases—especially in Europe—that did not fit the guidelines of any of the religious and political groups. Within a few months the Selfhelp group had assembled a list of almost 400 donors whose contributions made it possible within the first year to assist in 500 emergency cases, mostly in Prague and Paris, with a total amount of about $10,000.[37]

Apart from these social concerns, the New School also became an important center of communication among emigrés and was involved from the beginning in antifascist activities. Alvin Johnson not only was a member of the advisory councils of the Emergency Committee, the National Refugee Service, and other aid organizations but also belonged to the American section of the World Aid Committee for Victims of Fascism, founded by Willi Münzenberg in France, the American Committee against Fascist Oppression in Germany, and the Solidarity Committee for Awarding the Nobel Peace Prize to Carl von Ossietzky. Although the members of the Graduate Faculty defined themselves from the beginning as immigrants and remained aloof from all exile groups, from their politics, and from the bickering among them (only Staudinger and Kähler had closer ties early on to the German Labor Delegation composed of German Social Democrats), the rooms at the New School became the most important meeting place of various political exile organizations as well as a cultural center where many poetry readings and theater productions were put on. As early as the mid 1930s the composer Hanns Eisler was invited to teach at the New School. This cultural link took on a permanent official form in 1940 when Johnson invited Erwin Piscator, former director of the Berlin Volksbühne, to build a department of dramatic arts—the Dramatic Workshop—on whose studio stage an interesting combination of classical and avant-garde theater took place in the 1940s. Tennessee Williams and Arthur Miller worked on film scripts here, and Marlon Brando, Harry Belafonte, Rod Steiger, and Shelley Winters began their acting careers at the Dramatic Workshop.[38]

3. The Rescue Action of 1940–1941

With the German invasion of France in May 1940 and France's capitulation a few weeks later, the refugee problem once more became critical. With possibilities in the United States for finding jobs for the expected new wave of refugees unchanged—or worse because of the imagined or actual saturation of the academic market—it was once more the New School that stepped into the breach and offered to take in over 100 scholars within a few months. In a combined rescue action with the Rockefeller Foundation, another fifty scholars were brought to America, thirty-four of whom also ended up at the New School.

Contrary to its ambivalent stance in 1933, the Rockefeller Foundation now expressed the suspicion right after the war broke out that the United

States might soon be the only haven for the many European intellectuals fleeing the advance of Nazi troops, in particular since there was no guarantee that the Scandinavian countries would not be drawn into the military conflict as well. These fears were to prove justified all too soon with the German attacks on Denmark, Norway, Holland, and Belgium beginning in April 1940. Plans for renewed help were immediately begun at the foundation, and a functioning program was in place by May.

The scenario was based on a total Nazi victory in Europe, which would halt all intellectual work and research, leaving the United States as the only country where free thought and independent research would remain possible for the next five, ten, or perhaps even twenty years. Even before the exodus of intellectuals from all over Europe became a reality, a project was drawn up to bring to America about 100 academics from Britain, 75 from France, and smaller groups from the other countries. In view of the anticipated costs, the directors quickly reduced these numbers to a maximum of 100, particularly since the foundation was already committed to taking care of almost sixty scholars as part of a previously adopted program to help intellectuals driven from Germany.[39] The new action focused once again on rescuing social scientists because similar positive influences were expected to come from them as had come from the immigrant generation of 1933. In the collapse of European civilization that was taking place now, the planners at the Rockefeller Foundation saw another chance to advance American culture and civilization.

A few influential American social scientists were to be consulted confidentially on the selection process and the actual execution of the project. "Thus we could be ready if the final tragedy occurs." It was clear to the Rockefeller people that, once their plans became known, the "elbow-out attitude" would immediately flare up again at the American universities, but they hoped that the storm would blow over quickly because, first of all, the emotional climate would be different after a total Nazi victory in Europe than it had been in 1933 and, second, the West European scholars— most of whom were not Jews—would fit much better than many of the German refugees into the American academic milieu. Also, the idea was not so much to find permanent positions for the new refugees at universities as to build up major, independent research centers where the scholars would be able in quiet seclusion and "without publicity" to analyze the most recent events in Europe and provide urgently needed help in guiding future American policy.[40]

These plans represented a total revision of the foundation's refugee policy. Up to now the Rockefeller Foundation had wanted to play only a subsidiary role by providing financial help for salaries after a university or college had decided to hire a scholar. Now it initiated action on its own. By early June of 1940 it had already compiled a list of European scholars it felt strongly should be brought to the United States. Among them were the internationally renowned economists Ragnar Frisch from Oslo, Jorgen Pedersen from Aarhus, and Jan Tinbergen from The Hague. The implementation of the second step, finding universities willing to take scholars, immediately ran up against the same obstacles the earlier efforts had encountered. The Rockefeller people were told by Stephen Duggan, the chairman of the Emergency Committee, that the universities had not changed their attitudes toward refugees and were unlikely to make a significant commitment to the foundation's actions. Alvin Johnson was the only one to support the program; in fact, he had already begun to work along similar lines himself and proposed to the Rockefeller Foundation to bring "a fairly indefinite number of foreign scholars, not less than one hundred," to the New School without delay, if he could raise the necessary funds.[41]

With boundless optimism and eloquent persuasiveness he tried to convince the Rockefeller people—at the time he was unaware of their own preliminary activities—that the United States had barely begun the real work of help and could do far more if it were only willing. There were 60,000 college and university teachers in the United States, he argued, and the 400 scholars placed so far through aid organizations plus a maximum of 200 who had found jobs without such aid added up to just 1 percent of this number. Consequently, there was no reason, despite all the pessimistic talk of colleges and universities being overrun by immigrants, why at least twice the number already placed could not be absorbed.[42]

Because of the resistance the Rockefeller people had run up against elsewhere, they eagerly responded to Johnson's offer. All of a sudden Johnson seemed to them to be the only person really able to handle the refugee problem with the necessary aggressiveness and ingenuity, being far "better fitted for the task than anyone and vastly superior to Mr. Duggan" of the Emergency Committee. No one had "so unselfishly or so effectively served the refugees" as he, even though he was, as was duly noted, already sixty-six years old.[43]

In July the president of the foundation endorsed this new program, and by early August grants and travel costs were approved for the first seventeen scholars. This group included not only Frenchmen but also some Germans who had been driven from their country in 1933, among them Adolf Löwe (after naturalization in Great Britain in 1939, he changed his name to Adolph Lowe), his student Fritz Burchardt, and Wilhelm Röpke. The fact that of the three only Lowe ended up in America whereas Burchardt was able to stay in England and Röpke in Geneva may be a sign that in this first phase of the program the intentions were still largely prophylactic, namely, to save qualified individuals before the German troops overran all of Europe and blocked all routes of escape.

The speedy and successful start of the joint rescue program was accompanied by some serious worries within the Rockefeller Foundation about Johnson's strategy. Since part of the agreement was that the arriving scholars were to be hired for a maximum of two years, during which time they would become acculturated enough to take care of themselves independently, there was concern that the New School might be taking on more than it could handle if these expectations did not work out. In addition, the foundation suspected that Johnson did not always have a temporary stay in mind but wanted to keep permanently a number of scholars who fit into the research program of the Graduate Faculty.

Given the faculty's history to date, this was not an unfounded suspicion, for the faculty itself had originally been conceived as merely a temporary springboard for many of the scholars. In fact, however, only Karl Brandt had left the faculty, which had in the meantime grown to fifty members. The suspicion grew even stronger when Johnson announced his plan of placing the expected refugees in a new Institute of World Affairs that was to be founded in imitation of the Kiel Institute and to continue the work done by that group in the 1920s. With the arrival of Lowe, the most important people of the Kiel group were now assembled at the New School.[44]

Thus the Rockefeller Foundation could already see the danger looming on the horizon that after two years it might find itself responsible for the Graduate Faculty with its 50 permanent and 100 temporary members as well as for an annual debt load of several thousand dollars. In the following months, discussion of the joint emergency program was constantly accompanied by inquiries from the foundation about the degree to which the new scholars had emancipated themselves from the New School, until Johnson finally declared indignantly that he had no intention of putting his exile university into the hands of the Rockefeller people.[45] After this the foundation refrained from bringing up the subject again, although it did, as anticipated, in many cases have to go on financing scholars beyond the first two years. In several circular letters to the new scholars involved, Johnson kept mentioning the limited possibilities at the New School.[46] At the same time, however, with the help of $250,000 Doris Duke contributed toward the founding of the Institute of World Affairs, he was able to remove several scholars from the Rockefeller Foundation's payroll. In addition, the France Libre movement of General de Gaulle financed some of the new French scholars.

The overall results of the emergency program should certainly have sufficed to reassure the donors within the foundation, for they proved unfounded the suspicions long held about Johnson's strategy. Of the approximately 100 scholars originally figured on, 89 were actually invited, and 52 came to the United States. The proportions of their distribution are interesting: Thirty-four were placed in the New School alone; three went to Columbia University; two to Yale; one each to nine different universities in the United States and Brazil; and four found jobs at various research institutes, such as the National Bureau of Economic Research and the Brookings Institution. Of the thirty-four scholars who went to the New School only one, Adolph Lowe, soon received a full professorship. Johnson had brought Lowe over from Manchester before the emergency program was organized and had never made a secret of his desire to keep him. Of the other thirty-three, seventeen could be placed in other colleges and universities within the following two years, and three French scholars gave up their grants because they were paid by France Libre. That meant that after the initial two-year period had elapsed, only thirteen were still at the New School under the auspices of the emergency program of 1940, and the Rockefeller Foundation kept granting extensions and paying their salaries until the program finally ended on June 1, 1945.[47] Most of these individuals were French, and they returned to France after the end of the war.

In view of the more than 1,000 requests for help the New School received between August 1940 and March 1941, and in comparison with the New School's independent activities, the emergency program financed by the Rockefeller Foundation represents only a small effort. Parallel with this program, the Graduate Faculty had gone ahead with its own original plans and brought 100 scholars and other endangered intellectuals over from Europe. An important facilitator in this project was a new Emergency Rescue Committee for political refugees in France. This committee had been founded by representatives of the American section of the independent socialist "New Beginning" group around Paul Hagen, and Johnson had been asked to be on its board. In the person of Varian Fry, whom the committee had sent to Marseille, the New School thus had a direct line of communication with Europe.[48]

Johnson had also turned to other foundations—like the Guggenheim and New York foundations—and to labor unions to finance his own aid projects. Clearly, some salaries were taken, too, from a separate, rather large research fund contributed by the Rockefeller Foundation and intended for a so-called Peace Research Project that members of the faculty had embarked on after the outbreak of war.

The majority of those who arrived after 1940 became involved in one way or another with this project, which evolved by 1943 into the Institute of World Affairs, an institutionally separate entity from the Graduate Faculty. As in the years after 1933, some persons were now hired who were not scholars in the strict sense of the word and had not entered the United States with the nonquota visas issued to scholars. They came instead with special entry permits that Roosevelt had made available since the summer of 1940 for threatened political refugees in that part of France not yet under German occupation. Among this group were Ernst Hamburger, the former party leader of the Social Democrats in the Prussian Diet, and Ernst Rinner, the former editor of the reports from Germany for the exiled Social Democratic party, the SOPADE in Prague. These men were asked to do preparatory work for a major study of "social and economic controls in Germany and the Soviet Union." A fellowship was also obtained from the Emergency Committee's Rosenwald fellowship program for Ruth Fischer, the former chairperson of the German Communist party, and now an ardent anticommunist, to allow her to write about the development and structure of the party prior to 1933.[49]

The integration of such a large group made up of different nationalities, especially under the extremely tense conditions of the time, was far from easy. The French contingent, largest in number after the Germans,[50] refused to work with the Germans under one roof. To be sure, there may have been some grounds for this touchiness because the Germans had largely set the style and intellectual climate of the faculty over the past eight years and were to continue to dominate. But perhaps more important was the fact that the French and Belgian scholars thought of themselves as exiles waiting to return to their home countries, whereas the Germans, having been in the United States for some time, had almost all become American citizens. Although both national groups had suffered the same fate, profound differences and conflicts soon developed that could not be smoothed over in spite of Johnson's efforts. The more the French contingent isolated itself, the more bluntly nationalistic its attitude became. Not only did the French scholars refuse to work with others in the Graduate Faculty, as in the Peace Research Project that was just getting underway; they also objected to learning English and teaching in this language. In spite of all of Johnson's patience, they could not be incorporated into the adult education program of the New School, and that in turn led to complaints from the German side that the courses offered in French attracted hardly any students.

Matters did not improve until the organization France Libre, founded by General de Gaulle in exile in London after the French defeat, and the Belgian government in exile made available $75,000 annually in support of the French-speaking scholars. This money made it possible to build a program separate from the Graduate Faculty. In February 1942 the newly founded Ecole Libre des Hautes Etudes began offering courses in French and was immediately recognized by de Gaulle as a French university in exile whose academic degrees were to be accepted as qualification for the highest offices in a future liberated France. This soon gave rise to disagreements among different French scholars. The Ecole Libre increasingly saw itself as the intellectual arm of the Gaullist wing of France Libre because its faculty included a core group of Gaullist scholars associated with Alexander Koyré, a philosopher and direct representative of de Gaulle, as well as the anthropologist Claude Lévi-Strauss and the Russian-born political scientist Boris Mirkine-Guetzévitch. But other colleagues did not share this political outlook, and this soon led to disagreements. In addition to the dissension with the German group, new internal lines of conflict opened up, causing continual friction and further paralyzing the organization of the Ecole Libre, which had apparently been chaotic from the beginning. This caused some more moderate scholars—the social historian and former socialist Paul Vaucher, for example—to move gradually closer to German colleagues of similar outlook and to take some part in the work of the Peace Project. The Gaullist core, which obviously disapproved of the entire intellectual direction of the New School, went on cultivating its nationalistic hermetism and making frequent verbal attacks on the Graduate Faculty[51] until its return to France in 1945. What remained of the Ecole Libre split off completely from the New School one year later and continued to exist in modest size as a kind of institute of French culture in New York.[52]

4. Resistance of the State Department

As compared with the difficulties that had to be overcome during the first wave of immigration in 1933, the emergency program of 1940 was set up and initiated quickly because the organizations involved by now had a full functional administrative apparatus as well as the necessary experience. They also had money at their disposal, and the New School guaranteed initial jobs for the new arrivals. This bright picture was clouded by a change of attitude in the State Department toward the refugee problem. Although Johnson had informed the State Department of his plans before embarking on his rescue action and had been assured that the visa division and consulates would do all they could to support him, immigration policy from the summer of 1940 on went in the exact opposite direction.[53]

In those dramatic months nobody could doubt any longer that the political and racist persecution spreading to all of Nazi-occupied Europe could mean death for many refugees, nor could anyone question the desperate need of this flood of refugees, caught in the trap of unoccupied southern France, to escape to the United States. Yet at this very moment United States entry regulations were becoming tighter and tighter. Affected by this new strictness were not only the thousands of ordinary refugees who waited in lines at the doors of American consulates for entry visas issued under the regular quota system but also those—including the scholars—entitled to nonquota visas.

Like a large part of the xenophobic public, United States foreign policy from 1933 on had never welcomed the refugees. Although personally committed to the cause, President Roosevelt had not been able to promote it effectively. He had to take into account not only public opinion but also strong pressure from the southern wing of his own Democratic party. The southern Democrats controlled the congressional committees that dealt with this question, and the more sympathy the White House showed for the refugees, the more restrictive a line the southern Democrats took toward them. When Roosevelt initiated the International Refugee Conference at Evian in 1938, the House of Representatives immediately established the House Committee on Un-American Activities under the chairmanship of Texas Democrat Martin Dies. This committee was to examine the possible danger of fascist and communist infiltration posed by European refugees, and it soon became an important mouthpiece for restrictionists and anti–New Dealers, stirring up widespread hysteria about the security risk the German and European refugees supposedly posed.

These two fronts further hardened in the summer of 1940. On Roosevelt's initiative, a so-called Emergency Visitor's Visa Program was set up for exceptionally endangered political refugees, and an Advisory Committee on Political Refugees directly responsible to Roosevelt was charged with carrying out the program. The State Department saw to it, however, that these persons were subject to the same procedures as all other applicants. This ruling came from a Special War Problems Division in the State Department, created in January 1940, under whose command the visa division, too, was placed. This new bureaucratic apparatus and the consulates as well openly showed their displeasure at the presidential committee's intrusion into their affairs and undermined its work. The situation became even worse when the southerner Breckinridge Long was appointed to head the new division. Long had just returned from his position as ambassador to Italy and made no secret of his fascination with authoritarian governments. It is hardly surprising, then, that he thought refugees from fascist countries were automatically suspect and lumped "communists, extreme radicals, Jewish professional agitators, refugee enthusiasts" together as one undifferentiated enemy class.[54]

The procedural tightening of entry policy took the form, among other things, of time-consuming checking of applications in Washington rather than by local consulates as had been the previous practice; requesting two affidavits—that is, American sponsors—rather than one as up to now; and adhering to rigid monthly quotas for each consulate. Long also instituted his personal defense program, which can be summed up in the expression "delaying tactics" and was aimed at complicating the process of obtaining entry for refugees. Convinced as he was "that nobody has a right to come into the United States," he urged the consulates to put up all conceivable obstacles, and his recommendation was apparently more than welcome at many consulates.[55]

This background helps explain the countless difficulties the New School ran into in implementing its rescue program. As early as December 1940 Johnson had to complain to Long for the first time that some consulates were suddenly questioning the New School's right to hire nonquota persons. Long promised to look into the matter although he had received an inquiry from Marseille four weeks earlier, asking whether the New School had permission to hire scholars and whether it would be in a position to pay their salaries. Even this exchange of letters was somewhat disingenuous, for four weeks before that, in early October 1940, the Lisbon consulate had been informed by the Rockefeller official there of the New School's status and the rescue action for scholars that was about to get off the ground, and the Lisbon consulate had telegraphed this information to the American consulates in France.[56] These time-consuming inquiries dragged on for months and kept occurring despite Johnson's repeated urgings that speed was essential for the success of the rescue action.

Although the State Department had originally pledged its support, Johnson had to travel to Washington again and again to justify his rescue program before the visa division. The fate of scholars was often decided on the basis of vague suspicions, and the slightest hint of political questionability reported by European consulates could be damning. The United States consulates in France often accepted information from the Pétain regime in Vichy at face value. In the case of the French philosopher Louis Rougier, the consulate had nothing definite to go on but thought there was a "strong possibility" he was somehow associated with the Socialist party, and it consequently wanted to deny him a visa. But even when there were no political suspicions whatsoever, requests were often handled in a far from speedy manner, with the visa office first writing to Johnson to ask if the hiring of a particular scholar was really so crucial and why he did not want to employ United States citizens. In this way the State Department was able to delay decisions, for it took some time before the board of appeals to which the New School turned—and where urgent cases of this sort were piling up—could render a decision. Presumptuously, according to Johnson, Long and his officials took it upon themselves to decide on pedagogic and scholarly matters that were none of their business and of which they had not the faintest understanding.[57] Similar complaints about the work of the consulates came from the Rockefeller office in Lisbon, along with an urgent request to the central office to get the State Department to remedy the situation.[58]

Nothing went smoothly now for the New School. It soon became a regular pattern for the visa division to refuse all entry applications from Johnson, so that appeals had to be filed. It was obvious that the bureaucrats wanted to prevent increasing European influence at this emigré university. Johnson persevered and did not hesitate to call on old friends in power, such as Felix Frankfurter, who had in the meantime become chief justice of the Supreme Court, and Adolf Berle, who was undersecretary of state in the State Department itself. But when Johnson tried to change the obtuse policy of the visa officials not through regular channels but from above, the officials reacted by casting aspersions on and denouncing the New School in their interviews with the new arrivals. Representatives of the State Department asked some scholars who had just come to New York from France if they knew that the place where they were going to work was headed by communists. These machinations did not stop until Johnson threatened to request a public hearing on these attempts at sabotage.[59]

But Johnson and his friends had no influence on the policies of the consulates. There, depending on the personal whims of a particular consul, applicants could sometimes be treated with petty chicanery. One of the more harmless forms this could take is illustrated by what happened to Alexander Pekelis. Born in Russia, Pekelis had first fled to Germany in 1919 and had lived in Italy since the mid 1920s, teaching the sociology of law in Rome. He lost both his job and his newly acquired Italian citizenship when Mussolini enacted his anti-Semitic measures of 1938. At the consulate in Lisbon, Pekelis was told that the more than $25,000 of family assets he had in bank accounts in New York would not be enough to support him and his wife and three children. Only when he was able to supply proof of his job at the New School and an additional affidavit from Max Ascoli was he granted an entry permit.[60]

In the case of Hedwig Hintze, widow of the famous German historian Otto Hintze and herself an expelled scholar, the foot-dragging of the Rotterdam consulate precipitated a tragedy. Hintze had taught at Berlin as a lecturer (*Privatdozentin*) and expert in French history until 1933, when, being Jewish, she lost the *venia legendi*. The consulate first questioned her right to a nonquota visa because she did not have papers proving that she had held an academic position. When the New School found an earlier Berlin colleague of hers now living in the United States who supplied a sworn statement on this point, the consulate dredged up another reason to stall, claiming it had to check on whether she had done anything against the law in Germany. She never arrived at the New School; shortly after her encounters with the consulate she committed suicide to escape deportation to Auschwitz.[61]

The pettiness of American bureaucrats was responsible for the death of the French medievalist Marc Bloch, too. He was granted a nonquota visa but then tried in vain for almost a year to obtain an entry permit for his adolescent children. In July 1941 he gave up trying, returned the New School's invitation, and resigned himself to staying in France with his family. Three years later he was executed as a member of the French Resistance.[62] Emil Julius Gumbel, a mathematician from Heidelberg who had earlier written a history of the German Freikorps (volunteer corps) and other rightist associations, found himself in similar circumstances and apparently escaped Bloch's fate only by leaving his family behind. He arrived in New York in October 1940, but it took more than ten months before his family could follow him, his wife via Lisbon and his son by way of Casablanca. First they did not have the necessary French exit visas; then they had to wait for permission to get Spanish and Portuguese transit visas. By this time the United States entry visa was no longer valid and—typical of the vicious circle in which so many in unoccupied France were caught—it was not renewed until constant pressure from Gumbel forced the visa division in Washington to go through the entire bureaucratic process again.[63]

A last, sarcastic appeal by Johnson to the president of the Carnegie Foundation, who was also a member of the appeals board that reviewed cases in which entry was denied, sheds a telling light on American immigration policy after 1940:

> What does depress me profoundly, however, is the rate of speed at which these matters seem to be handled. . . . Within the last three weeks, two of our appointees have died in concentration camps while waiting for visas. At this very moment two others, one in Lisbon and one in southern France, are literally on the point of starvation. What will it avail the national interest as expressed in Section IV (d) [of the Immigrant Act] that eventually an enlightened Appeal Board will have a chance to consider these cases, if by that time the men be dead?
>
> This is one of the most astounding administrative procedure that has ever come to my attention. Under such a system it is possible for a case to shuttle back and forth among the primary, the secondary, and the tertiary instances for six months, or for the duration, or for eternity.
>
> I am not going to speak about humanitarian aspects. This world is so full of misery that the greatest conceivable success of the New School's program could have no appreciable effect on the state of human happi-

ness. We went into this program primarily not for the sake of European scientists but, with the sympathetic support of other educational institutions, for the sake of American science and the national interest which it serves. It is this interest which is being cheated by the procedure which has been described to us. Of course, the country must be protected against spies and other undesirable elements. But it begins to seem no less important to protect the country against persons who are totally devoid of understanding of the place of science and scholarship in American life and in the war effort itself.[64]

6 / Contributions of the Emigré Scholars at the New School

It is amazing that significant scholarly work was produced at the Graduate Faculty despite its chronic financial problems and its provisional state. The relatively homogeneous character of the faculty and the experimental nature of their research interests seem to have combined with the institutional chaos in a fruitful symbiosis. The spectrum of approaches and research traditions brought from Europe by the refugee scholars gathered at the New School included much that was new to American scholarship. This applies in particular to the field of economic theory; but original contributions were also made in other disciplines of the social sciences, contributions that influenced American academic discussion to varying degrees.

The work and impact of Leo Strauss has already been cited, as has that of Erich Hula and some others. Another name that should be mentioned here is Max Wertheimer, the founder, along with Wolfgang Köhler and Kurt Koffka, of Gestalt psychology. It is true that this school, which focuses on the processes of perception, failed for a long time to attract much attention in the United States because behaviorism was so firmly entrenched here. This may have been due in part to the deaths of Wertheimer and of Koffka in the early 1940s. But in the long run the effect of Gestalt psychology on modern social psychology, on the psychology of learning and motivation, and on other areas can hardly be ignored. Because of Wertheimer, the true intellectual father of this approach, the New School became the first center of Gestalt psychology in the United States. Although he did not publish much after 1933, Wertheimer's stimulating ideas soon attracted a considerable following of students. Despite his marked quirkiness, his charisma and broad educational background left a lasting imprint on the intellectual climate of the New School during the few years he was there. His students Rudolf Arnheim and Georg Katona, who had emigrated with him, started their academic careers at the New School, Arnheim in the psychology of art and Katona in the psychology of advertising. And with Solomon Asch and Mary Henle, students of Wertheimer and Koffka, teaching there for many years, the New School remained an important center of this branch of psychology.[1]

Another noneconomist whose work became influential is Arnold Brecht. Although Brecht was already over fifty when he arrived in New York and had a long career behind him holding top offices in the German government, he built up a notable second career at the New School as a political scientist. The transition was a more natural one for him than for many of his colleagues who had emigrated at the same time and, having studied law, often switched to the related field of political science. As director of the constitutional department of the Reich Ministry of the Interior for many years and then as Prussia's representative in the Länderkammer of the Reichsrat, and there responsible for budget problems, Brecht had written a number of studies on questions of administrative and constitutional law and, in the years after 1918, on current political problems. Some of the topics were the events leading up to the truce ending World War I, election law, problems of constitutional reform, and federalism. He also drew up the procedural rules for the Reich ministries in the 1920s.[2]

Continuing in this practical and scholarly vein, Brecht produced several books and numerous articles in the United States. Drawing on an immense amount of reading in international literature, he wrote on themes that range from the philosophy of law to various specialized problems of the modern constitutional and administrative state. All these studies came together in the 1950s in Brecht's monumental *Political Theory,* one of the first systematic presentations of the discipline of political science and a historical account of the approaches, values, and methods employed in this discipline. When it was published, the work received the Woodrow Wilson Foundation award for the best book of the year in political science, and it has long since become one of the standard works in its field.[3]

Brecht's academic knowledge and his practical experience soon made him a valued and frequent guest professor at Harvard University as well as an important consultant in the Washington administration both during and after the war. He was also to act as adviser to the United States occupation administration in Germany, a subject we will return to later. The reputation he soon gained in the American academic world is reflected by his election, as early as 1942, to the chairmanship of a special committee for comparative international administration set up by the Social Science Research Council and, in 1946, to the vice-presidency of the American Political Science Association.

Of note, too, is the work of the sociologist Albert Salomon. Salomon's numerous writings, together with those of Hans Gerth, a fellow refugee, did much to familiarize Americans with Max Weber's work. Salomon always remained overshadowed, however, by Talcott Parsons, who had originally introduced Weber to American readers in the 1920s.[4] Parsons, convinced of the immutability of the existing social order, was fascinated by Weber's work. Like Marxist theory, it introduced historical and economic dimensions into sociological analysis but, unlike Marx, did not question the framework of the existing order. Salomon was not able to modify this understanding of Weber much. His presentation of Weber's thought is essentially descriptive and retrospective and seems to have been affected in part by a profound loss of self-confidence caused by exile, an experience that left him with little of the energy he had displayed as an activist in the Social Democratic movement. In Germany, he had held a professorship at the Hochschule für Politik in Berlin and, from 1931 on, served as director of the Pedagogical Institute at the university in Cologne. He also edited *Die Gesellschaft,* the Social Democrats' leading theoretical publication, while its founder and publisher, Rudolf Hilferding, was serving in the Weimar government. Together with Jakob Marschak, Salomon helped lead the economic and political study group of Social Democratic students. In this period the idea of shaping the future and changing the status quo had guided his practical and theoretical work. But the year 1933 and exile from Germany were shocks he never overcame. On top of everything else he contracted polio a few months before his planned departure, a long and dreary illness that left him slightly disabled physically. Because of his illness he was not able to assume the job his former dissertation adviser, Emil Lederer, had arranged for him in the summer of 1933 until more than a year later, in September 1934.

For a long time most of his scholarly efforts went into presentations of the new thinking developed earlier in Germany by his spiritual mentor Max Weber and his friends Karl Mannheim and Emil Lederer. Over the years they did broaden into comprehensive lectures and studies on the history, of sociology, especially French authors, but their roots in social and cultural philosophy kept them from gaining a wider reception in pragmatically minded American sociology.[5]

The hiring in 1943 of Alfred Schütz introduced phenomenology into American philosophy and sociology. Given Schütz's background, the fact that the New School gave him an appointment shows once more the experimental and unorthodox character of the Graduate Faculty. Schütz had studied law and economics in Vienna under Kelsen and Ludwig Mises but had decided after earning his degree not to pursue an academic career. He worked instead for various private banks as a legal adviser and expert on matters of international economics, work that he continued to do full-time in New York after 1939 for business firms that had also emigrated. At the same time, however, Schütz maintained his academic interests, studying in depth first Max Weber, then Henri Bergson, and eventually the founder of phenomenology, Edmund Husserl. In his essay "Der sinnhafte Aufbau der sozialen Welt" [The tangible structure of the social world] of 1932, he made a first effort to combine theoretically the systems of Weber and Husserl. Implicit in this effort was an appeal to the social sciences not to regard philosophical methodology and empirical analysis as mutually exclusive. From Husserl's philosophy Schütz took over and introduced into social theory the term *Lebenswelt* ("world of daily life") to stand for the unanalyzed everyday life.

Husserl's philosophy was an important vehicle for Schütz for giving a more solid epistemological basis to Weber's sociology. The subject of investigation was the everyday life of active people together with the cultural norms and cognitive determinants that shaped all interpersonal processes. Human beings, Schütz taught, did not perceive an objective reality but in the process of communicating with others constructed their own realities within their consciousness. During Schütz's Vienna years this integrating approach had been directed against the pure metaphysics of the German philosophical tradition; now it once again offered a new perspective from which Schütz could critique the reduction of thinking to the pragmatism and behavioral psychology prevalent in the United States.

The logical positivism of the Vienna circle fit in better with the pragmatic tradition of American philosophy, and its representatives—like the Austrian neoclassical economists—built successful academic careers in America. Rudolf Carnap, who taught first at Chicago and later at Princeton, is an example. Schütz and his phenomenological sociology, on the other hand, did not attract much attention at first. He began and ended his academic career in the Graduate Faculty, where he eventually became a full professor in 1953. Only in the 1960s and after Schütz's death, when a younger generation had lost interest in functionalist sociology as taught by Talcott Parsons and Robert K. Merton, did Schütz posthumously acquire a larger following. A part of this younger generation was attracted by the neo-Marxian analysis of society, but others were less interested in objective social structures than in the world of subjective human experience. For these students Schütz became a guide, and by now numerous studies have appeared that have picked up and elaborated on the ideas in his work.[6]

But despite the originality of one or the other of these scholars and even though they made important contributions in their fields, they did not have much impact on the overall character of the Graduate Faculty or on how it was perceived by the outside world. It was the economists who gave it its decisive character. They were the intellectual core of the faculty from the very beginning, for after 1933 they were not only the largest group there but also a relatively homogeneous one, unlike the representatives of the other disciplines. The dominant influence they had both on internal discussion and on the outward impression the Graduate Faculty made was increased by the fact that they arrived at just the right moment, namely, when the ways of thinking and the approaches to research they brought with them met with a special receptivity in parts of the academic world at the time of the New Deal.

Given this situation, it is not surprising that the first public seminars Johnson asked the new faculty members to put on just a few weeks after their arrival in December 1933 and early January 1934 had as their themes "Laissez Faire—Interventionism—Planned Economy" and "Has Capitalism Failed?"[7] Johnson was intent from the beginning on spreading the message of the reform economists he had brought to the United States. His primary purpose was, of course, to demonstrate the caliber of his University in Exile, but at the same time he wanted, discreetly, to put some pressure on the newly arrived scholars to learn English quickly so that they could hold their own in the American academic community. There was a danger that the exclusively German faculty would not pay much attention to such elementary aspects of acculturation, and, indeed, the un-English "New Schoolese" spoken and written during the first phase must have been quite an obstacle to communication with the outside world.

Questions of economics continued to dominate the weekly general seminars during the school's first years, and these seminars remained a regular institution at the school until after 1945. Not only were the interdisciplinary methods developed in Germany practiced here, but, because the discussions were open to the interested public, the seminars also offered a chance to exhibit some of the characteristic work of the University in Exile to the outside world.

And, finally, the German scholars had a chance to become more widely known through the publication *Social Research,* which was launched in early 1934. Like the founding of the University in Exile, the quick start of this publication again illustrates Alvin Johnson's astonishing energy and optimism. Whereas someone like Emil Lederer, going on his many years of experience as an editor in Germany, considered the idea of starting a new magazine a pure fantasy and thought it would take several years to realize the project, Johnson set to work in November 1933 intent on publishing a first issue in January 1934. Only by publishing its own journal would the Graduate Faculty acquire an adequate public voice, for, Johnson argued, Chicago and Harvard had not become true universities until they started publishing the *Journal of Political Economy* and the *Quarterly Journal of Economics,* respectively. Every member of the faculty therefore had to agree to write one article a year, and the journal did in fact appear from spring 1934 on, as planned. With almost 800 subscriptions, it soon developed into a respectable organ for emigré scholarship.

As Johnson wrote in the preamble to the first issue, the central task of the journal was to be the "cross-fertilization of cultures." The scholars associated with the journal, he continued, had brought with them from Germany a critical approach to the social sciences and unusual methods, but their future subjects were the problems of the modern world as a whole, beyond national borders.[8] In many respects *Social Research* may be regarded as the continuation of the *Archiv für Sozialwissenschaft und Sozialpolitik,* which had ceased publication in 1933, and of the Kiel Institute's *Weltwirtschaftliches Archiv,* journals on which this circle of emigré scholars had had a great influence both personally and intellectually in the 1920s. And as in the first meetings of the general seminars of the Graduate Faculty, it was the economists who determined the themes of the new publication during its first years.

The ideas the economists of the Graduate Faculty brought with them from Germany had many points of contact with the work of American colleagues of the institutionalist school. Both groups doubted that an uncontrolled market system could function well; both saw economic reality in the larger context of society as a whole; both thought in terms of a process over long periods of time and did not share the neoclassicists' static concept and theoretical indifference toward historical developments; and, from all this, both derived economic and political conclusions that were later summed up in such concepts as "indicative planning." But there were also some obvious differences between them that bring into sharp relief the nature of their respective theoretical assumptions.

Whereas the institutionalists' analysis of the Great Depression and their recommendations for a strategy to combat it were based on the theory of underconsumption, the German reform economists' analysis of the depression relied more on the theory of disproportionality. These approaches indicate profound differences in the assessment of crises in modern market economies and of the character of modern industrialization. The institutionalists had shown in many studies, as had the German reform economists during the 1920s, in what ways the neoclassicists' assumptions about the harmonious functioning of the market had been made obsolete by the dynamics of development in industrial capitalism, but Thorstein Veblen and his followers had been unable to define logically and causally the factors responsible for this process. The institutionalists had no consistent theory that could explain the functioning of societal mechanisms. They had never made clear the analytical foundations that their pronouncements were based on. Veblen's descriptions spoke only vaguely about a process of "engineering," and John R. Commons, for example, dealt only with institutional improvements in such areas where capitalism had in the past failed to produce adequate social results.

The institutionalists regarded modern technology as the central motor of the capitalistic process, but this idea remained undeveloped. Veblen analyzed and criticized the organizations of private enterprise but not the system of modern technology and the dynamic processes of change, the economic cycles and crises, and their consequences for the labor market. His successors did not even go this far. In Veblen the Marxian heritage still played a major role, but Mitchell, Clark, Tugwell, and the other institutionalists had long since, in the 1920s, eliminated Marx from the epistemological foundation of their thinking and replaced his influence with John Dewey's pragmatism. With that they renounced an understanding of the modern dynamic growth process. The pioneering Marxian schema of expanded reproduction in which the Ricardian theory of capital accumulation was connected with Quesnay's *tableau economique* of a stationary circular flow of goods and which for the first time developed a concise model of technologically induced dynamic and disproportionate economic growth remained unnoticed. Instead, optimistic and activist ideas of using planning initiatives of some sort to regulate social processes dominated their thinking. The problem of technology played a role only to the extent that the economic process was assumed—by its very nature, so to speak—to go through various stages of technical development in industry and that economic crises, frictions, and other deviations from prescribed paths of growth were due to a lack of coordination in the circular flow of goods and money.

Nor had the planning postulates of the institutionalists before 1933 gone beyond generalities, for they did not clarify what authorities and instruments could be used to effect planning. To the German reform economists, on the other hand, it seemed only natural, given the traditions of governmental intervention in economics in Europe, that important functions of macroeconomic guidance should be assigned to the state. There were no such traditions in the United States, and the institutionalists therefore very slowly concerned themselves with the politicoeconomic role of the state. Instead, they set their hopes on the big corporations, which they also criticized, however, because of their unchecked accumulation of power. The agencies of the New Deal that sprouted up like mushrooms and the new economic administration that took over in Washington after 1933 changed some of this but still did not produce a model for more comprehensive economic and political planning. Also, there were still instrumental shortcomings. Because there was at that time neither an overall economic accounting nor a compilation of statistics on the gross national accounting, the institutionalists, in spite of Mitchell's creation of the National Bureau of Economic Research in 1920, were unable to draw up budgets that could define the goals and directions of a planned development.[9]

The German reform economists had some supplemental and corrective perspectives to offer, for they had been preoccupied with the very problems the institutionalists had stopped short of. By delving into the unsolved questions of technical change and its effect on the growth dynamic and by developing their theory of fiscal planning, they had been working out instruments with which causal connections between social and economic processes could be analyzed and from which operational strategies could be derived. Their studies, begun in the 1920s and later brought to conclusion in the United States, supplied some central points that modified the previous naive debate on planning in the United States. Beyond this, they were also able, on the basis of practical experience and knowledge acquired in Germany, to contribute some far-reaching suggestions in the area of international economics, a field that had hardly been touched on in America. Many of their analyses during World War II were in fact to contain important recommendations for setting up a German and European postwar order after the Hitler period.

1. Growth Dynamic and the Theory of "Technical Progress"

The earlier Kiel school provided the basis for these studies, and its members were also to determine the public image of the New School after 1933. Their research had received its decisive impetus during the debate in Germany on the economic and social side effects that automation had had after World War I and especially after 1924–25. The introduction of the assembly line had been responsible long before the Great Depression for ending the Weimar Republic's brief period of prosperity and plunging it into chronic unemployment with over one million people out of work.

As early as 1926, in an article on the possibilities of a theory of business cycles,[10] Adolph Lowe had first suggested this causal connection, thereby arousing considerable interest. For him, the causes of economic cycles and crises were to be sought not in the process but in the system itself, in the underlying structure of production with its "independent variable" of technical progress. These ideas were picked up by Lowe's students and colleagues, by Alfred Kähler and Fritz Burchardt, as well as by Hans Neisser and Emil Lederer. Technological progress—today we speak more cautiously of "technological change" because it can no longer be taken for granted that transformations in technology mean progress—and the resulting labor market problems and instabilities in the development dynamic were to be the subjects of their future research. In the course of this research, they would formulate some important ideas on growth theory, which up to then had been approached mainly through the quantitative aspects of the accumulation of real capital.

The neoclassicists had had nothing to say about this problem because they concentrated only on conditions of economic equilibrium, tacitly assuming that perfect competition ruled the market. They accepted the old Walrasian model of households and individuals dealing in goods and services they bought from and sold to each other in the context of a completely surveyable market, so that at the end of a fictive production period—real time factors, such as the lag between production and sale, were ignored—the markets were cleared and the mechanism could start all over again. In this scheme business cycles, depressions, unemployment, and other interferences were regarded as short-term frictional or externally caused deviations from the path of equilibrium. The neoclassicists explained the persistent recessions in the 1920s, for instance, with the "monetary theory of the business cycles" developed shortly before in Great Britain. This theory postulated that the capacity of the banking system to inflate the money supply beyond deposits, that is, "credit expansion" below the equilibrium interest rate, had upset the market equilibrium. It is not surprising that many of the Austrian neoclassicists—like today's monetarists—were vehement defenders of a strict gold standard that left the banks hardly any leeway in setting policies of money supply. Friedrich A. Hayek, the most brilliant of the Vienna economists, recognized the static implications of this view and accepted economic cycles induced by monetary factors as a necessary price of progress.[11]

The difference between the reform economists of the Kiel school and the neoclassicists surfaced in arguments presented by Lowe and Hayek at the 1928 gathering in Zurich of the German Society of Economists (Verein für Sozialpolitik). This was the first time the problem of business cycles had been publicly discussed. The neoclassicists reiterated a variation of the traditional assumption that flexible interest rates acted as a regulator of investment and therefore of employment, and Hayek took the new monetary theory of business cycles as his point of departure in analyzing economic cycles. Lowe countered that such approaches did not penetrate beyond the "peripheries" of theoretical reflection and were not very productive in exploring the causes of the cycles, just as the monetary angle could at best be of secondary use in explaining certain aspects of the cycles.[12] Basically, the argument focused on whether the factors affecting economic cycles and growth were endogenous or exogenous and how they could be influenced.

The neoclassical market model at that time disregarded the fact that in modern industrial economies the different production sectors are intertwined in rather problematic ways (horizontal disaggregation), something Marx's reproduction schema had first suggested half a century earlier with a simple two-sector model. This made the Walrasian schema essentially obsolete as a reflection of actual reality. Eugen von Böhm-Bawerk, one of the spiritual fathers of the Austrian school, had been aware of this danger and had, in response to Marx's model, formulated his so-called model of roundabout production. With this approach he tried to refute the Marxian notion of rigid structures with a marginalist explanation of progress in production (vertical or temporal disaggregation). In this concept the real creative force was roundabout production rather than capital equipment. Capital figured as a flexible intermediate product, originally of nature and labor, which in a linear process tended to the ultimate goal of consumer goods. Interest and saving functioned as the variable that determined the choice between present lower- or future higher-order goods. Essentially, it was the consumer who decided on the direction that production would take. The Austrian model leaves unexplained the reproduction and expansion requirements of the stock of fixed capital goods, which are at the very center of a horizontal model of production.[13]

But the real structure of an economy was—and is—anything but flexible, just as industrial relationships can hardly be regarded as an elastic process of vertical sequences. This was the argument taken by the representatives of the Kiel school as well as by Emil Lederer, whose paper criticizing Böhm-Bawerk was, not coincidentally, to appear as the lead article of the first issue of *Social Research* in 1934.[14] Using the slogan "Technical Progress and Unemployment," these scholars were the first in over fifty years to revive the old, classical question first articulated by Ricardo, J. S. Mill, and Marx about the interrelationship among capital accumulation, technical progress, and employment, a question that had long been relegated to the background by the victorious sweep of neoclassicism. It is this theoretical rethinking together with the economic and political strategies that grew out of it—in Germany as well as in the later exile period in America—that constitutes the crucial and at that time unique contribution of the reform economists, and for this reason economists working along similar lines today sometimes refer to them as the "new classicists."[15]

The neoclassicists did not associate problems or negative effects with technical progress because they assumed that such changes were accompanied by changes in wage and interest levels. Technical innovations could not displace workers permanently because, according to the neoclassical model of static allocation in which the price formation of production factors was defined in the same way as the price formation of goods on the markets, jobs lost because of increased efficiency of production would be compensated for somewhere else. First of all, the instruments of innovation had to be produced, and, second, technical progress would result in lower costs and prices, thus increasing demand. Depending on the elasticity of income, this would lead to the reabsorption of the workers in the same industrial sector or in other branches. In neoclassical theory permanent unemployment therefore arose only as a consequence of monopolistic demands on the part of the unions for increased wages, an argument the followers of this theory have never tired of repeating to this day.[16]

To counter this optimistic theory of compensation put forward by the neoclassicists, the reform economists pointed out that a market economy did not automatically lead to a balance of economic processes and that in an age of mass production prices did not react with the flexibility the neoclassical model took for granted. It was therefore the task of economists, they claimed, first to analyze closely the structure of technical production in order to determine the effect of technical change on employment in different sectors. The second task was to devise planning instruments that would lead to a "stabilization of economic fluctuation," that is, to remove the "tension" that was "growing sharper and sharper between the technical and the social order."[17]

And, finally, the argument reiterated over and over by the neoclassicists since the mid 1920s, namely, that wages had to be lowered to overcome growing unemployment, was relegated by Jakob Marschak to "the realm of intellectual epidemics" that periodically affect economic theory and practice. Lederer expressed similar sentiments when he wrote, "the primitive notion that it is *always* possible when there is high unemployment to restore equilibrium conditions by lowering wages belongs on the junk heap of economic theory." At the same time, however, these economists also criticized the theory of purchasing power advanced by the labor unions because demands for higher wages, too, would merely mean a shift in purchasing power. Marschak and Lederer therefore rejected the manipulation of wages as a means to combat technological unemployment because they did not regard the latter as a consequence of distorted factor–price relationships.[18]

Although the discussion of that time did not produce final answers concerning technological unemployment or develop a systematic theory of labor displacement, it nevertheless formulated the crucial questions for approaching this problem, which is still unsolved today. It also came up with some important suggestions for possible answers. In contrast to most models of the time, models based on the theory of demand, the analysis of the processes of labor displacement and compensation the reform economists developed was based on a theory of capital. In this they went back to the classical line of argument, which, as Neisser wrote, defined the capitalistic process as a race between labor being displaced by technological progress and its reabsorption through capital accumulation.[19]

Emil Lederer's *Technischer Fortschritt und Arbeitslosigkeit* [Technical progress and unemployment] of 1931 was a first systematic analysis of this subject. It had evolved from a project of the International Labor Office in Geneva to study the current global economic crisis, a project in which Lederer participated as the German expert. Drawing on Marx's theory of accumulation and Schumpeter's neoclassical notion that the investing impulses of individual, risk-taking entrepreneurs affected long-term economic development, Lederer tried to show under what conditions technical progress frees labor, that is, disrupts full employment, and thereby leads to economic crises. His theory of stagnation in specific economic branches bears an obvious resemblance to the Marxian law of the diminishing rate of profit and took as its starting point the varying rates of innovation—like the introduction of new types of machinery—in individual, dynamic branches of industry. Such innovations led to a reduction of labor not only in affected factories but also in static, antiquated factories because those innovations would cause a capital transfer to the more dynamic areas. Capital accumulation did not for Lederer automatically mean growth and employment; instead, the pace and direction of investment were crucial. When the demand for labor chronically lagged behind its supply in spite of capital accumulation, as in periods of rationalization, unemployment became "structural."[20]

Lederer's work was soon supplemented and expanded by studies Lowe had suggested to his students, among them Fritz Burchardt's examination of the schemes of the stationary circular flow in Böhm-Bawerk and Marx and Alfred Kähler's dissertation.[21] The latter appears from today's perspective as an important milestone, for Kähler not only presented an outstanding analysis of the theoretical discussion up to that time but also furnished pioneering work toward a multisector model for determining growth, technical transformation, and employment. In this he did not necessarily go along with Lederer's stagnation theory. For him, the assumption that technical innovation led to a reduction in labor was just as debatable as the possibility of the unemployed being reabsorbed. In his mind, the theoretical controversy centered exclusively around the conditions and circumstances of the compensations, which could be determined only by means of a comprehensive description of the economic processes and by taking the factor of time into account.

For this description Kähler developed a matrix comprising eight sectors to demonstrate the interdependent production relations among the different branches of industry. This model was to show the displacement of workers by machinery under maladjustment of those sectors as well as the conditions necessary for a successful compensation.[22] Kähler's study was of political importance because it made clear that wage changes play only a passive role in technical transformation and that wage reductions cannot stimulate new investment—as adherents of neoclassical theory hoped—and thus lead to economic upswings and growth. His presentation of the circular flow in a national economy can be regarded as an early version of a closed input–output model. As previously mentioned, Wassily Leontief was to receive the Nobel Prize in 1973 for his analytical elaboration on such an input–output model and its application to macroeconomic planning.

How integral the problem of technology and growth was to the approach of the Kiel school is shown by Hans Neisser's work. Whereas Kähler's study concluded with the cautious question of whether technical progress could still be held in check in an economy based on competition or whether it would necessitate some "overall economic interventions," Neisser's analyses, taking account of the global economic crisis, already pointed toward concrete, therapeutic economic policies. Since the mid 1920s he had carried on a debate with Fritz Sternberg on the latter's theory of underconsumption and imperialism. In this debate he had focused, using the classical reproduction schema, on the structural problems of modern industrial economies and their conditions of equilibrium. In a concurrent study of 1928 on the exchange value of money (*Der Tauschwert des Geldes*), he also stressed the theoretical implications his like-minded colleagues' thinking on labor displacement had for income and purchasing power. From this he derived the conditions for possible planning strategies. Since the reform economists, like their classical predecessors, assumed that displaced labor could be successfully reabsorbed only through long-term capital formation, while at the same time a misdirection of capital investment as described by Lederer had to be avoided, ways needed to be found of coordinating technical innovations and of monitoring their secondary effects on other sectors of the economy. This is what Neisser's first multicausal analysis tried to do. His point of departure for this analysis was that changes in the volume of the labor force and capital formation were two mutually independent factors. The analysis further assumed that demand for labor was less a function of wage level than of expected sales. Economic policy should therefore take into account monetary stimuli, the structure of demand, the volume of existing capital, and the long-term processes of capital formation being initiated as well as their multiplicative secondary effects.[23]

The planning initiatives of the reform groups were to become known as "active anticyclical interventionism," a term that is today associated more with the name of Keynes. Whereas the neoclassical economists regarded credit as an outside interference in the flexible, self-adjusting industrial system and therefore rejected monetary stimuli to rev up a stagnant economy, the reform economists saw credit in exactly the opposite light. Neisser's book on the exchange value of money had furnished the necessary background for this view. The book's importance in the history of theory lies in the fact that it overcame the decades-old failings of German monetary theory. Until well into the 1920s, monetary theory in Germany had been dominated by Georg Friedrich Knapp's "state theory" or by the Austrian school's subjective evaluation of money; that is, it had been preoccupied with questions of definition based on either state validation or the special commodity quality of gold. To be sure, Schumpeter had published his famous essay "Das Sozialprodukt und die Rechenpfennige" [Money and the social product] during the inflationary phase of World War I. In it, he introduced a new definition of the old quantity theory rejected by the two schools just mentioned. He had also developed there a concise theory of the circular flow of money in the modern economic process, but this essay was largely ignored at the time. Neisser then picked up this thread and argued convincingly for recognizing the quantity theory. With this contribution he put an end to the still dominant theoretical separation of the circular flow of money and of goods and stressed the active role money played in economic growth. He also placed more emphasis on the effectiveness of demand and thus, for the first time in German monetary theory, presented a well-founded plea for a planned manipulation of the money supply.[24]

To the reform economists the question of credit appeared in a completely different context than it did to the neoclassicists. For them, credits could only be derived sociologically from the inner structure of production. The question of credit accordingly was the result, not the cause, of economic dynamics. They could therefore without hesitation recommend public pump priming to counteract business cycles. This was not all that original an idea because it was also discussed during those years by Keynes and others.[25] But the reform economists went beyond the Keynesian model. For them, active anticyclical interventionism meant the allocation of resources, initiated by monetary measures, to achieve certain ends. In other words, it meant directing consumption and investment—the two most important components of aggregate demand—to keep in check the "fatal factor of disruption" inherent in technical progress, for these economists recognized that there was not only cyclical unemployment but also structural unemployment.[26]

The "new classical" approach of the reform economists was further developed in many studies during the years of emigration. By inquiring into technological unemployment they introduced a qualitatively new paradigm in the United States, but in this they were to remain outsiders for some time. As much as ten years later, Neisser noted that this kind of research was a neglected "stepchild" in American economics.[27] An article by Alvin Hansen written in 1931 and obviously based on discussions he had had in Kiel during a trip to Germany remained for many years the only contribution by an American on this subject. Hansen and some of his colleagues had recognized the problem of job losses resulting from technological change, but in view of the rapid advances in productivity and the expansive growth during the prosperous 1920s they examined only short-term layoffs followed by new employment. Thus David Weintraub came to the optimistic conclusion that in those years approximately 90 percent of those who were laid off found new jobs within a few months.[28]

At the New School Lederer and Kähler, after 1933, picked up the earlier discussion. Lederer's book on technical progress and unemployment had been attacked from the neoclassical perspective by Nicholas Kaldor, who once again attributed long-term unemployment to the "rigidity of money wages." Kaldor did admit that Lederer's conclusions, if they were correct, would be of fundamental, almost "revolutionary importance" from a theoretical as well as a practical point of view.[29] This caused Lederer to elaborate on his previous ideas and give them a firmer base in many concrete examples. He once again presented his theses and added some important conceptual clarifications, first in several articles written for the journal *Social Research* and then in a considerably expanded second edition of his book *Technischer Fortschritt und Arbeitslosigkeit* [Technical progress and unemployment], which the International Labor Office published in 1938 in three languages. He declared that the entire question of technology was a problem of the growth process and that traditional economic concepts were no longer adequate to grasp it. Traditional economic thought assumed that a static economy was the norm and then defined dynamic developments as oscillations around this base line. Countering this view, Lederer developed in rough outline a growth-oriented system exhibiting a "harmonious dynamic," a kind of steady-state growth, distinguishing between labor-saving improvements and new inventions.

Lederer was apparently influenced here by his new experiences in the United States and the high level of automation and broad supply of goods he saw there. His stagnation theorem, as a kind of displacement multiplier, had indicated the conditions under which rapid technical progress through rationalization within specific industrial sectors could turn into an obstacle to economic growth. With this, Lederer's distinction between technical improvements and inventions now supplied the necessary basis for a possible reabsorption of workers laid off because of the rationalization of work processes. The rapid pace of growing capital intensity could lead to destruction of the whole industrial structure in modern societies if there were no coordination between labor displacement by improvements and the expansion of new industries through increased new inventions. The capitalistic dynamic thus not only led to development but could at the same time spell destruction.

Here the question of adequate public intervention and control surfaced. Lederer was convinced that private business was capable of correcting mistakes in development, but he thought there was reason to believe that out of a traditional reluctance to do so it would be less effective than would a planned economy at counteracting crises and disturbances.[30] Here the first effects of Lederer's adjustment to his new social world are apparent, for he was now much more restrained than in 1931 in his arguments for a planned economy, having earlier considered the "social control" of the capitalistic dynamic crucial to the survival of European nations.

Kähler, too, continued his earlier research at the New School. He picked up the work begun in his dissertation and now tried to add empirical support for the model he had developed on the theoretical level. In the first essay he published in *Social Research*, he demonstrated with reference to German and American developments that postwar rationalization was not a linear continuation of prewar trends of technical change but was qualitatively new. Postwar rationalization brought more profound changes and transformed economic structures more rapidly than anything before had done and, Kähler argued, contributed significantly to the duration and severity of the Great Depression. He did not share Weintraub's optimistic assessment that the increase of productivity during the 1920s had given rise to only brief layoffs. Instead, he pointed out that although production capacity had risen steadily during this period the size of the work force had continually decreased and that the curve of productivity had risen faster than the curve of production. With this he furnished an important indicator—one that is used today by a German research institute, for example—for measuring labor displacement caused by technical change. He was also instrumental in refining the accuracy of growth theory, for in the 1940s he scrutinized not only technical progress but also, among other things, the qualifications of the work force and the effect of better education on growth potential.[31]

In spite of their originality these theoretical studies of the 1930s never received the attention they deserved. The neoclassicists remained convinced that the free market supplied its own automatic and harmonious processes of adjustment, and the New Dealers of the institutionalist camp, though interested in the questions of practical planning raised by the economists at the New School, had not much use for the underlying detailed theoretical reflections. But the most important reason why the New School economists' work was ignored was probably the victorious sweep of Keynesian economics, an approach that seemed to offer a much more immediate strategy for conquering unemployment than the structural policies of the reform economists and did so without challenging the existing social order. Some other contributing factors to the lack of recognition may have been Lederer's unexpected early death in 1939 and the fact that Lowe and Neisser were not yet at the New School at this time, so that the incentive was lacking for Kähler to pursue the discussion more actively.

Only today, in view of the present worldwide crisis, the revolution brought about by microprocessors, and new, structural long-term unemployment, is the significance of those early studies being recognized, and they are generating growing interest. Among the younger economists in Germany and in the United States, as well as in other countries, a kind of renaissance of the Kiel school is taking place as economists try to combine the short-term Keynesian theory of effective demand with the classical theory of a long-term accumulative process and the structural change that goes along with it.[32]

2. Economic Planning and the Keynesian Model

In all of their work the reform economists had openly wondered whether the problems of economic interventions that technical progress would create in advanced industrial societies were still solvable in a free-market system or whether permanent planning would not become necessary. This political question absorbed these economists at least as much since the beginning of the 1930s as did the theoretical analysis of economic dynamics, for the redefinition and elaboration of classical theory had also—in view of the depression—led them to reflect on the practical consequences of their theoretical insights. The starting point of their reflections was that concentration and monopolization tended to result in ever larger units of capital, which, in their eyes, had long since rendered obsolete the regulating function of the market as hypostatized by traditional economics.

In a heated debate on monopolies carried on around 1930, the reform theoreticians had pointed out that the pressure of fixed costs led to inflexibilities in large capital units, inflexibilities that greatly insulated these capital units from movements in price, wages, and interest. Emil Lederer spoke of a "false circle" of production that created an inner ring of large enterprises immune to the market and representing a potential aggravation of economic crisis of unknown dimensions. In a depression, such enterprises would have to keep prices high because fixed costs remained the same even with declining production, with the result that these sectors of the economy would set off a cumulative process of aggravating the economic crisis.[33] Lowe saw in the rapid rationalizations of the mid 1920s gigantic misinvestments and capital destruction because the fruits of advances in productivity were wasted by a monopolistic price policy. The blessings of technical progress had not led to cheaper prices and greater mass demand. Under the existing system of cartels of raw material producers—which accounted for roughly one-fourth of German production—those blessings resulted instead in greater profits for the monopolies. As a consequence, no streamlining had taken place in the area dominated by the cartels; that is, unproductive, marginal enterprises were not eliminated. At the same time falling demand undermined the market for consumer goods, and, because prices were not lowered, the necessary compensation process did not take place.[34]

In the debate on how the current depression was to be overcome the reform theoreticians favored "active anticyclical intervention," by which government would stimulate effective demand. But on the whole their attitude toward this approach in fiscal policy alone, later recommended most prominently by Keynes, remained rather skeptical because it was designed merely for short-term intervention and disregarded the underlying structural problems. The policy model of governmental deficit spending was aimed solely at raising demand during the economic crisis, taking for granted the existence of a functioning market system. It also failed to recognize that private production and government decisions do not affect identical segments of the economy.

The reform economists saw these problems in a much sharper light. Their stronger interest in the underlying structural factors logically led them toward more far-reaching political conclusions. Instead of intervention designed only to counteract business cycles, they demanded a comprehensive, goal-oriented politization or control of production decisions. Lowe wrote at that time that anticyclical policy amounted to "barking at the moon and a failure to understand the interconnections between the capitalistic economy and the capitalistic state if the state tried to emancipate the political sphere without transforming the economic structure." He thought "ill-conceived" an intervention theory that, for lack of more specific goals, embodied the danger of further accumulation of power in the hands of big economic units and interests, interests to which even the governmental bureaucracy would succumb. His last plea to be published in Germany therefore was a call to work on "the fundamental task of setting the switches for a new economic system."[35]

The reform theoreticians did not define their perspectives more concretely until they were in the United States and until Keynes's standard work, *The General Theory of Employment, Interest, and Money,* appeared in 1936. In the fall of that same year Lederer and Neisser published the first two reviews of Keynes's work in *Social Research.* These were followed by several essays by Gerhard Colm.

The thrust of these articles was that Keynes had not developed a general theory at all. The oscillation of his thinking around effective demand as an explanation of what caused economic upswings and downswings was just as monistic and therefore questionable as the neoclassical perspective, the New School economists argued. They did stress that Keynes's macroeconomic approach was an important step toward a theory of economic dynamics, and they perceived a similarity in outlook to their own in Keynes's assertion that wage level had no directive influence on investment—as the neoclassicists claimed—and therefore was secondary for the level of employment, but otherwise they could see nothing in Keynes's book that was incompatible with orthodox doctrine. The central difference between Keynes and the neoclassicists lay only in their different evaluations of the conditions favoring investment. Keynes's hope that government could stimulate demand and thus create a climate favorable for investment, which would in turn lead to greater employment, could be, but did not necessarily have to be, realized. Not only immediate, short-term effects on employment levels were important, the critics claimed, but also the longer perspective of what kind of investment was stimulated and what sectors of the economy were affected. If this aspect was disregarded there was a danger that the initial upswing caused by measures designed to counteract unemployment due to business cycles would at the same time raise structural unemployment.

Criticism was also leveled at Keynes's optimistic vision of continuous economic development interrupted by only brief and easily correctable downturns. Keynes could arrive at such a view only, his critics argued, because he largely ignored the interconnections of production among industrial branches and sectors. To be sure, Keynes distinguished between demand for consumer goods and for production goods, noting that they did not follow parallel curves, but nowhere was there a breakdown either of the goods making up total supply or of total demand. The decisive figure affecting demand for consumer goods—total national income—was nowhere broken down specifically. Instead, different kinds of individual income were aggregated into a gross national product. This disregarded the different quality of the components of income—wages, interest, capital gain—and consequently also ignored the assignment of social roles that go along with the different kinds of income, so that the uses to which income is put appear completely undifferentiated.

The criticisms these New School economists leveled at Keynes anticipated some questions whose full significance is being recognized only in today's discussion of economic policy, now that the optimism of Keynesian policies dominant during the 1960s has waned. The early critics had

113

pointed out that the quantitative increase in demand, which was supposed, according to the multiplier principle, to have an overall stimulating effect on the entire economy, was not all that mattered but that qualitative aspects also had to be taken into account, among them: problems of disproportionate growth, the fact that structural changes do not affect all industrial branches at the same rate, technical immobilities, and, at that time also, the strivings toward autarchy on the part of some industrial countries (tariff and currency exchange policies), as well as the lack of markets for the products of the old industrial countries. Keynes did not consider these real-life factors and their long-term effects, his critics pointed out, so that his theory was unlikely to be of use in guiding long-term growth. While acknowledging the great intellectual accomplishment of the British economist, Lederer nevertheless concluded: "Keynes has failed to consider those very changes in facts which lead to the perplexities this book is intended to discuss."[36]

Behind this more technical criticism there were also broad philosophical differences bearing on the social role of the state, differences that can be traced back to contrasting intellectual backgrounds. Keynes, according to Lederer, aimed at stabilizing the market system, thus remaining within the tradition of the eighteenth-century liberal utopian concept. The underlying experience that inspired the theoretical thinking of his German critics, however, was the collapse of the Weimar Republic. They did not share Keynes's optimism about human rationality in the economic sphere, a rationality that would supposedly lead people to coordinate their behavior adequately with government initiatives. Thus it was not merely a matter of economics when Gerhard Colm asserted that the state should not just respond reactively in trying to overcome depressions but had to take active measures to assure lasting full employment.[37]

No doubt this interpretation of Keynes offered by the German reform economists is somewhat extreme. After all, Keynes himself had not excluded the possibility—at least abstractly—of significant intervention in the spirit of his critics. As early as the mid 1920s, in his essay "Am I a Liberal?" he had forcefully argued against the course modern capitalism was taking and the increasingly rigid dogmas of neoclassical thinking, and he had called for a new order "which deliberately aims at controlling and directing economic forces in the interests of social justice and social stability." For this "New Liberalism" new wisdoms would have to be invented that would be annoying, dangerous, and disobedient to those who had set the tone in academe up to then.[38] In view of this personal confession the goals of Keynes's *General Theory* cannot be stated as unequivocally as the New School critics did. It is true that Keynes stressed the "conservative" nature of his reform ideas, which aimed at getting rid of institutional obstacles in order to coordinate interest levels, rates of investment, mass consumption, and full employment. But he was quite aware that massive fluctuations in employment levels might lead to a situation where investment decisions could no longer be left "in private hands without danger." A "comprehensive socialization" of investment might turn out to be the only means to achieve full employment.[39]

However, such statements should not obscure the differences between Keynes and the German reform economists. Keynes himself made it clear that his analysis applied only to the short term while the technological structure was explicitly accepted by him as given. His theory was meant to solve only a short-term depression; in the long run, he assumed, the forces at work within the market model as analyzed by traditional theory would prevail. As Lowe later commented aptly, "in spite of drastic breaks with tradition, . . . the General Theory as a logical construct is a product of neoclassical thinking. What distinguishes it from the orthodox version is a different set of motivational and institutional premises rather than a different technique of analysis."[40]

By contrast, the German reform economists' structural analyses focused on the long-term process of growth. Economic slumps and unemployment were for them not short-term aberrations but constant side effects of technical change and of structural upheavals resulting from this change, side effects that had far-reaching consequences for the entire social system. The planning they advocated therefore was not restricted to directing that core area of long-term economic processes. Rather, they also demanded more comprehensive planning and intervention, such as the broad measures discussed in Germany before 1933 under the slogan *Wirtschaftsdemokratie* ("industrial democracy"). Keynes's *General Theory*, in any case, did not formulate an anticyclical economic policy, that is to say, a consistent policy for stabilizing the economic process, but recommended establishing more favorable conditions, primarily for investment demand, during economic recessions. The planning concepts of the reform economists, on the other hand, were aimed at creating a coordinated set of tools for dealing effectively with economic disproportionalities, that is, for eliminating the processes that disconnected production, employment, and prices. At the same time their strategy for avoiding economic crises aimed at stabilizing the political system, which the German economists perceived to be much more labile than did someone like Keynes.

These ideas were, of course, influenced by the negative experiences of the Weimar Republic. This was the first time that democratic participation had become a real possibility in Germany, and that possibility aroused the opposition of the old elites accustomed to ruling in the earlier Kaiserreich. In this context planning also meant limitation of social and political power. The urgency of the planning concepts of the time and the social goals they implied became evident in the end phase of the Republic, when the groups opposing the Republic were able to use the economic crisis as a means to upset the political system.

Living in Great Britain with its very different social structure, Keynes felt no need to reflect on such political consequences. The fact that private production and decisions affecting fiscal policy did not affect identical segments of the economy in his model represented no problem to him because British society had very different habits of democratic civility and established procedures of compromise. Adolph Lowe in particular had encountered this aspect of British society during the 1930s. His temporary isolation from his earlier colleagues and the different social climate in which he found himself influenced the perspectives of the work he did in Manchester. The skepticism that he had already voiced before 1933 about the role of the state in economic interventionism found new justification here. Within the British class structure, which was not all that different from that in Germany, he found considerable conformity and ability to compromise. Enhanced by more democratic access to education and less insuperable class barriers, these factors accounted for England's stability, a stability achieved without extensive government regulation of conflict.[41] These experiences continued to influence Lowe's further economic studies. This work, done in the 1950s and sixties at the New School and focusing on instrumental analysis, resulted in an important modification of his group's previous theoretical thinking about planning.

Against this background, Lowe saw in the Keynesian policy model nothing more than a variant of social conformity. In this model the state, which in market theory is the *Nachtwächter* ("night watchman") standing outside economic transactions, now entered into the economic process. It could be an important intervenor, but without the power to set limits on private decision making it could have only a subsidiary, corrective influence. Convinced of the functionality of the capitalistic system, Keynes concentrated on increasing the efficiency of the market processes on which the neoclassicists centered their analyses. The German reform theoreticians, by contrast, wanted to regulate or influence economic processes in the long run primarily by changing the framework of the political order.

Questions of planning and social order were also central to the work done at the New School during its first years and decades. The general seminar, in which all members of the Graduate Faculty participated and which was the nucleus of their academic life, gave rise to even more comprehensive, interdisciplinary sociological discussion of this topic. If before 1933 the discussion had been largely dominated by criticism of monopolies, it now centered on the question of how "chained capitalism" could be transformed into a "balanced capitalism." In terms of political structure, this included above all else a clarification of the relationship between economic and political democracy. The German experience with industrial democracy was insufficient for this. First of all, there had never been anything like democratic participation in the economic process; and second, the numerous government measures of the Weimar Republic, such as fixing work time or compulsory arbitration were intended to bring about sociopolitical improvements only, not necessarily to improve the functioning of the economic system.

The work of the New School economists therefore aimed at the interrelation of economics and democracy, going beyond sociopolitical measures and the right to have a voice in decision making in individual companies. It was instead to focus primarily, as Alfred Kähler explained, on positive regulation of production and distribution in order to maintain the economy in a dynamic equilibrium. This implied more than a "liberally managed capitalism" of the Keynesian stamp; it meant instead considerable governmental investment policies and growth control.[42] What is remarkable here is that as early as the mid 1930s ecological reasons were cited for such planning preferences.[43]

Eduard Heimann in particular examined the philosophical aspects of planning and its theoretical relation to democratic government in his discussion of Marxism. He had been having growing doubts since the 1920s about the Marxist vision, according to which the working class as a historical force would bring about socialism. For Heimann that meant social freedom in a just and nonauthoritarian society. In his book *Soziale Theorie des Kapitalismus* [Social theory of capitalism] of 1929, he had made it clear that social transformations were not brought about so much by any particular economic class as by individual willingness to assume responsibility and collective ability to work toward a goal. A large, enlightened, and informed majority had to support emancipation movements and their future goals, or, Heimann warned, the result would be not freedom and security but merely a change in rulers.[44]

Heimann picked up this thread in the United States. Using historical materialism as a foil again, he showed how a growing gap had opened up in the socialist movements of Europe between traditional Marxist vision and actual political strategies. This in turn had led to a contradiction between the original socialist promises and real goals. The socialist example of the Soviet Union made him doubt whether democracy and socialism could be combined within the old categories of thought. The collectivization of the agrarian sector had been a morally and economically justified move, Heimann felt, but it had been imposed from above and in violation of the will of those affected. Planning could thus take the form of despotism. This showed that economic interventions should be accepted not as political principles justified in themselves but only as functional means to realize goals accepted by consensus. Even though collective planning had taken on a largely totalitarian character in the Soviet Union—as well as in Italy— Heimann still saw it as an antitotalitarian instrument. For him it did not mean control and shaping society from above; instead, it served as a democratic way of directing growth to maintain decentralized production and a pluralistically organized social infrastructure.[45]

These themes came up again and again in many seminars, conferences, and articles after 1933. Just a few weeks into the academic year, a first symposium on the topic "Planned Economy" was held at the Graduate Faculty, and of the 157 articles published in *Social Research* during the following years up to the outbreak of the war more than half were devoted to economic questions; in most of these, planning problems were discussed. In addition, several special volumes were published, among them *Political and Economic Democracy* of 1937 and the collection of essays *War in Our Time* (1939), which also centered on these questions. Other colloquia, on topics like "Struggle for Economic Security in Democracy" and "Functional Fiscal Policy," also show how perennial a discussion topic this was at the New School.[46]

The continued concentration on this area by no means reflects an intellectual and retrospective self-preoccupation on the part of this immigrant group, as has repeatedly been claimed.[47] Unlike the theoretical analyses of the problem of technology, these studies by the New School economists evoked considerable interest. As we will show later, these economists found an attentive audience at academic meetings of their discipline, and the symposia at the Graduate Faculty attracted many American colleagues. In 1937 Heimann helped organize a symposium in New York that presented the most comprehensive assessment of economic planning to date in the United States. Of the forty contributions presented there, three were by Heimann himself. A list of the literature that had appeared on the topic was also compiled. This comprehensive international bibliography shows that the work done at the New School was preeminent; of the articles from American periodicals cited, those from *Social Research* outnumber those of any other scholarly periodical.[48]

These facts give some indication of the position the New School economists quite rapidly acquired in their new world. To be sure, during the first years of the New Deal, planning was viewed with real optimism, and this facilitated the academic adjustment of the German economists. Just how much uncertainty reigned among American intellectuals in this area is shown, for example, by W. C. Mitchell, who considered Bismarck's social and economic policies the most successful attempt at constructive planning to date.[49]

On the whole, however, the explicitly theoretical studies on planning published by New School academics during the 1930s did not meet with much interest in the United States. The numerous books and articles by Heimann in particular encountered difficulties in spite of the author's efforts to promote them. In his writing, the necessary practical recommendations were lost in the mass of European philosophical and intellectual background presented. Heimann may have been a stimulating participant in the internal discussions of the general seminar, but in public he became more and more of a loner who was "very little in touch" with his new surroundings.[50]

The prevalent new optimism and the search for new ways not only reflected John Dewey's slogan "Learning by Doing" coined at that time but also gave rise to numerous new organizations and publications that were devoted to questions of planning and that critically examined the New Deal experiment. Thus the National Planning Association was formed in 1934, and the National Economic and Social Planning Association launched a publication called *Plan Age*. Established research organizations, too, like the National Bureau of Economic Research and the Brookings Institution were doing work in this area. The Rockefeller Foundation, too, established a special priority for research on "Economic Planning and Control" within its social sciences program and allocated almost $2.4 million to it.[51] It must be pointed out once again, however, that the optimism of the New Dealers was shared by only a minority and that the more conciliatory Keynesian model was able to assert itself over these initiatives in theoretical planning.

3. Fiscal Policy as Active Economic Policy

Thus the theoretical discussion about economic planning carried on by the New School economists remained largely Platonic. There was one area, however, in which their planning ideas had a lasting impact during the 1930s and 1940s. This was due to Gerhard Colm, one of the most interesting younger experts to come from Germany. Not only did he make important contributions to contemporary fiscal theory—which, it is hardly an exaggeration to say, he revolutionized—but, having been called to work in the highest levels of the Washington administration, he would also have a considerable impact on the shaping of American fiscal policy after 1939. Colm's concept of fiscal policy differed from the Keynesian model in important ways. Its goal was not so much to correct short-term oscillations through reactive government regulation as to plan the long-term course of the economy with the help of the national budget. And, as a fiscal expert in the Bureau of the Budget and an adviser to the president, he was able to some extent to put his ideas into practice in the 1940s.

In his habilitation thesis *Volkswirtschaftliche Theorie der Staatsausgaben* [Economic theory of government spending], Colm had shown the traditional underpinnings of public fiscal policy to be erroneous as early as the 1920s.[52] Though this branch of economics had been neglected in most countries, it was quite highly developed in Germany. Obviously, Colm's work in this area made much more of a mark in the United States, where the study of public finance was still in an archaic state according to the unanimous assessment not only of German experts but of American observers as well.[53] The American tax system at the beginning of the New Deal still reflected nineteenth-century liberal ideology that regarded taxes simply as money withdrawn from productive use in the economy. This attitude proved to be a great hindrance to combating the Great Depression in the first years of the New Deal.[54] Many of the study commissions set up by the administration and by Congress after 1933, as well as private studies, show how deficient knowledge in this area was felt to be in the United States. In the old textbooks these problems were not mentioned at all.[55]

Because of this desolate state of affairs, Colm's first articles on public finance in *Social Research* apparently met with great interest, for he was soon among those scholars at the New School who were invited to contribute to various other publications and periodicals,[56] and his first independent study published in the United States on the tax policy of the New Deal attracted immediate attention.[57]

Unlike conventional fiscal theory, which focused almost exclusively on the state's revenues and regarded taxes primarily from the point of view of how they could be obtained with a minimum of difficulty, Colm in the 1920s had turned his attention to government expenditures—as the title of his book indicates—and their economic consequences. Even before the outbreak of the Great Depression the procyclical fiscal policies pursued by all the industrialized countries had led him to doubt the theory that claimed national budgets were subject to market laws and thus should be strictly balanced. Instead, he tried to show not only that the state as a "third pillar" was an integral part of the economic process, along with the producers and the private households, but that it also formed a separate economic system. Unlike private enterprises, which are interested only in their own individual economic success, the state had to fulfill a multidimensional function aimed at stabilizing the economy and the social system. Contrary to accepted economic theory, this was in no way an arational view, Colm claimed, for there existed "another rationality of selecting goals" without which modern markets could not function at all. With this argument he not only challenged neoclassical assumptions but at the same time advanced a consistent theory of interventionism based on means and ends. First of all, he showed that governments had been practicing economic interventionism consistently since the nineteenth century. The only new element in his approach, he claimed, was a clearer analysis and definition of the effects of the government's actions on the economy as a whole. The other thrust of his book was against the conservative consolidation of power that went along with the state's acting like an "upright householder." According to Colm, the national budget should instead serve as an instrument for implementing policies to control economic cycles and structures and thus become the motor of macroeconomic activity.[58]

In many different articles published in the United States, some of them coauthored by Fritz Lehmann, Colm put in concrete terms what this new definition of government tasks implied. It was even more important now than it had been earlier in Germany to quash the misconception that the government's assumption of a growing role in the economy was a slippery road leading to the total state or an unpatriotic debilitation of the country.[59] These voices never asked where tax revenues came from or how public expenditures were used. In addition, it was necessary to correct the widespread opinion that a rise in public expenditures was synonymous with an unproductive policy of encouraging consumption. In Colm's opinion, traditional concepts, such as the "gross national product," were obscured by a veil of "greatest confusion," for there was no asserting from an economic standpoint what was preferable, the private production of, say, whiskey or publicly funded improvements of the educational system. The dilemma of conventional statistics, according to Colm, was that calculations of social productivity regarded everything that had a price as if it were all of equal value. From this perspective—which has a new relevance today—he argued for a more precise definition of the social product that could be used in making macroeconomic decisions, a definition that would differentiate among economic, social, and infrastructural components.[60]

In order to clarify his criticism Colm distinguished between various historical types of state. Succeeding the liberal, night-watchman state, a second type, the social state, had arisen under capitalism. In the name of social justice it attempted to use the tax system to reduce excessive differences in income and introduced other measures to help the socially disadvantaged. After World War I a third type could be distinguished, a state that was taking an increasingly active part in the economic process (war socialism). For the American audience Colm called this type, somewhat euphemistically, the "partner state." Finally, new tasks confronting the state since the outbreak of the Great Depression in 1929, tasks deriving to a considerable extent from demands by diverse organized groups for public protection of their interests, had resulted in the most recent type, the "control type of state," which already pointed beyond the limits of the capitalistic epoch.[61]

One problem apparent to Colm was that the public, the politicians, and the experts as well were still thinking in terms of the outdated types. The large private companies, on the other hand, had long since begun to resort to long-term planning as a strategy for survival. Bringing about the necessary changes in perception in this area was another purpose of Colm's many publications. He wanted to structure the budget in such a way that it could act as a "built-in stabilizer" and maintain full employment within balanced economic development. This idea was also advanced by Keynes, but Colm defined it differently.[62] Unlike Keynes, he did not think that the state should stimulate effective demand during economic crises. He considered a precise definition of goals more important, namely, a definition of where future development should be headed and by what means it should be supported. Colm accused the New Deal politicians of having given up advance planning because, in the most recent crisis of 1937, they had once again and "without any clear idea" of the consequences lowered taxes for business. It had become obvious since the Great Depression, Colm argued, that such reductions were unlikely to solve anything because production decisions were based on expectations of future developments. Washington practiced a diffuse "pump priming" instead of developing a long-term growth strategy with enough flexibility to permit quick short-term reactions. This was the first time that Colm recommended what he would try to translate into official policy after the war when he worked as an economic adviser to the president. What he wanted was for the administration not only to prepare an annual budget but also to publish "economic projections" for longer periods, perhaps five years, projections that would indicate the course the government was planning to take and the priorities and means for pursuing it.[63]

The future direction of the economy should not be completely left up to private enterprise—which was motivated solely by its own profit—especially since miscalculations on the part of the large capital forces could no longer be absorbed by the market but were instead passed on to the public in the form of increased social costs. Beyond this there were entire areas of the infrastructure that profit-oriented enterprise ignored and that up to now—unlike in Germany—had not been counted among the tasks government was responsible for. Colm was thinking here not just of the road network and other communication systems but also—and this deserves to be called almost visionary—of measures to protect the environment, conserve energy, and so on.[64] Germany had been exemplary in this respect in the 1920s, constructing urban central-heating networks, making housing projects more pleasant by planting parks near them, and organizing leisure-time activities—all this not just for sociopolitical reasons but also, as was explicitly stated, to create jobs.

In this connection Colm also attacked the orthodox notion that the national budget had to be balanced, a notion that had remained un-challenged even by the Roosevelt administration during the first years of the New Deal. He argued that a balanced economy was more important than a balanced budget. The latter would only have a negative, reinforcing effect during each phase of the business cycle. What was more important than the balance of revenues and expenditures was that the two sides of the budget be based on the same economic projections and that a goal-oriented fiscal policy distinguish clearly between—and coordinate—the budget's short-term effects of spending and its long-term effects on economic programs.[65]

Apart from defining the function of the national budget in the economic process, Colm continued to work on a normative definition of the factors determining the level of public spending. This debate had a long history in Germany and had been revived in the early 1930s by Colm's colleague at the New School, Arnold Brecht. Brecht had added to the old "law of the expansion of government activity accompanying economic and cultural progress," as it had been formulated at the end of the nineteenth century by Adolph Wagner, a new, by now classical "law of the parallel progression of public spending and population density," which offered a partial refine-ment of Wagner's law. Working with observations gathered in the 1920s when he was in the Reichsrat as the Prussian government's official reviewer of the Reich budget, Brecht based his law on a comparison of taxes in different countries. His immediate aim was to justify the fact that state spending was higher in Germany than in the less densely populated and less urbanized France, and he was partially motivated in this by criticism from Allied reparation creditors who claimed that Germany's public ex-penditures were excessive.[66]

These kinds of considerations, which the German experts on public finance brought with them, were ahead of American thinking by several decades. The first American empirical study of the levels of public spending was not published until the 1950s, and it referred back specifically to Colm and Brecht, thus representing a kind of reanalysis of the work of the New School economists.[67] What Brecht and Colm had done after their emigra-tion was to try to verify, in the context of the American situation, the trends that had begun to emerge in Germany. In this, Brecht used as the decisive determinant his law of population density—dense population being a given in Germany but not in the United States—whereas Colm took as measures of state spending the degree of industrialization and personal income, factors already implied in Wagner's law. By using these indicators, he arrived at a more realistic picture of the characteristics of American government spending.[68]

The search for such indicators was not motivated by an abstract interest in economics and fiscal policy. Rather, he saw them as connected to crucial sociological questions. Increasing industrialization and the consequent rise in standard of living went hand in hand with greater demands for public services, which, if not met, could lead to loss of loyalty to, and possibly to paralysis of, the political system, something Colm and his colleagues had personally experienced in Germany. Thus Colm emphasized the fact— which still seemed startling at the time—that social spending, interpreted in the broadest sense, was higher in rich countries with less objective need than in poor regions. The cultural paradox in America was that the great abundance of material goods was accompanied by a growing deterioration in the quality of life. The private enterprise system claimed most of the national resources, so that barely enough money remained for public infrastructure, schools, hospitals, roads, and so on. The sociological consequence of this development was that people adapted more and more to the things offered them as consumers, since there was no institutional support in the area of education and leisure-time activity to encourage a more creative way of life.[69]

Colm's stature did not go unnoticed long in Washington. He was first asked only to join a group of experts who were to work out the criteria and measures necessary for a solid financial and economic policy, but his wealth of knowledge and great vision soon led to the offer of a permanent job as financial expert in the Bureau of the Budget.[70] Here he found an almost boundless field of activity, for not only American public finance but also public accounting practices were still at an archaic stage. The Budget and Accounting Act of 1921 legally required for the first time that something like an all-inclusive annual federal budget be submitted. The Bureau of the Budget was set up for this but was hardly equipped to do the job in the following years; or, as Colm put his criticism,[71] the act of 1921 had set up an apparatus but had not stated how this apparatus was to work. This did not change until the Reorganization Act of 1939, which placed the bureau directly under the president. Now the budget became a unified government program with clearly defined goals. This reorganization represented a major break with the past and introduced an economic orientation into the budgetary considerations of the U.S. government.

Colm was able to make his first and most lasting marks in the drawing up of the emergency or extraordinary budget. Such a budget—which consists essentially of revenues and expenditures for one-time projects that are credit-financed or will pay for themselves over time—had in Germany been a separate entity from the regular budget ever since the 1880s. Nothing comparable had existed in the United States before 1933. At the beginning of the New Deal, Roosevelt had promised to lower taxes and at the same time declared that he would initiate a comprehensive reconstruction program. Since these two goals were mutually incompatible, an emergency budget had to be drawn up, which included the new government initiatives to be financed through public loans. This extraordinary budget, intended as a provisional emergency measure, became a permanent institution and was publicly criticized as a violation of classical accounting principles.

Here Colm was able to provide some needed theoretical elucidation. First of all, he explained that the figures of the emergency budget were much less certain than those of annually recurring appropriations. Thus a separation between the two budgets was not a violation of accounting principles but rather contributed to greater accuracy, since the budget entries should be as specific as possible. But what mattered even more to Colm was to show how such a differentiation allowed the state to pursue active economic policies. In an age when all governments were forced to intervene more and more in the economic process, new forms for government management had to be found. The extraordinary budgets offered Colm an effective way to make these initiatives transparent, and they could also be used in support of the longer-range projections he recommended. For unlike the regular budgets, which included only the current appropriations for the year in question, the extraordinary revenues and expenditures—amounting generally to sizable sums—indicated some longer-term directions because they could be carried over from year to year. When the emergency budget was changed into a regular extraordinary budget, Colm was therefore one of the proponents of "no-year appropriations" to be codified in the extraordinary budget and resorted to later. These no-year appropriations provided for some flexibility of action, although Arnold Brecht warned that no such special powers should exist in a proper national budget policy. According to German budgetary law, for instance, only specific annual amounts could be included in the budget even in the case of major one-time projects that extended over several years, although some special carry-over rules allowed for a certain degree of long-time projection.[72]

Colm also argued for setting up an interdepartmental finance committee that would plan necessary economic strategies for the president. Such a committee did not come into existence until the Full Employment Act of 1946, although the Office of Economic Stabilization established in 1941 may be regarded as a precursor.[73] During this favorable phase—because it was still relatively open—of restructuring budgetary policies, Colm was also involved in working out a comprehensive national budget that was to set overall political and economic priorities for new government activities. From it, the progress of government initiatives and their net effect on the economy could be determined. In 1944, for the first time, economic projections were submitted to Congress instead of budgetary reports as in the past. Colm had long been calling for such projections because they indicated future government plans beyond the accounting year. Finally, as a member of the team of experts in the Bureau of the Budget, he did much of the work to correct previous shortcomings of the statistics used to estimate national income, statistics for which Simon Kuznets had laid the groundwork in the early 1930s.[74]

Politically, this kind of work represented a constant balancing act, always accompanied by the worry that one might expose oneself to suspicions of being an enemy of democracy. The director of the Bureau of the Budget repeatedly requested Colm as well as other financial experts to stick to aspects of budget planning that were related directly to government activity and to avoid all ideological statements. Effective corroboration was supplied by plans the conservative British government was formulating at this same time to insure full employment after the war. These plans called for an active fiscal policy similar to the one Colm and his co-workers were proposing. Still, they remained cautious and made sure that their work was released to the public only with great discretion, and they constantly reiterated that planning, far from being subversive, was becoming increasingly crucial for the preservation and functioning of a free society in the age of modern technology.[75]

This work culminated in the Full Employment Act of 1946, which Colm had a major hand in shaping and which incorporated important elements of his earlier financial and economic thinking. Nevertheless, Colm thought the new law fell far short of providing for a future, goal-oriented policy of economic planning. Years later one of his colleagues from this period expressed his admiration for Colm's amazing political effectiveness and attributed to him an unqualified leading role in creating that "magna carta of economic planning."[76] The act was meant to introduce new planning principles and new procedures into economic policy. For this purpose a Council of Economic Advisers in the Office of the President was created. This council was charged with working out the long-range economic goals for the reports the president was to submit to Congress at least once a year. The reports were to state among other things what level of production and what volume of purchasing power were necessary to assure full employment for the coming year, whether changes in government policy were called for, and what concrete steps should be initiated. This represented no guarantee of full employment and economic stability, but at least adequate tools for reaching this goal were established.[77]

A newly created economic committee made up of members of both houses of Congress was to consider the reports and pass them on to the legislature. An aspect not to be underestimated was that the president's new economic reports were meant to have a significant function in the economic education of the public. In them, financial and political perspectives were presented that figured in none of the textbooks of the time. These reports were consequently published in large editions and distributed to select audiences in the public, especially to universities and colleges.

Because of great uncertainty about the handling of technical details, much was kept rather general, and some procedures were left without precise definition. Still, it is clear that the plan for economic projections realized one of the medium-range strategic goals Colm had formulated in the 1930s. From now on, budgetary decisions would no longer be based on past developments but would be made with a view to the future and be oriented toward politically defined macrogoals that budgetary policies would help achieve.

The projections on the development of the economy as a whole were to have an "announcement effect," according to Colm, that private business could take into consideration in its decision making. Since private enterprises planned their own business policies but refused to admit that planning made sense in the larger context of the whole society, he also regarded the projections as a basis for a future "concentrated economy" that would allow individual interest groups to coordinate long-term planning.[78]

But the Full Employment Act, which seemed for the first time under the New Deal to promise an economic policy based on more varied perspectives, turned out to be stillborn, for with Roosevelt's death the previous openness of politics changed. Truman rejected the "mandate for planning" (Colm) contained in the act. To be sure, the presidential council, whose staff included Colm, submitted the first longer-range projections and estimates in the following years, but the administration made no use of them. On the contrary, the controls of the wartime economy still in effect were reduced and a liberal course taken. Restraint was urged on employers and unions in price and wage policies, but the expected improvements in the market economy did not materialize as the returning soldiers were reintegrated into the work force, and inflationary developments could not be avoided. By the end of the 1940s prices had risen by a third, and the rate of investment was rising considerably faster than the rate of private con-, sumption, resulting in the first serious postwar recession in 1949. In that same year the council submitted its first five-year budget for the period 1950 to 1954, but there was no response from either the White House or Congress, especially since the Korean War in the making elicited different economic and political priorities in Washington.

With Eisenhower's election and the change to a Republican administration in 1952, the personnel of the council was replaced, too. Keynesian economists who had no interest in long-range planning and consequently no longer worked out all-inclusive budgets predominated there now. No sooner had a clear, goal-oriented political strategy been developed under the New Deal than it was revoked. In 1952 Colm left the president's advisory staff in a resigned mood and became chief analyst in the National Planning Association, with which he had been collaborating closely since 1945. Here he produced numerous publications in which he continued his analyses of active planning for the entire economy, and he also gave many public lectures in the United States, Germany, and Western Europe, soliciting support for these ideas.[79]

4. Writings on National Socialism

At the New School the reform economists were not occupied exclusively with developing and completing research on economics begun in the 1920s. Like many other emigrated social scientists they also soon began to study the developments that had led to the victory of national socialism.[80] This is another indication of the breadth of their analytical approach, for the problems their analysis focused on here had already been central to some of their earlier work, as in Emil Lederer's sociological studies of the middle class and Gerhard Colm's study on the "masses." Of course, the emigrant scholars' analyses of fascism were also an attempt to come to terms with their own shocking experiences. In the very first issue of *Social Research,* European intellectuals' reaction to the victory and nature of national socialism was summed up by Giuseppe Antonio Borgese, a student of Benedetto Croce and future son-in-law of Thomas Mann.[81] Another reason—probably the most urgent for the New School economists—for publishing so many studies of fascism after 1933 was that their authors wanted to call attention to the fascist threat, which the American public was hardly aware of or regarded with indifference. Although many of these studies were occasioned by current events, they, like those of the former Frankfurt Institute of Social Research, nevertheless represent important attempts to understand fascism from the sociological perspective of that time.

In a programmatic article that served as the basis of discussion in the first general seminar on this topic, Paul Tillich set the stage for future analyses. Against the background of United States experience, where the Great Depression had been no less severe than in Germany but had not given rise to authoritarian tendencies, he outlined a broader spectrum for possible analysis than the previous sociological theories of fascism had provided. In addition to the growing social tensions in modern industrial society, the disintegration of liberal middle-class identity, and the increasing susceptibility of the fragmented modern masses to all kinds of ideologies, Tillich saw other factors contributing to the victory of fascism. These were the separate historical developments in Central and Eastern Europe, the fact that nationhood had come too late to Germany, and the German tendency to mythologize and absolutize the state, whose leaders believed that only authoritarian rule would lead to success and to acceptance by Western European neighbors.[82]

The new type of "totalitarian state" outlined by Tillich did not, however, anticipate the analysis of totalitarianism first put forth in the mid 1930s in the wake of Stalin's purge trials and revived after 1945 during the cold war, an analysis that equated bolshevism with national socialism/fascism. Most of the emigrés at the New School at that time rejected this view, and Jakob Marschak no doubt expressed a general conviction when he termed the assumption that these two types of dictatorship were identical a "miserable platitude." He saw only "formal similarities" between them.[83] A similar assessment is suggested by the fact that Colm and Lowe, for instance, did not, after their flight from Germany, preclude the possibility of working in the Soviet Union.[84]

The later orthodox theory of totalitarianism did have a few adherents, among them Arthur Feiler and Max Ascoli. But their work, which was based exclusively on the institutional forms political rule took in Germany, Italy, and the Soviet Union, was not representative of the group as a whole. When in the mid 1930s a collaborative research project on the rise of fascism was begun—to be only partially realized—Feiler and Ascoli remained isolated and had to publish their study separately.[85]

More representative of the general view of the emigré scholars was the writing of Eduard Heimann. His studies grew out of an earlier critique of the historical shortcomings of the socialist movement. He picked up his previous basic ideas again in the United States in several articles and then in his major book *Communism, Fascism, or Democracy?* (1938). In his view, Adam Smith and Karl Marx, or classical liberalism and socialism, were largely in agreement in their analysis of society and the concept of man. The philosophic split and the resulting misdirected political strategies came about only after the European world refused to analyze more closely the shifts in power and market conditions brought about by modern large-scale industry on the one hand and the subjective needs of human beings on the other. Though liberalism had constructed a *homo oeconomicus* with an immutable urge to maximize material satisfaction, Social Democratic parties, particularly in Germany, had given in to the "slothful illusion" of hope, assuming that everything would run in the right direction on the material level. Then bolshevism had made short shrift of dialectics and, taking advantage of the revolutionary situation during the war, had built up a dictatorship. Fascism had finally descended on Europe as a punishment for the "betrayal" of the ideals of human spontaneity and of the democratic concepts of order and freedom, a betrayal of which both the passively tame German socialists and the professional revolutionaries of hard-line bolshevism were guilty. Not unlike the philosopher Ernst Bloch at that same time, Heimann saw in fascism a just retribution for European socialism's abandonment of the passion that had informed the old fight for freedom and its retreat instead to a "formal rationality" that handed political destiny over to natural evolution. Such a stance banned human subjectivity from the "rational democratic processes."

Heimann thus regarded fascism not so much as a step in the development of capitalism as an irrational rebellion on the part of the middle class—which the socialist movement had carelessly neglected—against the diminishing of the concept of human nature. While conceding—like Tillich—a certain historical justification to bolshevism as an educating dictatorship in Russia's preindustrial society and seeing in its rule a legitimate bulwark against capitalism, which had begun to spread to that country, he considered the fascist dictatorship of the middle class an incarnation of inhumanity. Because its prioritization of values was no different from that of capitalist big business—which, however, represented an objective threat to the social position of the middle class—fascist dictatorship channeled economic fears together with irrational needs into specific political defense strategies and made scapegoats of rationalism and its supporters, namely, the labor movement, intellectuals, and other, arbitrarily selected minorities. The fact that fascist dictatorship borrowed techniques of governing from bolshevism was accidental in itself, but it did partially explain why the European labor movement was unable to develop, let alone carry out, a realistic defense strategy.[86]

Heimann attributed a considerable share of responsibility for the victory of fascism to the socialist movement, and, no doubt aware of the implications and possible misunderstandings his analysis could give rise to, he stressed more than once that his study was in many ways nothing more than a variation of his earlier thoughts from the 1920s. Repeatedly referring to his growing doubts about socialism after 1918, he tried to forestall the suspicion that his "present lack of sympathy for the socialist movement could be attributed to his American surroundings."[87]

Emil Lederer's major study of fascism, *State of the Masses*, published posthumously in 1940, is a concise indictment of the socialist hopes that came to such an abrupt end with the unchallenged assumption of power by the National Socialists. Of all the New School intellectuals Lederer had probably had the longest and closest contact with the German labor movement. In his *Einige Gedanken zur Soziologie der Revolutionen* [Some Thoughts on the sociology of revolutions] of 1918 he had still painted a highly optimistic picture of well-organized, politically aware "masses," presenting their goal-oriented, collective actions as a realistic path for profound social change.[88] No trace of this optimism remained after 1933. For Lederer, social tensions no longer produced class struggle and revolutionary citizens but fostered only a growing, directionless radicalization. If this took the form of revolution, it could lead—and this was for him the lesson of fascism—to results very different from those expected in the past and from the utopia promised by Marxism. In earlier revolutions the masses had been the crucial driving force, but they had dissolved after their goals were achieved or after their attempts had failed. Fascism, by contrast, had transformed mass movements into a permanent institution. In a totalitarian state crowds became amorphous collectives of different groups, held together solely by perpetual action and by an appeal to the most primitive, irrational collective instincts.

Lederer continued, more so than Heimann, to adhere to the rational world view he had held in the past, but he was at one with Heimann in criticizing the fundamental assumptions of Marxism. By putting economics above all else, Marxism had failed to take sufficient account of the individuality of human beings and had thus constructed the utopia of a classless society, a utopia that was, however, no longer rationally acceptable. For Lederer this was no reason to abandon the idea of socialism; instead, he searched for ways of redefining it. Since there was no such thing as a *volonté générale*, or a conscious, homogeneous, and goal-oriented proletariat, Lederer argued, the socialist premise that the solution to class conflicts would automatically end social problems and usher in freedom was unhistorical and unrealistic. On the contrary, he saw in the institutionalization of an evolutionary class conflict of whatever nature—the great "agent of life"—a basic principle necessary for the progress of a free and dynamic society. By contrast, he argued, the totalitarian mass state remained static because its "ideas," that is, the emotional appeals designed to evoke mass loyalty and unity, remained always the same. Lederer's calls for a "realistic socialism" tried to drive home the idea that only the coexistence of different social groups makes up a true society, that only a sufficient stratification could prevent the mass state, and that evolution was the only way in which progressive social transformations could come about. Only as long as the diverse interests within modern societies were not glossed over by a vague ideology of community could the emotional susceptibility of the masses be contained and kept in balance through rational discourse, regardless of what political system was in place.[89]

Since Lederer's work remained unfinished, these ideas are not further elaborated. There are only vague suggestions, as in the idea of "concerted action," of how these theories of democracy would affect the evolutionary process in a society made up of diverse interest groups. Surely it is also questionable whether fascism can be regarded as a classless society and the amorphous masses as "actors" who bring a dictator to power and keep him in power.[90] Lederer's book did not, in fact, meet with much approval among his German fellow emigrés. It is unlikely that Franz Neumann was motivated by rivalry when he wrote in his *Behemoth:* "Were Lederer's analysis correct, our earlier discussion would be completely wrong. Social imperialism would then not be a device to ensnare the masses but an articulation of the spontaneous longing of the masses. Racism would not be the concern of small groups alone but would be deeply imbedded in the masses. Leadership adoration would be a genuine semi-religious phenomenon and not merely a device to prevent insight into the operation of the socioeconomic mechanism." Lederer's "basic error," he felt, lay in equating class structures with social differentiation, which prevented him from seeing the true character of fascism or national socialism. Although Neumann criticized Lederer for not asking who benefited ultimately from the manipulation of the masses under fascism, he nevertheless conceded that Lederer had raised some important new questions. Also, Neumann added, the inadequacies of the sociological analysis of fascism at the time had to be taken into account.[91]

Although Lederer failed to ask what concrete interests the ruling elites had in creating a fascist state, his book still deserved credit for suggesting that socialist discussion needed to break with the old Marxist notion of the historical role of the proletariat. The reality of capitalism and the technical means of mass manipulations now available made that perspective obsolete, and greater attention had to be given instead to the basic, subjective needs and emotions of human beings. His book led the way toward a further analysis by asking what historical conditions and unsolved economic problems had unleashed the manipulated masses and their ability to destroy all social life down to the family. Implicit in this question was an urgent political appeal to the United States and the Western democracies to take a stronger stand against foreseeable military aggression, which was bound to be the final outcome of the Nazi creation of a common fascist identity in Germany. By the time the book appeared one year after Lederer's death, edited by his former student Hans Speier, these last warnings had been rendered obsolete by the outbreak of the war.

Adolph Lowe's brochure *The Price of Liberty,* written in Great Britain and published there in 1937, in some ways complements Heimann's and Lederer's books. Lowe wrote from a different perspective and with an entirely different aim. Produced under the impact of the failed Weimar Republic, this brochure demonstrates more than any other comparable work what new horizons had opened up for German leftist intellectuals in Western democracies.[92]

Lowe started out with the question of why a class society as riddled with feudal relicts as Great Britain's had proved to be so much more stable than Germany's in the face of economic crisis. The only answer he could find was that in England a broadly based "spontaneous conformity" had built up over many centuries of slow but constantly advancing social change. One of the marks of this conformity was the voluntary self-restraint exercised by classes, groups, and individuals. In spite of all the plutocratic elements and class antagonisms that existed, some degree of social mobility, a more open educational system, and other institutional factors contributed to consensus and pursuit of a middle course. In pursuing this middle course, the individual members of society considered social stability more important than the total satisfaction of class and group demands.

Similar observations by other German intellectuals also show how profoundly they were struck by what they called spontaneous conformity—a term that did not necessarily imply total harmony in the society—not only in England but in the United States as well. Albert Einstein, for example, noted enthusiastically that in America the "we" was more important than the "I." Because custom and convention were stronger than political programs, cooperation and an effective division of labor could arise more easily and with less friction, especially since the sense of social responsibility of the owning class was more highly developed in America than in Central Europe. Later, Hannah Arendt was similarly surprised to find political freedom coexisting with social inequality in the United States. Social protest there did not contain an implicit demand for an entirely new social order but could support the political status quo while criticizing it.[93]

By contrast, Lowe saw entirely different forces at work in Germany, where democratizing processes had always consisted of short-term measures imposed by the state in response to national catastrophes, such as the Prussian defeat of 1807 and the collapse of the Kaiserreich in 1918. Because political emancipation had failed to take place, the German middle class had since the nineteenth century cultivated an intellectual and individualistic extremism that had a disintegrating effect. The marginalized labor movement could not counter that tendency, and social cohesion was preserved only through the old bureaucratic and absolutist state apparatus. In this connection Lowe also sharply criticized the Humboldtian ideal of education, which at the time was so highly revered in Anglo-Saxon and American intellectual circles. True, the German university system had encouraged great freedom of thought and fostered the development of the individual personality; however, it was anything but democratic and far from interested in producing politically responsible citizens. The Social Democratic and leftist liberal educational policies of the Weimar Republic had sought to change that. Those policies had, however, plunged the universities into a profound identity crisis, from which they emerged more and more as centers of the counterrevolution.

Not surprisingly, Lowe's conclusion concerning the ability of democratic societies to resist the fascist challenge is summed up in the following assumption: "Spontaneous conformity is the only mode of life through which a large-scale society can reconcile the conflict between freedom and order." But, he goes on, this can be achieved only over time and through education, which has to be more than just the cultivation of autonomous personalities and has to be equally committed to bringing about the formation of a new social and intellectual order, an order Lowe defined as a true "social democracy." In the following decades Lowe was to continue to publish, along with his economic writing, articles on education and educational policy.[94]

Soon after the publication of *The Price of Liberty*, Lowe was forced to recognize that one aspect of the social conformity of British society was that foreigners were not allowed to become integrated. Although he had become naturalized on the day the war started in 1939, he was, in particular at this time of early war hysteria, treated as an outsider. This was why he accepted Johnson's renewed invitation to come to the New School a few months later. Franz Neumann, who also had spent his first few years of exile in England, had similar experiences. He, too, found that British society, stable and solid as it was, proved so intolerant that he soon gave up all hope of ever being allowed to become an Englishman. He decided to move on to New York in the same hope of being able to feel there that as a human being, an intellectual, and a political scientist he was an integral part of at least the socially uniform world of the United States.[95]

These more theoretical analyses of fascism were complemented by a great many empirical studies of political developments primarily in Germany, most of which appeared in *Social Research*. With these articles the New School scholars tried to inform the American public and warn against the growing danger of national socialism. A few other publications, such as the large collection of articles published under the title *War in Our Time*, had the same aim. This title was a deliberate allusion to the slogan "Peace in Our Time" that Neville Chamberlain had coined after the Munich conference of 1938, with the change exposing the illusion contained in the original phrase. The contributors to the volume emphasized that the Munich agreements on the German occupation of Czechoslovak territories had not brought Europe closer to peace but had only escalated the state of "not-yet-war." Using figures taken from the German national budget and military expenditures, including appropriations entered under cryptic titles, Colm and Kähler showed not only that Germany had systematically rearmed itself far beyond the Nazis' proclaimed defense capabilities but that the arms buildup had been achieved at the expense of the well-being and basic needs of the country. In all likelihood, Colm and Kähler concluded, Germany would resort to conquest and exploitation of foreign territories to compensate for the economic crisis that lay ahead. Working along similar lines, Heimann pointed out the economic and military motives of Germany's policy of autarchy. Lederer studied the militarization of production, and Hans Speier the propagandistic preparation for war. Max Ascoli expressed more hope—prevalent in the West as well as among some of the German emigrés—that the people would grow increasingly rebellious against fascist oppression.[96]

The same motive of enlightening the American public lay behind the decision to publish a first complete translation of Hitler's *Mein Kampf*, a project undertaken in 1938–39 by the New School. Before that, the only version available in English had been an abridged translation authorized by the Nazi government. This abridged translation gave no indication that the most vituperative passages had been cut. In a didactically clever form the new, complete version showed graphically, by using different type, what had been omitted in the earlier edition and at the same time made clear through careful commentary that Hitler's slapdash piece of work should not be dismissed as crude propaganda but should be recognized as the blueprint the Nazis had been following and would continue to follow.[97]

The abridged translation of 1933 had sold very poorly. This new edition, however, was received with great interest after Germany's attacks on Austria and Czechoslovakia. Within the first year of its appearance ten printings were sold, and after the United States entered the war the army used this complete version, "because of its excellent translation and annotation," as a standard work in the field of psychological warfare.[98]

Hans Staudinger and Werner Pese wrote a detailed study of the translation, showing that *Mein Kampf* had to be read as a projection of the policies later pursued by the National Socialists. The book was an authentic expression of Hitler's goals precisely because it had been written at a time (1924) when its author was still a nobody who could ignore political and tactical considerations. Granted, very few Germans had actually read the book, but its absolutist claims and the emotional pitch of Hitler's rantings reflected the basic mood of many segments of the German people after 1918. Among the conclusions Staudinger and Pese reached—and this is why the study was not published at the time—was that only total defeat and a prolonged occupation of Germany would succeed in eradicating the Germans' susceptibility to national socialism. Sweeping changes in social and economic structures and extensive reeducation were essential to achieving that end.[99]

Working along similar lines, Hans Speier and the psychologist Ernst Kris supervised a major research project on the manipulative effectiveness of Goebbels's propaganda. Among the many studies done in this connection and published in book form and as articles in various American periodicals, two books stand out in particular, a voluminous study entitled *German Radio Propaganda* and a glossary of *Nazi Deutsch*. Both convey a powerful impression of the militarization and irrationalization of thinking and language under the Nazis.[100]

Finally, some of the New School scholars joined a wider circle of emigré intellectuals and like-minded Americans in trying to reach the American public in other ways. With Alvin Johnson as their spokesman, they took part after the Munich conference in Hermann Broch's and Giuseppe Borgese's plan to draw up a common manifesto that would not only spearhead the publicity battle against fascism but also encourage, in view of the Western countries' passivity, a reexamination of these countries' democratic principles. The planned manifesto was not to be like other collections of essays propounding various antifascist or democratic ideals. Instead, the aim was to produce a collectively conceived program for an international order after the defeat of fascism. After a number of conferences, the manifesto was published in the spring of 1941 under the title *The City of Man: A Declaration of World Democracy*. It was signed by seventeen prominent persons, among them not only Broch, Borgese, Thomas Mann, and Alvin Johnson but also Frank Aydelotte, director of the Institute for Advanced Study at Princeton; Christian Gauss, dean at Princeton; Gaetano Salvemini and William Elliott from Harvard; the theologian Reinhold Niebuhr; and the writer Lewis Mumford.[101]

In spite of its utopian aspects—the vision of universal peace and a future world democracy—this is an important document for a couple of reasons.

First, it was the product of a far from common intellectual and political collaboration between emigrés and Americans, and, second, it reflected on the future role of the United States in world politics. Because the appeasement policy of England and France had been partially responsible for bringing Europe to the verge of destruction, the manifesto declared, the United States with its enormous economic resources was the only country left capable of stopping fascist barbarity and defending the ideals of human rights and international peace against Hitler's dream of world conquest. But the manifesto also made it clear—as the politically committed emigrés and other new American citizens would never have dared to do on their own—that America as it existed was not ready for the task, for democracy there, as in the European countries, was in a severe crisis. For the time being, social realities that conflicted with democratic principles—the plutocratic dominance of the dollar, the oppression of the blacks, and a far from democratic educational system were cited—hardly justified the United States' assumption of the necessary international leadership role.

5. Peace Research and the Institute of World Affairs

Immediately after the outbreak of war the studies of fascism at the New School gave way to a large project entitled "Peace Research," which was to develop planning perspectives for a German and European postwar order. But this project was overshadowed very soon by more pressing, more important tasks because the Washington administration now turned to the New School with massive needs for information relevant to the more urgent problems of the war. For instance, immediately after its founding in the winter of 1939–40 the National Defense Commission requested a series of analyses of the causes that had led to the rise of national socialism and of the economic conditions that had made the German military successes possible.

Because of the United States's political isolationism since 1918, American political science in the 1930s was lacking in internationally oriented research institutions and had hardly a clear understanding of world politics.[102] The outbreak of World War II made both these failings instantly clear. Only now did people realize how much they had closed their eyes to the fascist dangers looming in Europe and Japan. They also began to realize that the United States, if only because it was such a huge economic power, would no longer be able to stay out of world politics.

All of a sudden international expertise was much sought after in politics and in academe. Interest now turned directly to the New School, whose large faculty had not only brought European experience to America but whose work had always been international in perspective. Some of the faculty had even had practical experience during the demobilization years in Germany after World War I. This biographical background had been reflected in the political tenor of their writing in the United States since 1933, but it was only after the outbreak of the war that their appeal to America to come out of its isolationist shell gained much attention. Suddenly, Alvin Johnson noted, officials from the administration and the army came knocking at the doors, asking for information, analyses, and assessments concerning Europe.[103]

After 1939 the emigrés at the New School were probably the academic group most frequently consulted by U.S. government officials. The Rockefeller Foundation now contributed substantial sums to the Peace Project as well. This made it possible for the first time for the Graduate Faculty to undertake extensive group research with sound financial backing and to build up a common research apparatus.[104] The Rockefeller appropriations were no doubt made partially to conform to Washington's expectations. The Board of Economic Warfare, for instance, which had been established after the war broke out, was very much interested in the experiences of the New School people. It would have liked to hire some of the scholars who had just come from France, but because of their status as "enemy aliens" it could not employ them directly, so projects were assigned to them indirectly through the Rockefeller Foundation.[105] This method of financing was used not only for the studies on Nazi propaganda already mentioned but also for projects on the institutional aspects of the armament industry, on the recruitment of the government elite in Germany, on the role of women in the work force, on resource allocations, and on wage politics, to mention only a few examples.[106]

Of course, the New School was proud to have the largest staff of experts on international matters in America. The more obvious it became that the United States would have to enter the war, the more often the New School was consulted by American as well as British experts, and even the Soviet press agency Tass asked for their findings.[107] But at the same time doubts and frustration were beginning to grow at the New School because the Peace Project was more and more in danger of having to take a back seat.[108] In a programmatic appeal entitled "War and the Scholar," Alvin Johnson tried to explain to the interested public that, although the scholars should indeed contribute toward winning the war, their prime task was "to win the peace."[109] For him the events of 1918, when the Allies had won the war but lost the peace, stood as a warning. The central goal of research at the New School should therefore be to develop strategies that would provide a rational basis for future peace negotiations and prevent them from once again turning into a competition for satisfying short-term national interests.

From the early 1940s on, the New School considered founding its own international research institute for this purpose.[110] This institute was to be administratively independent of the Graduate Faculty and was to take over the tasks of the original Peace Project. Here the scholars could begin work on plans they had long wanted to develop. At the same time the new institute would be an important refuge for the European scholars waiting to be rescued in France. Unconstrained by national interests, so Johnson expected, this community of intellectuals in New York had the unique potential to outline plans for a peaceful postwar world.[111]

But financial obstacles stood in the way. The Rockefeller Foundation was willing to help pay for salaries but denied further requests to cover associated administrative costs. What apparently aroused opposition was that the shaping of future plans so crucial to American foreign politics was to be left entirely to emigré circles. The Rockefeller people approved of the intentions and plans as well as of the personnel, whom they knew from experience to be "first-rate in every respect,"[112] but they thought it would be preferable to pursue this project at an American university.[113] However, behind this argument was probably less concern for national security interests than petty jealousy on the part of American institutions. After all, the Rockefeller Foundation had by now worked together with the initiators of the planned institute for twenty years, most of whom had in the meantime become American citizens.

It was not until Doris Duke, the tobacco heiress, donated $250,000 and thus guaranteed funding for a few years that the institute was established in 1943. The name "Institute of World Affairs" indicated the scope of the envisioned program. Given the dimensions of the world crisis, it was felt that the economic, social, political, military, and philosophical aspects of possible peaceful solutions could not be considered separately. Nor could the problems be geographically limited, even though Europe, the prime victim of German brutality, was obviously to be the focus of any analysis. The choice of name also emphasized the connection with the former Kiel

Institute and the research begun there before 1933. It was no coincidence either that Adolph Lowe, who had been more directly involved in the demobilization problems after World War I than anyone else in the group, was appointed research director of the new institute.[114] Because the studies undertaken at the Institute would be used to help determine the future postwar order, an obvious attempt was made to place them in the context of research that had been going on over the past decades. One major reason for this was to forestall possible attacks by the public—to which the New School had been subjected enough as it was—against this major new program. The New School also wanted to forestall similar objections on the part of the Rockefeller Foundation and possibly of other academic institutions. The foundation actually contributed more than $100,000 over the next few years for associated costs of various studies. It did so because research centers at other universities seemed to be slow in getting started. Some research on international linkages was initiated here and there, but it rarely went beyond the scope of the papers prepared by the New School group.[115]

At the inauguration of the Institute, Lowe made it clear that a stable peace could be built only on a sound economic base. Here he drew on theoretical studies he and his colleagues had begun in the 1920s. These studies indicated that unregulated growth dynamics and the increasing separation of production and employment had caused sociopolitical instability in various countries as well as international rivalries in an increasingly unstable world market. Technology and unregulated capital accumulation, with their side effect of creating job losses, were now considered the crucial variables in an analysis of postwar conditions. The scholars therefore concluded that the most important element for achieving international stability was full employment along with a high standard of living, and these goals were to be attained through globally determined and internationally coordinated economic policies. The shaping of the postwar period, according to Lowe, should not be left to the diplomats, as it had been after 1918. What was crucial now was not so much a matter of foreign policy as of creating a new, comprehensive economic and social order.[116]

What was strikingly new in this approach was that victory over national socialism and the establishment of democracy in Germany did not constitute the sole problem of the future. The German question was just one aspect, granted an important one, in the Institute's work toward a lasting peace in Europe and the world. Hannah Arendt, for one, noted approvingly that the New School scholars were thinking about Germany "in terms of Europe."[117] They in fact saw themselves not as exiles exclusively interested in Germany but as new partners in the American academic community.

In this the New School group differed from many political emigré circles and displayed a refreshing lack of German national pathos. Nor did it, like these circles, generate abstract and utopian schemes for a future social order in Germany and Europe. Such schemes had already been produced aplenty by the leftist spectrum of the Weimar Republic, and even then little attention was given to the question of how they could be realized. This was particularly true of various socialist conceptions that aimed at the total abolishment of capitalism. The question of how such a transformation was to be achieved—possibly by revolutionary means after the future military defeat of Germany and with the support, or at least the toleration, of the victorious "capitalistic" powers—a question that raised again the unsolved problems of the November Revolution of 1918, was left largely unanswered.

As the New School scholars' writings on fascism in the 1930s had already attested, the hope cherished during the Weimar period that the working class would carry the banner of democratic progress had been abandoned after the events of 1933. But rather than lapsing into resignation as some of their friends and colleagues at Max Horkheimer's Institute of Social Research had done, the New School scholars developed an outlook in which the concept of "social conformity" became the key feature of stable societies. It was this concept that provided the central strategic direction of their planning for international peace.

The Institute of World Affairs was not seeking national political solutions or radical (and unrealizable) social transformations. It sought instead the creation of a stable, internationally coordinated postwar economy free of the conflicts spawned by excessive growth and exploitation, and it pinned high hopes on the incipient cooperation evident in the anti-Hitler coalition. Lowe saw a "lucky omen" in the fact that the Institute had been founded at the very moment when the foreign ministers of the three Allied powers were meeting for the first time in Moscow to discuss the establishment both of an international organization to maintain future peace and security and of a European advisory commission to formulate a common postwar policy. His suggestions for building a European postwar order looked not only to England for inspiration but to the Soviet Union as well. Lowe and his colleagues thought a kind of convergence of the two supranational societies essential, with Great Britain taking on more socialistic traits and bolshevism being forced to become more democratic. Socially, nationally, and internationally, these two powers were to be the pillars of a "new kind of conformity." Otherwise, it was feared, there could be no stable European peace; and the future German state, occupying a middle position both geographically and in the unsolved tensions it had inherited from history, would suffer the same fate the Weimar Republic had after 1918. This meant a rejection, on the one hand, of all the theories of totalitarianism that were increasingly in vogue in the United States as well as among leftist emigrés and, on the other, of strategies of German deindustrialization, such as those discussed in connection with the Morgenthau plan.[118]

The basic elements of a future peaceful order in Europe were thus defined. The first condition was that Germany's defeat would have to be total, unlike after World War I. Those responsible for the war—the systematic holocaust was at this point still unknown—were to be punished in order to preclude the possible reemergence of the stab-in-the-back legend. Further satisfaction of the desire for revenge, understandable as this desire was, was rejected since it would only endanger future peace. Under the leadership of the United States, which would have to accept its global responsibilities as a world power, worldwide economic connections were to be established through internationally planned resource allocation and, above all, through credit operations. The Germans were to make reparation for the destruction they had wrought—not, however, in the form of monetary payments but rather through an integrated, complementary exchange of goods to be internationally coordinated. Because Germany was lacking in raw materials, what the planners had in mind here was the contribution of "know-how" and labor, either directly or in the form of goods.

These considerations placed the European problem in the wider context of a global economic order to be newly organized. On the level of the national economies, the scholars could draw on their own earlier research of the 1920s, which had worked out tools for achieving stable economic growth and full employment. There were, however, no comparable models for an international economic policy. What was required was a kind of global New Deal designed to protect the world market against erratic oscillations in exchange rates, prices, credit availability—in short, in the terms of trade. The United States with its abundance of raw materials and its accumulation of world currency reserves was to provide the necessary stimuli here. In this connection ideas were put forward that were later partially realized in the Marshall Plan.

The longer the war lasted, it was assumed, the harder it would be to turn the war economy back into a peace economy. The reintegration of returning soldiers into the work force and the readjustment of production carried with them the dangers of excess capacity and unemployment, dangers that could, however, be averted if unneeded goods were made available on credit to regions destroyed by the war. Repayments were to be made to international funds, which would in turn finance progress in other disadvantaged regions, in particular the Third World. According to the concluding overall vision, no battle against fascism could succeed in the long run as long as the anti-Hitler coalition was unable to prevent worldwide depressions and inequalities—today we would say underdevelopment—and guarantee full employment within a socially just international order.[119]

After 1943 these problems were scrutinized in greater detail in many fact-finding studies. These studies did not intend concrete political suggestions but were empirical studies that could then serve as a basis for later decision making. Only a small part of this research evolved into voluminous publications. These appeared in a series of books by the Institute of World Affairs published by Oxford University Press (later by Cornell University Press). Most of the work done at this time was commissioned by the U.S. administration and, for reasons of secrecy, took the form of papers mimeographed in only a few copies to be sent to Washington or to interested research teams. But even in these technically oriented analyses it was quite obvious what political end they were meant to serve. Also, all specialized studies were interdisciplinary in approach and were conceived of as no more than puzzle pieces in a large, overall project.

The largest project no doubt was a collection of twenty papers entitled "Germany's Position in Postwar Reconstruction," produced under Lowe's and Staudinger's direction. The main section contained an urgent warning against repeating the mistakes of the Versailles Treaty, with its dilettantish, unilateral dispositions on reparations. Short-term interests and a desire to punish on the part of the victors had then further destroyed international economic relations and contributed to the instability of the young German democracy. More farsighted experts, like Keynes, had pointed out immediately after 1919 that huge, unilateral reparation transfers were unrealistic. On the one hand, the debtor, Germany—to the satisfaction of conservative political elements there, which refused to make their peace with defeat—would hardly be able to raise the requested sums. On the other, the creditors had no economic need for a rigid capital transfer that would put their own production at risk. In spite of this, the reparation demands were kept up into the 1930s, and the United States was partially to blame here. It had withdrawn from European affairs without signing the Versailles Treaty and had then rigorously insisted on repayment of the war credits earlier extended to England and France. This forced these countries in turn to demand payments from the German Reich. The vicious circle was closed when the Americans, following the Dawes Plan in 1924, loaned some of their accumulated capital to Germany. So huge amounts of foreign currency accumulated in the Reichsbank, making it possible to meet the reparation obligations but saddling the German economy with additional, cumulative interest debts amounting to billions of marks. To break out of this vicious cycle of international capital flow, the European countries engaged in aggressive dumping of export goods, each trying to better its position at the expense of its trading partners as well as of its own workers, who saw the purchasing power of their money reduced. Europe, led by Germany, thus tumbled into that dramatic deflation which further aggravated already disastrous developments in the domestic economies.[120]

The results of the Germany project, in some cases, also provided concrete suggestions for the future occupation powers. The stated intent of the studies had been to derive operational strategies for a future Allied policy from a historical and descriptive examination of what had happened after the Versailles Treaty. Thus Ernst Fraenkel's paper on the Allied occupation of the Rhineland from 1918 to 1923 showed what kinds of problems military occupation gives rise to. This had been the first time in modern history that a civil administration had been replaced by a foreign military authority. From the historical analysis of this occupation policy, which was put into effect without regard for the legal and administrative traditions of the occupied territory and without an executive base of its own, conclusions were drawn for the future treatment of Germany: Without legal justification based on existing legal traditions and without the structure of an administrative apparatus of its own, an occupation force could not achieve cooperation with the vanquished; therefore, no reconstruction policy could be successful.[121] Along similar lines, a collective project headed by Arnold Brecht focused on an international comparison of administrative institutions. Out of this project grew a first draft of a constitution, formulated by

Brecht, for a future European federation. Other papers examined the federal structure and the voting patterns in Germany before 1933. Also of great importance were studies on the forced population transfers under the Nazis after 1938 and on anticipated problems of remigration after the war.[122]

Finally, a major part of the project was devoted to European and global economic problems. A comparative examination of developments of production, the structure of demand, and employment levels in the United States, England, and Germany and the interconnection of these countries' trade policies after World War I was used as background for taking a closer look at the goals of future economic strategies, such as complementary exchange of goods, the direction of credit flows, reconstruction aid, and the elements of a coordinated policy of demand. In this context problems of planning and control also moved into the foreground. Comprehensive studies showed what planning initiatives had thus far been put into practice in England, Germany, and the Soviet Union and what their effects had been. As a preliminary conclusion of this research a model of a "mixed economic order" was proposed. This did not, however, add anything qualitatively different to the conclusions the New School group had arrived at earlier from their research on technical change and finance theory.[123]

It was also characteristic of these plans for a postwar order that they did not originate in an isolated academic milieu. Some of them had been worked out in direct cooperation with American public agencies. Arnold Brecht's papers on administration, for example, were written in cooperation with the Public Administration Committee of the Social Science Research Council. A number of other analyses were directly commissioned by Washington. Thus the papers on "Social and Economic Controls," focusing on the American war economy, were written for the Office of Foreign Economic Administration.[124]

Although the New School group did not lack lines of communication for making their research known, they were under no illusions about the concrete effectiveness of their work. It had been obvious to them from the start that the strategies they worked out would be realizable only if they had the support of a common Allied policy or at least of a common basic attitude for dealing with the postwar world. The actual course of international politics, however, soon took a different direction. Roosevelt would have been the most likely of the Big Three leaders to be able to reconcile within the anti-Hitler coalition the conflicts that had surfaced even before the end of the war. But after his death, the vision of the New School group came to naught. "Contrary to our expectations," Lowe and Staudinger wrote in their final report on the reconstruction project, no "fundamental agreement was apparent, during the two years in which the Project was in progress." Many of the drafts thus remained mere intellectual "guesswork."[125]

This was and is the fate of most intellectuals: They can advise, recommend, and urge; they can work out and offer strategies; but they do not make the decisions. Despite their profound disappointment about the different course political developments took after 1945, the New School scholars' intellectual efforts and work load did not diminish in the period that followed, for the Peace Project had been only one aspect of the research the Institute of World Affairs was engaged in. International economic problems in particular continued to be analyzed. Hans Neisser, for example, had some time ago begun empirical research on an international level on the division of labor in the process of industrialization and on its consequences for world trade. In collaboration with Franco Modigliani, a former lawyer who had fled from Italy and then studied economics with Marschak at the New School, he was able to continue this work on a new, mathematical basis. In the following years this topic culminated in some of the first empirical works on international trade.[126]

Neisser's work was complemented by studies that asked what effects an accelerated war economy had had in different countries on the qualification level of the work force and what frictions were likely to arise in the labor market when the economy returned to peacetime conditions. This research culminated in another major publication that examined the growth potential of providing training for workers and proved an important milestone in growth theory as well as in the modern economics of education.[127] Finally, there was another study along the same lines that examined the industrialization problems of the Third World and their effects on national labor markets.[128]

With the end of the New Deal, the beginning of the cold war, and then the McCarthy era, funding for this kind of research began to dry up. The work of the Institute was more and more at odds with the dominant political climate. It was no longer appropriate, for example, for Arnold Brecht to recommend at a conference of the State Department that America make known to the world that its fundamental opposition to the Soviet Union was based only on the disregard for human rights there and did not extend to the economic system.[129]

Thus, when Lowe asked to be relieved of his duties as director of research in the early 1950s in order finally to have time for his own research after years of predominantly organizational work, the Institute could barely sustain itself.[130] Many of the previous younger faculty had moved on to pursue careers at other institutions, and because of America's new role in foreign politics, internationally oriented research had long since found a secure home in American academe. The tiny New School could no longer compete in these circumstances. The fact remains, nevertheless, that it and its Institute of World Affairs had for years provided decisive stimuli for awakening American interest in this new field of research.

6. Initiatives toward a Theoretical Synthesis

It was not until long after World War II, during the 1960s, that Adolph Lowe's epoch-making *On Economic Knowledge: Toward a Science of Political Economics* was published. This book and the somewhat later, special study *The Path of Economic Growth* were the culmination of decades of collaborative research carried on by Lowe and his colleagues at the New School.[131] Both books drew on work started as early as the 1920s on technical change, problems of growth, and economic planning. It may seem inappropriate to extend the label of scholarship produced by German scholars in exile to publications that appeared so much later, but Lowe's *On Economic Knowledge* illustrates not only the continuity of individual as well as group research but also some shifts in outlook brought about by the American experience. This is why it is justifiable to include these late works in this study, although its scope is basically limited to the period up to about 1950. At that time the Graduate Faculty had become a completely American institution of higher learning, and the emigré scholars had long since become integrated as American citizens.

It should also be taken into account that Lowe alone among his colleagues had been unable to continue work he had started earlier after his flight from Germany, and it would be almost twenty years before he was able to return to it. He had been forced to put aside a project planned before 1933 on the "theory of a growing economy." This project was to complete and then bring together in systematic form preliminary studies of business cycles and growth theory dating from the 1920s. At the University of Manchester, Lowe's new academic home after he left Germany, the economics faculty was dominated by the orthodox neoclassicist John Jewkes, who soon relegated Lowe to the political scientists. As his contribution on the causes of national socialism has already shown, Lowe's publications from these years demonstrate that he was more interested in the areas of political theory and intellectual history than in economics in the strict sense. At the New School he was busy with other tasks until the end of the 1940s, handling organizational matters as research director of the Institute of World Affairs and thereafter helping to edit the unpublished papers of his friend Karl Mannheim, who had died suddenly in 1947.[132] It was thus not until the early 1950s that he was able to return to his original scholarly projects. Several lengthy papers, which picked up the topics of his work from the 1920s, simply summarized the discussion, now discontinued again, of the technology problem. These papers seem to have served primarily to clarify his own thinking in anticipation of further research.[133]

His perspectives had broadened in the meantime. There were no doubt many reasons for this, among them the fruitless discussions in Germany before 1933 about combating the worldwide economic crisis, the situation he was forced into at Manchester, his activities there as a political scientist, and the dominance and intolerance of the neoclassicists he experienced after 1933. In any case, starting in the mid 1930s, Lowe began to formulate his first fundamental reflections on the place economics should occupy in the wider context of modern social science. These reflections centered not just on his criticism of the dominant paradigms in academic discussion of economics; they were also a kind of reassessment of his own previous work both as an official in the economic administration after 1918 and as an academician since the mid 1920s. His thoughts found a first expression in his book *Economics and Sociology* of 1935. The subtitle *A Plea for Co-operation in the Social Sciences* programmatically sums up Lowe's and his group's old point of view and at the same time indicates the future direction of Lowe's own work after years devoted to specialized problems.[134]

As the English sociologist Morris Ginzberg noted in his preface to the book, this was a question that had been raised again and again since the days of classical economics. But although the interdependence of social phenomena within the social totality was perfectly apparent, the social sciences had not been left untouched by the modern trend toward division of labor, so that the thinking of economists had become reduced more and more to analyses of a narrow model world, a model that took in only parts of the real world and did so abstractly.[135] It was against this hermeticism of "pure theory," in particular as practiced by neoclassical economists, that Lowe's call for a realistic "economic sociology" was directed. What he had in mind were the old moral and philosophical ideas of the classical econo-mists, who still strove toward universal knowledge in the Enlightenment tradition.

The demand to break down the barriers the neoclassicists had erected was not all that original. It had long been a theme of the historical school of economics in Germany and of modern sociology. But Lowe went farther by calling into question the basic tenets of neoclassical economics, the a priori nature of its deductions, the rationality principle of "economic man," as well as the notion of a harmonious market and its underlying assumption of perfect information and mobile production factors. Lowe claimed that the reality on which the old economic models were based had long since changed. He pleaded, instead, for a realistic theory based on actual experi-ence and recognizing that the economic process was constantly evolving and therefore generating new data and basic constellations.

This is as far as Lowe went in this particular work. His one aim here was to enable economic analysis to evolve into a reality-oriented etiology. He did not ask at this point what would have to be done and what means employed to counteract or possibly even prevent negative developments observed in the real world. The book consequently concluded simply with the statement that an understanding of modern dynamic processes de-manded the cooperation of the different branches of social science. The "partial analyses" supplied by conventional economic theory and its "in-strumental rules," which applied only to individual components, could not shed much light on complex social and economic processes. To be sure, such analyses were necessary and justified, but only once the processes and mechanics of the economic system in its entirety were understood.[136]

Lowe himself wondered whether such ambitious aims would not lead into a realm of "unlimited possibilities" and uncover merely the "rules of chaos." But his previous work on business cycles and technical change convinced him that, even if the neoclassical perspective with its notions of harmony and its hypotheses of equilibrium was abandoned, one would still find regularities that did not constantly seek a state of equilibrium.[137]

Lowe returned to these questions in his book *On Economic Knowledge*, and now he attempted to find the action-oriented answers that, he was convinced, a realistic theory would come up with. He started out with a comprehensive, historical overview of economic theory from Adam Smith through Marx and the neoclassicists and on up to Keynes, discerning in their work the progressive coming apart of a system that had originally been conceived of as rigidly closed. Against this background he then formulated the thesis that the center of economic theory did not lie where it had been assumed to be since the time of the neoclassicists, namely, in "positive analysis." In spite of his former criticisms of Keynes, Lowe presented the Keynesian approach, with its definition of full employment as the highest macrogoal of economic policy, as an important step toward a new formulation of the kind of systematic thinking economics had abandoned. Keynes's approach supplied Lowe with some important clues for reviving political economics in the classical tradition. From this he developed a model for achieving definite goals in actual economic practice. The old "positive analysis" with its merely descriptive aim was now replaced by an "instrumental analysis" aimed at change.

This approach, that is, the discovery and regulation of an effective "functioning order," summed up ideas developed by Lowe and his Kiel colleagues since the 1920s on the purpose of economic theory, but it also offered new suggestions on how economic policy could solve problems. In the history of economic analysis it represents a revolutionizing of traditional economic thinking, of neoclassicism with its hypothetical-deductive methods, of Keynesianism with its concentration on short-term malfunctionings of the economy and its demand for reactive interventionism, and of the Marxist system as well. In spite of the strategic differences between these schools of thought Lowe saw a commonality in the fact that they all, like the natural sciences, started out with certain fixed assumptions, such as the inherent order of economic processes, the autonomous existence of economic subjects, and a universally valid code of behavior. Economic theorists postulated rigid economic laws of motion analogous to the laws of gravity. According to these laws, economic man made only rational decisions and had uniform needs, such as the urge to maximize value. These more and more ideologized fundamental assumptions had turned economics into an "ivory-tower theory" that bore little relation to real life, and its increasingly refined research methods therefore did not provide results of empirical importance or contribute to the accuracy of economic prognoses.

Instrumental analysis was directed, first of all, against the foundations—taken over from the natural sciences—of traditional economic thinking, which had regarded the rationality and extremum principle as an axiom needing no further proof. Lowe conceded that the economists' hypothetical and deductive models had at one point been of some empirical value.

During the liberal era of capitalism, for example, a number of external pressures—mass poverty, unrestrained competition, and the puritanical work ethic—had in fact caused the later dogmatized maximization principle to become a strategy of survival.

Second, instrumental analysis was directed against the epistemological value of traditional economic theory to the extent that the latter claimed to be an empirical science. The only reason why neoclassical thinking still figured so dominantly in economic analysis despite a much changed reality, Lowe argued, was that it reflected an ideal of autonomous man that was in keeping with the political and cultural value system of the West. Man had, however, never been autonomous. He had always been dependent on many social, cultural, institutional, psychological, and other factors. Advertising and technical as well as social immobilities were obvious examples in modern societies. Also, historical developments during the last centuries showed how questionable the concepts of social order underlying the market model had become. After all, paradoxically, the very accomplishments of modern capitalism—the growing prosperity of all classes, the limitation of competition, the organization of capital and labor, and the increasing interventions of the state—had undermined the self-regulation of markets and thus removed one of the central, axiomatic foundations of market theory.

It was these historic facts that Lowe tried to draw attention to in his book. Instead of the economic process postulated by neoclassical economics—a process isolated from society and directed at the one-dimensional and timeless goal of maximizing goods—Lowe proposed a "pluralism" of possible optima of production and distribution. Reaching them would not be merely an economic and technical matter but would require political and social decision-making processes beyond the scope of individual economies. To illustrate his case he pointed out that today's ecological dangers and the end of the growth euphoria would lead people to adopt very different systems of preference, to which conventional economic models with their rigid definition of man would be poorly equipped to respond.

Since it was impossible according to these models to predict unknown future developments from the facts and behavior inherent in an actual, existing situation, Lowe proposed to turn the problem around. Let the future state of the system be assumed to be known by defining in political terms the goals to be reached. That was what the term "political economics" in the subtitle of his book was all about. Examples of such politically postulated goals might be full employment, certain rates of growth,[138] redistribution of wealth between rich and poor countries, reduction of hazardous industrial wastes, and so on. It would then be up to instrumental analysis to determine how these goals could be achieved. Once that was known, the necessary behavior variables that would set the process in motion could be defined. In this way the unknown behavior of economic subjects would be revealed and determined through goal-oriented adaptation processes.

What Lowe recommended was partly put into practice in the Federal Republic of Germany shortly thereafter—though without reference to his reasoning—in the stability law of 1967. Its "magic square" named full employment, growth, price stability, and balanced foreign trade as future goals. But these goals were set merely as general directions for government economic policy in the Keynesian sense without being binding for other economic groups. And they were never attained. It almost seems as though Lowe anticipated these failings when he went beyond defining goals and the paths leading up to them and asked about the possibilities of imposing them. The last and crucial step of instrumental analysis therefore concerns the institutionalizing of a system of social controls that would range from harmless techniques of persuasion to complementary public investments and price, wage, or investment control and on up to rigid forms of compulsion.[139]

The significance of *On Economic Knowledge* lies in the fact that it tries to reconnect the economic core process with the essential components of the sociopolitical world of which it is a part. As the phrase "political economics" in the subtitle indicates, the book stands in the classical tradition of Smith, Ricardo, and Marx. But while for these writers endogenous and exogenous factors were still closely linked, this connection was gradually lost as economic theory developed over time. Lowe's model and his instrumental method tried to bring about by conscious guidance of economic developments what according to the classical school of thinking was achieved by the automatic feedback mechanisms of the market. Whereas the empirical usefulness of the neoclassical market model is measured by the ability of economists to make accurate predictions, the test of instrumental analysis lies in the success of its economic policies.

With the definition of instrumental analysis as a system of social controls, Lowe's thoughts on strategies for initiating stable developments leading toward a brighter future, thoughts he had started to formulate thirty years earlier during the Great Depression, had come full circle. At that earlier time his thinking had been entirely within the traditions of German economic scholarship. Even the transformation ideas of the reform economists and their preoccupation with institutions were not so far removed from these traditions because both pinned their hopes on the socialization—to be imposed from above—of large-scale enterprises. Lowe's new approach shows a marked shift in perspective. His system of controls now suggests a novel theory of "liberal," noncollectivist planning that offers a synthesis of old and new economic theories. It represents an attempt to combine the classical, neoclassical, Marxist, and Keynesian systems with new research methods in a way that would make it possible to regulate macroeconomic processes.

This planning model shows clear signs of Lowe's having lived for several decades in a new social milieu after 1933, and the insights he gained into the role of "social conformity" in the Anglo-Saxon countries also had a marked influence on his epistemological foundation. Lowe's instrumental analysis, which is equally applicable to market systems as to decentralized planned economies, throws a bright light on his acculturation to the political world of progressive American social sciences. Alvin Johnson once defined his American approach and that of the former German emigrés as follows: Their "cultural world premised order, evolving toward democracy. Mine premised democracy evolving toward order."[140] Apart from this aspect of reflecting exile experiences, Lowe's instrumental analysis also indicates a turning away from the planning euphoria of the earlier period of intellectual and political optimism. The belief in the promises of "socialistic utopia" originally shared by Lowe gave way as he grew older to a much more skeptical attitude toward the possibility of directing economic processes to bring about a just and free society.[141]

The broad, interdisciplinary approach that underlies Lowe's book was also attested to not only by the spectacular reception of the work but also by two symposia organized at the New School with top-ranking authorities as speakers. Along with economists of widely different views the participants included sociologists, philosophers, and even natural scientists. Discussion not only revolved around economic theory and practice but extended as well to the philosophical aspects of this *magnum opus*.[142] The work's controversial quality lay not just in introducing a new paradigm. That is, after all, not uncommon in the history of scholarship. *On Economic Knowledge* represents a much more fundamental break with the traditional normative basis of all schools of economic thinking. Even colleagues sympathetic to Lowe, like Kenneth Boulding, noted that he demoted the proud lead science of modern society back to its premodern status as handmaiden to politics. In doing so, reviewers pointed out, Lowe revived traditions reaching back to the Greeks, traditions according to which rational economic action derived not from the inherent logic of the principle of reason but from politics or, in other words, from ethics.[143]

Lowe himself had made no allusion to such a wider historical horizon. A criticism on this account, surely justified, came from his longtime fellow fighter Gerhard Colm, who had, with his model of economic projections, followed similar though not as far-reaching aims. Colm complained that *On Economic Knowledge* was like a glance into the entrance hall of a fantastic edifice but that it revealed precious little of the actual interior.[144]

Lowe described some of this interior in a further book, *The Path of Economic Growth*, which attempted to apply the instrumental method to that particular aspect of economic reality that had been at the focus of the author's and his colleagues' work from the beginning. The new traverse analysis developed in this book—that is, the scrutiny of the transition processes set in motion by changes in production techniques—marks the conclusion of decades of research on the problems of technology and growth. It should be mentioned in passing that during these years the neoclassical camp had begun to discuss similar questions, although the studies published by John Hicks in this area remain at this date an exception rather than the rule.[145]

Other models developed after World War II also reflect the inadequacy and failings of neoclassical economics. What comes to mind here are, apart from Lowe's and Colm's work, welfare economics, Leontief's input–output analysis, and Jan Tinbergen's theory of economic policy, among others. It is surely no coincidence that these approaches were put forward almost exclusively by European scholars who had come to the United States in the 1930s. In their work, too, we find pleas for more intensive discussion of economic goals. But, compared to Lowe's vision, they were much more technically oriented, and they largely stayed away from the discussion of appropriate social behavior patterns and controls that was of such central importance to Lowe.

7 / The Influence of
the New School Scholars
in the United States

1. The Traditional View of the New School

From the beginning, opinions differed widely among the interested public concerning the Graduate Faculty into which the University in Exile had evolved, its function as a collection point for German and European emigrés, and its scholarly significance. Even today this controversial reputation has not changed much, as the literature on the history of the academic exiles in the United States after 1933 shows. At the beginning of this book we cited Lepsius as an example of the general attitude in Germany. In this view, the Graduate Faculty had been an intellectual emigré center marked by originality but of no influence. Coser, by contrast, concluded in the United States that the group's outsider status was really an advantage because it allowed them to preserve unaltered the views they had formed in Germany and pass them on to a small, interested minority in the United States.

The intellectual positions of the New School scholars as outlined in Chapter 6 and the reception they met in the United States lend little support to the view that the Graduate Faculty led a ghetto existence. Gerhard Colm's works on public finance in particular can be cited in this connection. So, too, can the comparative international research of the Institute of World Affairs under the leadership of Adolph Lowe; the debate on technology and growth which has—beyond its role in the history of academic exile—experienced a significant revival just recently in the discussion of the causes of the current economic crisis; and, finally, the analyses of fascism during the 1930s that were of passing, but at that time overwhelming, interest. There is no need here to recall the significant contributions in other disciplines, like Max Wertheimer's Gestalt psychology, the comparative studies of governments and bureaucracies by Arnold Brecht and Erich Hula, or the phenomenology of Alfred Schütz.

The assessment expressed in that cliché arose in a strange way. Since previous research on the exile of German scholars has made almost no use of the archives of aid organizations or of numerous available posthumous papers, a picture has emerged that is based largely on numerous older personal reminiscences from various emigré circles. And in these circles the University in Exile was not viewed very favorably from the beginning. An unmistakable element of envy, ill will, and discomfort colors opinions about this flourishing institution in the accounts of those who were not accepted by it or who out of political self-identification as exiles watched the relatively easy integration of the progressive intellectuals of the Weimar years with suspicion. The economist Carl Landauer's reaction may be viewed as typical. He also came from the German reform socialistic tradition and was lucky enough to find a position immediately at the University of California in Berkeley after the Handelshochschule in Berlin was closed down. In California he heard with some vexation that Lederer had received an appointment at the New School. In his isolation in California he consoled himself by recalling rumors to the effect that conditions at the University in Exile were supposedly not very pleasant.[1]

Even greater reservations were harbored by some members of the former Frankfurt Institute of Social Research, which had first reestablished itself after 1933 in Geneva and Paris and did not move to space made available by Columbia University until the mid 1930s. The victory of national socialism had profoundly shaken the self-confidence of the Institute, and the increasingly political orientation of the core group around Max Horkheimer and Theodor W. Adorno—which was shortly thereafter to lead to the demise of the Institute—added further to a suspicious frame of mind. This, along with the group's intellectual isolation, bred a view of the New School as a rival institution. More will be said on this subject later. Similar resentments were to come, too, from the French scholars who found a home after 1940 at the Ecole Libre under the roof of the New School.[2]

The criticisms of various political emigré groups were of a different kind. The movement "Free Germany" in Mexico, for instance, recognized the great scholarly accomplishments of the New School—equating the New School accomplishments with the work of the economists there—but complained that these intellectuals hardly spoke as "German" scholars and apparently regarded their "departure" (*sic*) as permanent.[3]

In the circles of many former emigrés a negative image based on almost no detailed knowledge persisted until very recently. As late as 1984 Herbert Zassenhaus, a former Schumpeter student, maintained that other emigrés had avoided the New School "like the plague" because the research produced there never broke out of the "eggshell" of the Kiel or Frankfurt approaches and could therefore not be integrated into other kinds of thinking. In the family of the management scientist Julius Hirsch, on the other hand, the idea had taken root that the Graduate Faculty was a camouflaged establishment of the German social democracy that served to save only its own intellectual cadre.[4] Such farfetched notions would not be worth mentioning if they did not, even after several decades, convey something of the specific quality of emigré psychology at the time. Zassenhaus had studied with Lowe at one point in the 1930s before moving to Bonn to study under Schumpeter. Schumpeter arranged a scholarship at Harvard for him after he fled from Germany but then paid no further attention to him. Given Zassenhaus's rather depressing personal situation, the group spirit at the New School must naturally have presented a particularly striking contrast. The situation was even clearer in the case of Julius Hirsch. In the first years of the Weimar Republic, some of the economists later gathered at the New School had worked under Hirsch, who was undersecretary in the Reichswirtschaftsministerium (Department of Economics) at the time. Lowe had even accompanied him as an official aide to the World Economic Conference of 1922 in Genoa. This former working relationship had given rise to considerable intellectual tensions. But after war broke out and the Germans occupied Denmark, those old disagreements did not stop the New School people from trying to help Hirsch, who had been teaching at the University of Copenhagen since 1933. All that they offered Hirsch, however, was a position as visiting professor, and he apparently blamed his former subordinates for his precarious situation, which was no different from that of other emigrés arriving in the United States in those years.[5]

From the beginning the Graduate Faculty was also the permanent subject of criticism from conservative American circles. During the first years the isolationist public objected mostly to the concentration of so many foreign scholars in one institution. Attacks like those of a professor of German, himself of German extraction and friendly toward the Nazis, who regarded the emigrés at the New School as a threat to internal peace and a perversion of academic freedom, were still isolated voices at that point in time.[6] But after the outbreak of the war and later during the McCarthy era political denunciations based on an amalgamation of isolationist and pro-Nazi attitudes took a sharper tone. In one of the many private letters of complaint received by aid organizations, the New School was accused of being the breeding ground of a "pro-communist" or "near-Bolshevist intelligentsia."[7] The central FBI office in Washington, too, received many reports from its agents that attested to similar reservations among various sectors of the population.

But such defamations are more revealing of the hysteria of the public. Many prominent New Dealers like Adolf Berle, Rexford Tugwell, Alvin Hansen, and others were also constantly suspected of being socialists and communists who were supposedly trying, especially now under the conditions of a wartime economy, to use the New Deal as a vehicle to bring about a "dictatorship."[8] Nevertheless, FBI agents were several times placed at the New School in the guise of students to check on the substance of the "numerous complaints." But nothing was ever brought to light. The reports stated that everyone knew that most of the professors subscribed to "extreme liberal" views but that there were no communists among them and that nobody engaged in un-American activities; on the contrary, they were all convinced anti-Nazis.[9]

Such rumors, however, stayed alive, and as late as 1946 the chairman of the House Committee on Un-American Activities (HUAC) spoke disparagingly of the socialistic aims of this "strange institution."[10] Still, none of the members of the New School was called before the committee. Just as he had fought earlier against the Nazis on numerous committees, Alvin Johnson was among the first to try to put a stop to Senator McCarthy's rampage.[11]

Obviously, the New School members, and in particular the economists among them, were not in the mainstream of American academe. But this does not mean that they led a marginal existence. On the contrary, the quality of the Graduate Faculty was recognized and highly regarded beyond the intellectual circles that supported the New Deal politically. Some of these voices even spoke of a "time bomb" that was ticking away at the New School for America's intellectual culture. For there students were taught not only the necessary facts but also the methodological foundations for turning theoretical insights into political practice. The interdisciplinary and practice-oriented teaching, which did not shy away from questioning even the implicit ideas and assumptions underlying the research, was in sharp contrast to the limited, behavioristically oriented curricula of American universities. If the modern social sciences were dominated by European emigré scholars in general, the Graduate Faculty, which specialized in this area and had the numerically largest staff, formed a center that could not be overlooked.

The sociopolitical self-concept of these scholars, which ran counter to any kind of pure theory and isolated specialization, and their opposition to the claim of many colleagues that science was value-free were of considerable appeal to those who ascribed some measure of responsibility for the severity of the Great Depression to the lack of ethical norms in the economic world view, that is, in the neoclassical, abstract models. Some observers were also struck by the variety of the audience at the New School. There were not only young students but also people belonging to different age groups and social strata, sometimes including colleagues from other New York universities.[12]

Dorothy Thompson, a journalist who was particularly concerned about German and European matters, thought the Graduate Faculty to be not only the most important German "outpost of free and independent scholarship" but also the most significant group of German emigrés.[13] And Thomas Mann spoke not merely symbolically when he praised it as a "university of both hemispheres."[14] Even the Office of Strategic Services, which was established after the beginning of the war and out of which the Central Intelligence Agency was to grow, noted that the most capable German leftist intellectuals were gathered at the New School.[15] This was, at the time, less a political appraisal than a label indicating high quality, for the OSS, too, had hired German emigré scholars belonging to the left spectrum for its Research and Analysis Branch. In view of the inadequate knowledge of Europe in the United States, these scholars were expected not only to supply factual information but above all to provide needed critical analyses of what was happening in Europe.[16]

2. Influence of the New School as an Institution

It is possible only rarely to make precise statements about the impact of scholarship. Similarly, an assessment of the influence of the emigré scholars in the United States can be attempted only with certain qualifications.

There are, of course, a number of criteria, such as the hiring policies of American universities, the kind and distribution of publications the scholars wrote for, and so on, but it is doubtful whether applying these criteria can provide an accurate picture. The representatives of Austrian neoclassicism, for example, found an easy entry into American academic life. They received appointments, as already mentioned, at the most prestigious East Coast universities, and they made significant contributions to economic theory in America. But this in itself does not adequately answer the question of influence because it would suggest that all those who taught at smaller universities and colleges, who published less, or whose work was not at the center of current discussion had been much less influential. Following these criteria, intellectual impact would be measured by how successfully scholars adapted to the current consensus in their discipline and subscribed to its paradigms. For the historiography of exile such a perspective would also mean a relapse into old notions of assimilation. That is why Coser, for example, suggests other criteria in his book. He bases his assessment of the impact of emigré scholars in America on their personal interactions, the exchange of ideas with others, and the establishment of new intellectual networks—paying no special attention to famous academic institutions. The scholars' significance is not measured by whether or not they taught at Princeton or Harvard, whether they published with well-known publishers, or how often they were cited in the mainstream literature of their discipline. Instead, they are evaluated according to who listened to them, who adopted their message, and for what reason. In this kind of approach the historian of the influence of German emigré scholarship concentrates not just on what the Europeans brought along with them and were able to integrate unproblematically into the new social world but also on the social and cultural conditions that facilitated or hindered the reception of new and different ideas in the United States.[17]

From this perspective the outsider status of the New School stressed in the literature is limited to the institution alone, namely, the unique case of a tiny organization that became an institution of higher learning only as a consequence of the German immigrants who taught there. In spite of its limited possibilities and permanent financial problems, the Graduate Faculty quickly acquired a considerable reputation among academic circles in the United States. The fact that the original effectiveness of the school was not remembered in later years is not attributable to any fault of the scholars who were gathered there. In the field of economics, Lowe, Neisser, Kähler, and Staudinger continued their research well into the postwar years, but they shared the fate of American New Dealers from the 1930s and 1940s, as the abrupt end of Gerhard Colm's professional career in Washington after 1945 has already shown.

If the few years of the Kennedy period are disregarded, the New Deal era, including the wartime economy, marks a short, exceptional phase in the tradition of liberal economics in America. The new theoretical approaches discussed during those years gained ascendancy over the neoclassical paradigms only temporarily, and the suggestion that the methodological principles inherent in economic practice be scrutinized was not picked up by free-market economics, which held sway again after 1945. Not even the syntheses proposed by the reform economists, syntheses that aimed at developing the traditional models further by incorporating concepts and tools of the neoclassicists, sparked any interest in that camp. It is a sign of many neoclassicists' tendency to isolate themselves from other influences that Adolph Lowe's economic theory of liberal planning and Gerhard Colm's similarly conceived idea of economic projections found a few lasting followers only among outsiders. In the Federal Republic of Germany, by contrast, Colm's ideas were adopted by some Social Democratic economists in the concept of "medium-range fiscal planning" and were even tentatively put into political practice beginning in the late 1960s.

It may also be regarded as typical that the input–output analysis developed by Leontief during the war to coordinate production decisions in industrial societies first encountered widespread skepticism among academics and politicians alike. Interestingly enough, Leontief's further research after 1945 was funded only minimally by American research institutions and much more generously by international organizations.[18] A similar pattern can be observed, by the way, in the Federal Republic of Germany. When the former Institute for Business Cycles Research, now called the German Institute for Economic Research, sought to establish connections with international research projects and asked the German Ministry of Economics for financial support to conduct surveys for use in input–output analysis, its request was rejected by the administration then under the wing of Ludwig Erhard. Funding came instead from industry. A change initiating public support for research did not come about until after the Berlin Wall was built and long-range provisions had to be made for meeting political crisis situations.[19] In the context of the postwar "rollback" and the renaissance of neoclassicism, the work of the former

German reform economists in the United States clearly occupied an outsider position, but this limited view ignores important facts of the New Deal era.

Immediately after their arrival Colm, Feiler, and Lederer had been invited by the American Political Science Association to a discussion held in December 1933 on government regulation of the economy. It was hoped that these German scholars would be able to contribute some important ideas because, as the organizer of the event stressed, their approach differed from that of most economists in the English-speaking world. It is no coincidence that this first symposium ushered in a period of more concentrated research by American scholars on government regulation and planning.[20] Naturally, such topics also figured in the many conferences organized at the New School itself, some of which attracted top-notch participants. A conference on "The Struggle for Economic Security in Democracy" held in early 1939 was attended by Gottfried Haberler, Alvin Hansen, and Paul Sweezy from Harvard; Arthur F. Burns and John M. Clark from Columbia; Gunnar Myrdal from Stockholm; and Rufus Tucker from General Motors, to mention just a few names. The impression such events apparently made was noted by Gerhard Colm, dean of the Graduate Faculty at the time. "The symposium went very well. The auditorium was filled at every meeting and even overflowed at the evening meetings. This shows that the choice of topic met with interest. The panel of speakers was also well selected. We were generally pleased with our American discussion partners, and all Johnson said was: 'I'm bursting with pride for the faculty.' "[21]

In early 1935 the New School economists were also inducted into the American Economic Association in a striking show of support. This is especially noteworthy since at this point some first negative voices fearing competition made themselves heard.[22] Such expressions of displeasure could hardly have diminished when it became obvious that the Graduate Faculty would regularly present papers at future conventions and particularly in 1938, when the New School was represented by work from seven scholars at the Detroit meeting. Emil Lederer alone gave several talks on problems of measuring industrial growth and on modern social security.[23] It is probably also a sign of the school's reputation that Alvin Johnson was elected president of the association for 1936. Though he was not eager to take the job he accepted it nevertheless because of the prestige it brought to the New School.[24]

Members of the Graduate Faculty also contributed papers and took part in discussions at various other events devoted to economics. In 1935 Gerhard Colm was among the representatives of six universities invited by the National Bureau of Economic Research to work out closer forms of joint research on current problems of the economy. This meeting resulted shortly thereafter in the establishment of a Universities-National Bureau Conference on Business Cycle Research, which worked in two sections during the following years and concentrated on developing methods for calculating national income and on price policies. It was in this context that Colm presented his first preliminary ideas on the structure and statistical calculation of a comprehensive account of public revenues and expenditures. These ideas evoked immediate curiosity and interest, particularly because of the attention Colm paid to social factors in his figuring.[25] Later the committee set up a third section—which included Lowe and Neisser—to study business cycles. The composition of this team shows how prominent the influence of the European scholars was in the late 1940s, for the Europeans, including Lowe and Neisser, Haberler, Koopmans, Leontief, Marschak, Tinbergen, and others, accounted for half of the members.[26]

Another indication of how solidly the scholars of the Graduate Faculty had become established in American academe is shown by the invitations they received from 1936 on to teach as guest lecturers at other universities. After 1938 such engagements became a regular routine for almost all the members of the Graduate Faculty.[27] At the same time the presidents of several great universities, like Robert Hutchins of Chicago, and other figures in public life began to show great interest in joining the Board of Trustees or the advisory committee of the school. This illustrious circle suggests that the New School was anything but a hermetic ghetto of Europeans.

The Graduate Faculty was also proud of *Social Research*'s success. Not only did the publication quickly acquire a steady and rapidly expanding readership, but the daily press, too, devoted more space to it than to any other comparable periodical dealing with the social sciences in the United States.[28] In addition, the number of students grew steadily and resulted in a further spreading of influence. The University in Exile had started out with about 100 enrollees. By 1945 the number had climbed to 5,500.[29] Toward the end of the war more than 200 former students of the New School reportedly worked in the federal administration.[30]

Starting in the mid 1930s, Washington became interested not only in Colm's work on public finance but also in other research pursued at the

New School. Because of the paucity of background information, the Works Progress Administration (WPA), which had been created in 1935, initiated a project of translating monographs of interest written by German and other European scholars into English. Among these monographs were several studies by New School scholars, like Emil Lederer's paper "The Problem of the Modern Salaried Employee," which dated back to the year 1912.[31] Hans Speier's similar study of the political attitude of German salaried employees during the 1920s presents an interesting case. Speier had intended to submit it as his habilitation paper in Germany, but the Nazi rise to power put an end to those plans. Thus only a translation of the manuscript was published in the form of a mimeographed WPA monograph.[32]

After the outbreak of the war the Graduate Faculty and its research center, the Institute of World Affairs, were consulted more and more by Washington. In the spring of 1943, the New School noted with satisfaction that no less than twenty-six government offices had called on its experts. In addition, many members of the faculty contributed to the "war effort" by being involved in over twenty-five government and army committees and projects. And at the school itself, over 100 courses were being offered by the spring of 1943.[33] To mention just two more examples of the New School's success, Arnold Brecht was appointed head of a Council on Public Administration, which was at that time occupied primarily with questions concerning institutions of the wartime economy; and Hans Neisser was asked to work for the Office of Price Administration.[34]

New School faculty members were involved in public activities in other areas as well. Johnson, Lowe, Marschak, and Neisser were among the founders of the American Labor Conference on International Affairs, which had been proposed by American union leaders in early 1943 and to which scholars in the social sciences as well as some emigrated representatives of the German labor movement were invited.[35] Varian Fry was named secretary, and this appointment indicated the direction the future activities of this body would take. Until his expulsion from France, Fry, as head of the Emergency Rescue Committee in Marseille, had been involved in trying to save endangered German refugees, and the selection of the conference members bears his clear imprint. The idea was for the 13 million organized American workers to have some say in future American peace policies. Given the apolitical character of the American unions this was "an idea nothing short of revolutionary," as a German representative of the German Social Democratic party in New York reported to the party's board of directors in exile in London.[36]

The new organization's publication bore the programmatic title *International Postwar Problems,* and its few issues—publication was suspended after one year because of the scarcity of paper—seem like a German or European union periodical if one scans the list of contributors.[37] Hans Neisser also prepared a lengthy study commissioned by the American Labor Conference on possible reparation payments of the Axis powers, in which he warned against repeating the mistakes of the years after the Versailles Treaty.[38]

There are a number of other activities the faculty members engaged in that should also be included in an evaluation of the New School's impact. The Hebrew University in Jerusalem asked Adolph Lowe in 1939—he was still in Manchester at the time—for his expert opinion on the creation of its new social sciences department. Following this, the Graduate Faculty was invited to contribute one member to a committee charged with determining the final shape of the department. The Hebrew University obviously regarded the New York institution as a possible model.[39] The high regard in which the New School's opinion was held in matters of scholarly management is shown, too, by inquiries like the one from the National Economic and Social Planning Association. The association asked, first, whether it would make sense to set up a clearinghouse for research information in the social sciences that could serve as a data bank for universities and public offices and, second, how one should go about doing it.[40]

The scholars at the New School had reason to be satisfied with the response their work elicited. Praise came as early as the late 1930s from the National Bureau of Economic Research, which commented that American scholarship had benefited to an almost inestimable degree from the fruitful and original ideas the transplanted university had brought with it; "economics especially has been stimulated by the scholars assembled there." The chairman of the economics department of the University of Chicago, H. A. Millis, expressed the opinion that the Graduate Faculty's contribution to the development of the social sciences was more impressive than that of any other American university he knew and that this was so not just because of the different social background of its members. The articles published in *Social Research* also evoked interested attention, even from rival publications. The editor of the *American Economic Review* was impressed and surprised by how quickly the German economists had acquired detailed knowledge about the American economy and been able to incorporate it into their own methods.[41] If even half of the compliments received from American colleagues during the following years were true

167

and represented general opinion—as Max Ascoli, dean of the school at the time, reasoned—one could say "that our standing is high."[42]

In government circles the respect for expert opinions and reports prepared by the Institute of World Affairs also seems to have been considerable. The Board of Economic Warfare considered it "of great advantage to the government to be able to draw on the research talents of Dr. Lowe and his colleagues." This was not a mere expression of politeness addressed to the scholars of the Institute but a remark made to a third party.[43] Many references in correspondence between American organizations point up again and again how interested the staffs working on war economy planning, in particular, were in the comparative international studies of the New School. Some requests for information even came from abroad, like those from Canadian government offices.[44]

3. Impacts of Individual Faculty Members

In addition to the extensive network of contacts the emigré scholars built up and the following they won among colleagues, we find in the invitations faculty members received to teach at other universities and institutions further but less significant evidence of the Graduate Faculty's standing. If we were to base our assessment of the school's influence on these invitations we would be accepting the idea of the New School's outsider position and that the successful acculturation of its members depended primarily on how much they became integrated into other American institutions. Some faculty members did move to other academic institutions, but this says nothing about the circumstances or the significance of those who remained at the New School. Some of them had also received invitations to other universities but chose to stay. Adolph Lowe was invited to teach at Chicago—for years the Mecca of American economics—but he likened conditions there to those on a luxury liner and much preferred the work atmosphere and team spirit on the shabby "trawler" of the New School.[45] Loyalty to Alvin Johnson and his creation may also have played a role in some faculty members' decision to stay. The agriculture expert Karl Brandt, on the other hand, moved on to the Food Research Institute at Stanford in the mid 1930s, was recruited from there to become an adviser to the Department of Agriculture, and worked for the World Bank. But such a career summary reveals nothing about the concrete reasons for his leaving the New School, namely, his frustration at finding himself in a completely alien environment in the urban metropolis of New York, a feeling that soon gave rise to tensions with his colleagues.

There were other factors apart from such personal constellations that moved some members to leave the New School. We have already mentioned Gerhard Colm's career as an expert in public finance in Washington and, after 1952, in the National Planning Association. There he had a staff and resources at his disposal that the New School could not match. In addition, he had a chance there not only to continue his scholarly work but also to have a hand for a time in shaping a segment of American politics. Still, he remained close to the Graduate Faculty and often came to New York to attend lectures and discussions, and he continued to consult his old friends and colleagues on various specific questions.

In early 1946 he was asked by General Lucius D. Clay, commander-in-chief of the United States occupying forces, to help draw up plans for reorganizing currency and financial conditions in Germany. This was a job that tempted him, but he was also conscious of how Germans would respond if someone like him were to try to shape future political developments as a representative of the American occupation. How touchy a question this was is shown by the fact that, as soon as word spread of the job he had been offered, conservative emigré circles that had been close to former Reich chancellor Heinrich Brüning circulated a rumor that Colm was a supporter of the Morgenthau plan. Colm conferred first of all with his New School colleagues, who urged him strongly to accept because here was a chance to affect events in Germany and to prevent a repetition of the catastrophic developments after World War I. It was only after they promised to defend him against similar attacks in America that he agreed to take the new job.[46]

On his three-month mission to Germany Colm, together with his fellow emigré Raymond Goldsmith and the American banker Joseph Dodge, drafted the famous plan—known in the literature as the Colm–Dodge–Goldsmith (CDG) Plan—that was proposed in May 1946 and on which the later West German currency reform was to be based. A sign of how much the plan owed to Colm's extraordinary knowledge is that Clay always referred to it as the "Colm plan."[47]

By the time the currency reform was introduced in the Western zones of Germany in June 1948 not much was left of Colm's original intentions. Historians attribute the two-year delay to disagreements among the Allied occupying powers about where the new currency should be printed and about how the German debts should be dealt with. Or else they cite the difficulties of working together with German representatives who had developed a plethora of reform plans of their own.[48] But these circumstances account for only part of the delay.

One preeminent feature of the CDG Plan was that it combined ridding Germany of the inflationary masses of money left over from the Nazi period with an ambitious economic program and—even more importantly—with an equalization of war-damage compensation. This way, conditions were created for more democratic structures in Germany and for equal opportunities for different groups. This aspect of the plan reflected Colm's and Goldsmith's experience of German hyperinflation after World War I, which had led to a huge shift in wealth from money owners to owners of real capital and had been a major source of the instability of the Weimar Republic. The plan clearly also reflected the normative basis of Colm's work in economics. Economic insecurity, he declared during a talk on the perspective currency reform, was a hothouse for totalitarianism because, faced with the choice between insecurity and limitation of personal freedom, people were more likely to choose the latter.[49]

The sociopolitical components of the plan provoked a horrified response in Washington, where the New Dealers had less and less say after Truman became president. The State Department thought the plan was consistent with Joint Chiefs of Staff Directive JCS 1067, which defined the goals of United States occupation policy in Germany. It therefore approved the plan, but the conservative War and Navy departments, which were responsible for policies concerning Germany, rejected it, claiming it was "too radical and leans too far towards the accomplishment of social objectives extraneous to financial considerations." There was even an inquiry to the Buréau of the Budget asking what kind of political person Colm was.[50] The fear was that the rigorous taxation of capital proposed for Germany to equalize financial burdens might someday provide a precedent for similar demands in the United States. "A terrible thing not only for the capital but also for capitalism" was the sarcastic comment of John Kenneth Galbraith, who was working in the State Department and surveying the Washington scene during those months. "At meetings that summer in the Pentagon, Howard C. Petersen, a man of conservative instincts who was then serving as Assistant Secretary of War and who would later become a leading Philadelphia banker, could not control his alarm."[51]

In these circles even Colm's past suddenly appeared in an unfavorable light. Since the beginning of the war the FBI had begun compiling an extensive dossier on him as it did on all the emigré scholars. Although the dossier revealed nothing except that he came from Germany, he nevertheless appeared suspect to some now because he had been at the New School and had risen so quickly in Washington.[52]

Generally, the responsible departments were quite indifferent to what was happening in Germany, so that the local American military authorities had considerable autonomy in shaping occupation policies. In this case, however, the Office of Military Government for Germany, U.S. Zone (OMGUS) was advised that only general principles were to be developed for the reorganization of German currency "as recommendations"; under no circumstances should a concrete program be set up, such as the one called for by the CDG Plan. Nor was the request for a fund to equalize payments for war damage to be granted because it might possibly lead to a centralization of financial power or even to state socialism.[53]

Colm angrily rebuked the experts in the War and Navy departments for acting as though the plan had been designed to be carried out in the United States and for refusing to realize what the situation was like in Europe. But to no avail. All work on the currency plan was halted for the time being, and several months passed without progress. In Germany, the word from the commander-in-chief was that the significance of currency reform should not be exaggerated.[54] In spite of all this, General Clay again invited Colm, whom he admired greatly as a financial expert, to take part in the final phase of preparing the currency reform in the three Western zones. But the Council of Economic Advisers refused to give Colm leave for the two months he would have been away.[55]

The currency reform actually instituted in June 1948 failed to include the originally planned equalization of financial burdens between inflated monetary and real wealth, the progressive capital levies connected with it, and the protection of small savings. It therefore opened opportunities to propagandists from various camps for attacking the antisocial attitude of the Western democracies—a fear Colm expressed in his letters to Clay. For Colm the currency reform violated elementary principles of equality without which, he thought, democracies could not exist. Limiting the reform to monetary measures and cutting the money in circulation—as had been done during the currency stabilization after the hyperinflation in the fall of 1923—hurt only money owners whereas those with real property remained largely unaffected. Colm once more called attention to the social and possibly political consequences of such an unjust distribution of the burden. Clay promised he would urge the West German authorities to initiate immediately the equalization that was due,[56] but by the beginning of the 1950s a different course had long since been embarked on and a change in social structure as originally envisioned was no longer realistic and, in fact, no longer wanted.

Jakob Marschak's career in the United States is no less remarkable than Colm's, though entirely different. Mere words can hardly convey an adequate picture of his many-sided intellectual history. Having started out as a professional engineer in Kiev, Marschak, as a young man, was a Menshevist minister in the short-lived "pedocracy" of Terek in the Caucasus after the October Revolution. He then developed into a leading international econometrist who in his old age was president-elect of the American Economic Association. (His sudden death in 1977 prevented him from actually assuming the position.) The extraordinary breadth of his personality manifested itself very early when, immediately after his flight to Berlin in 1919, this convinced socialist studied with the conservative mathematician Ladislaus von Bortkievicz (before moving on to Lederer in Heidelberg) and at the same time took an active part in the socialist student movement. After 1924 he worked first as an editor at the liberal *Frankfurter Zeitung,* then on the staff of the labor union research center for economic policy in Berlin and, after 1928, on the government-commissioned economic reports prepared in Kiel. In 1930 he habilitated in Heidelberg even though as a Jew, a Socialist, and a Russian he had no chance of ever receiving a professorship in Germany. Even conservative colleagues who were critical of him nevertheless had to admit, as did Schumpeter, that he was one of the greatest talents among mathematical economists. After his flight from Germany, Marschak taught briefly at Oxford University before being appointed the first director of the Institute for Statistics newly established there.

When he was invited to the New School in 1938, Marschak resumed a fruitful intellectual exchange with old friends he had worked with in Heidelberg and Kiel. His assertion that the complex problems of economic reality could be approached "without tears" only by using mathematical tools was regarded rather skeptically by his New School colleagues. They argued that mathematics dealt only with quantifiable data and that therefore the great variety of human actions and motives was in danger of being schematized into rigid rules of behavior. Nevertheless they, too, considered econometrics an essential tool, especially for their structural and theoretical analyses of technical change. Hans Neisser and the young Italian refugee Franco Modigliani in particular made use of Marschak's work in this context. As Marschak's collaboration on monographs on the Russian economy written for the Peace Project shows, he himself was by no means determined to turn economics into a mathematical science but recognized fully the usefulness of historical and descriptive scholarship.[57]

Marschak's influence made itself felt even more among the wider circle of scholars than at the New School itself. His econometrics seminar soon attracted Tjalling Koopmans, Wassily Leontief, Paul Samuelson, and other participants. Sometimes even colleagues of opposite convictions would turn up, like Schumpeter from Harvard, who found mathematics difficult and was never able to feel at home in that discipline. The seminars sometimes grew into veritable symposia, so that at the suggestion of the National Bureau of Economic Research the course was moved for a time to the bureau's larger halls on Columbus Circle.[58]

In the United States, econometrics had caught on in all economic camps in the late 1930s, after having been dismissed as a mere eccentricity of a few specialists just a few years earlier at the beginning of the decade. Schumpeter, for instance, reported after his arrival at Harvard how "frustrated" he was by the difficulties of trying to promote this methodological branch, which was so much farther advanced in Europe. Nobody in the United States seemed to recognize that econometrics was more than the traditionally offered "mathematics for economists," which taught only what was needed for doing statistical research.[59] In view of this situation it is not surprising that Alfred Cowles, a businessman from Colorado Springs, founded a committee—later named after him—to advance econometrics in the United States. Cowles was moved to take this step when he saw, as treasurer of the recently (1930) founded international Econometric Society and as the financial backer of its journal *Econometrica*, how far ahead the Europeans were in this field.

In 1943 Marschak was appointed director of this Cowles Commission for Research in Economics and was for this work awarded a professorship at the University of Chicago, where the research facility had been set up. We mention here only parenthetically that Marschak was replaced at the Graduate Faculty by the young Abba Lerner from the London School of Economics. This marked the first time that the New School hired someone other than an exiled European scholar.

In addition to Marschak other, mostly younger, economists of various theoretical convictions but all equally interested in econometric questions were gathered in Chicago. It is striking what a significant role scholars who had fled from Europe, like Tjalling Koopmans from Holland, the Polish Marxist Oscar Lange, and the Austrian neoclassicist Gerhard Tintner, played in this circle. The group immediately tackled a large common project on the application of mathematical methods to the analysis of business cycles, a project that included preliminary numerical and statistical studies. Marschak also involved a number of recent graduates in the project, including Kenneth Arrow, Evsey Domar, Trygve Haavelmo, Lawrence Klein, Herbert Simon, and his own former student Franco Modigliani. Klein, Simon, and most recently Modigliani were later awarded Nobel prizes,[60] which gives a sense in retrospect of the caliber of the group.

Marschak published only very little of his own during this phase. Mostly, he wrote introductions to the studies of his co-workers, introductions that succinctly presented the essence of the topic in question and that should therefore not be underestimated.[61] Short pieces are typical of his production in general because the mathematical approach made more extensive verbal explication unnecessary. His co-workers commented unanimously that without his leadership the work of the Cowles Commission would probably not have produced the results it did.[62] Further evidence of Marschak's intellectual scope and the reputation he had gained in the United States were his appointments as a member of the Conference on National Income and Wealth and, in 1946, of the Commission on Scientific Aspects of Atomic Energy.

In 1949 Marschak passed the directorship of the Cowles Commission on to Koopmans but remained a member of the group. In the following years he turned to other, new areas of research, working first, from 1955 on, at Yale where the commission had moved and, from 1960 to his retirement in 1965, at the University of California at Los Angeles. Excited by John von Neumann's and Oskar Morgenstern's game theory, he began to study how large groups gathered information and made choices and decisions. These forays into highly specialized and theoretical fields demonstrate once more the experimental range of his unconventional, interdisciplinary thinking. Among the central criteria in his theory of groups and decision making were the importance of the communication process and the need for transparency to reduce uncertainty and misinformation. According to his friends, Marschak was the first to develop a systematic theory about the economic value of information. How far beyond the limits of his own field his thinking penetrated is shown, too, by the fact that the importance of his work on information processes and on the decision-making behavior of individuals was recognized at first not so much by economists as by psychologists and sociologists.[63]

A third example of the success individual members of the Graduate Faculty achieved is the career of the sociologist Hans Speier, who left the New School at the same time as Marschak and made his mark in an entirely different area. As an expert on German war propaganda he had been asked in 1942 to head the Foreign Broadcast Intelligence Service—part of the Federal Communications Commission—which analyzed European radio and news reports after the outbreak of the war. Speier's work there took a more active turn after the Allied landing in France in 1944 and with the foreseeable defeat of Germany, for now he was asked to act as propaganda adviser for the Office of War Information. From there, he became head of the Germany section of the Occupation Areas Division in the State Department when the war ended. In this capacity he spent several months a year in Germany between 1945 and 1948 to advise the United States occupation forces on questions of reeducation, on preparing publicity for the Nuremberg trials, and so on.[64] Speier's tasks were more informal in nature than the activities of his former New School colleagues, who were also working for OMGUS. Not only Colm but also Hans Simons and Arnold Brecht had been brought in because of their administrative and professional knowledge to help plan German reconstruction. Simons was at U.S. headquarters in Frankfurt after the establishment of the British and American bizone, working on plans for the future governmental and administrative structure of Germany, and Brecht was part of a team watching over the reorganization of the federal structure during the drafting of the West German constitution.[65]

During the first years after the war Speier had not yet considered leaving the New School permanently. He had been given annual leaves for his work in Washington, and Johnson had been proud to be able to make available a scholar deemed indispensable for these tasks.[66] Speier's association with the New School did not end until he received an offer in 1948 from the Rand Corporation in California to create and then direct a research department in the social sciences there.

This institution had been founded after 1945 by the U.S. Air Force to retain some of the many experts who had contributed to the "war effort" in different offices during the war and to use them in political planning for the postwar world. Rivalry among the different service branches probably played a role in this, for the navy had established a research institute of its own, the Center of Naval Analysis, as early as 1942, and the army had followed suit, organizing not just one but several research groups. Whereas these groups were working exclusively on military requests for research, the goals of the Rand Corporation were defined more broadly and were more ambitious in scope. The overall aim was to analyze the entire field of modern social science. However, first-rate people could be attracted only if the institution, like the universities, guaranteed them independence and academic freedom. The research policies and projects were therefore to be determined by a civil board of directors and a board of overseers, with the air force being represented only on an advisory council.[67]

As had been true in the research division of the Office of Strategic Services during the war, in the Rand Corporation, too, there was the strange situation of a large number of former emigrés who belonged to the leftist political spectrum working under its roof. Their experience as scholars and their knowledge of Europe were highly valued, and the air force never attempted to exert any influence on their work.[68] From today's perspective, the connection during and after the war between so many former leftist intellectuals and institutions like the OSS and the Rand Corporation may seem odd. We have to remember, however, not only that some of those hired may have been grateful to have found a secure livelihood but also that the United States had not yet acquired the negative image of an imperial superpower. The fact that the United States alone among comparable powers did not have a secret service during the war until the OSS was founded demonstrates once again its isolationist stance in the international politics of the time. It was thrust into the role of a global superpower by the need to fight fascism, and it came to Europe as a liberator. Despite the kind of criticism leveled at the United States by the group associated with *The City of Man,* for example, the leftist intellectuals pinned their hopes on the United States as the guarantor of a democratic international order of peace. Vietnam was not yet on the horizon.

Although the think tank of the Rand Corporation produced many studies relevant to military interests, in particular on the Soviet Union, its major focus was basic research on such topics as game theory and the beginnings of computer science.[69] Hans Speier put together a team to assess attitudes toward foreign policy among West German elites based on surveys conducted in the Federal Republic. On this team were John Herz and Otto Kirchheimer, both of whom had worked for the OSS earlier and whose special assignment now was the civil service and union leadership. The outcome of their research was later published in book form under the title *West German Leadership and Foreign Policy.* Together with Karl W. Deutsch and Lewis Edinger's *Germany Rejoins the Powers* (1959), this book probably conveys the most comprehensive picture available of German politics during the early 1950s.[70] In a parallel project Speier examined West German public opinion on the question of rearmament, including attitudes toward German military tradition and toward the recent past. Later he wrote at some length on the Berlin crisis of 1961 as well as on more philosophical questions.[71] By the early 1960s his involvement with the Rand Corporation had become limited to acting as chairman of the research committee. By this time the Rand Corporation was no longer being funded by the air force and was financed instead from general funds. In 1969 he moved to the University of Massachusetts at Amherst, where he concluded his academic career.

These three representatives of the emigré generation, who left the New School and subsequently held high positions in their different scholarly and political areas, are not the only ones whose work and lives made an impact on the outside world. After 1945 the political scientist Max Ascoli also left the New School. His marriage into the well-to-do Rosenwald family, which had for many years been among the financial supporters of the Graduate Faculty, permitted him to start his own enterprise. In 1949 he founded the liberal magazine *The Reporter,* whose publisher he was for the next twenty years.[72]

But the Graduate Faculty did not just pass on qualified scholars to other intellectual projects; its work and mode of operation also seem to have appealed to new, particularly younger, scholars. Otherwise, Abba Lerner surely would not have chosen to become Marschak's successor. And when Hans Neisser left the Wharton School of the University of Pennsylvania to fill the position left vacant after Arthur Feiler's death, the National Bureau of Economic Research had also tried to recruit him because it considered him "one of the best combiners of rigorous theoretical capacity and sense of reality." Neisser opted for the New School. The bureau could understand Neisser's wish to return to this circle of old friends, but it was not at all pleased to end up on the losing side in many other instances when it competed with the New School for academics on the "research assistant level."[73]

8 / Problems of Integration

1. Individual Exile Experiences

In retrospect Adolph Lowe once described himself and his colleagues as *Emigrationsgewinnler* ("profiteers of emigration"). An ironic characterization of this kind would not have been possible without the perspective of time, but there is still a kernel of truth in it. In the age-old history of politically, religiously, or otherwise motivated expulsions, scholars have always occupied a rather unusual position because scholarship, or science, by nature transcends national boundaries. Or, as the theologian Paul Tillich saw it from the perspective of his firsthand experience, the creative spirit is per se "the permanent emigre in the world."[1] Stating the case even more sharply, the American sociologist Louis Wirth declared the concept of "intellectual emigrants" a contradiction in terms because, he said, intellectuals are always nomads in the universe of the mind and should feel at home anywhere.[2]

Such optimistic appraisals made by Americans and the emigrants themselves in discussions during the 1930s are no doubt in part due to the relatively auspicious circumstances the United States offered after 1933, despite the isolationist climate of public opinion, the institutional obstructionism, and the xenophobic attitude of the universities. The scholars had not had the usual wait for a slot in the quota system when entering the United States, and unlike earlier immigrant groups they arrived with a strong and conscious antipathy for their homeland that only increased their desire for integration. Those who had come by way of various

European countries had also experienced how different the open society of the United States was from that of other countries. In addition, they were fascinated by the optimistic new spirit of the Roosevelt era. Its readiness to experiment carried on what had just been so brutally suppressed in Germany by the Nazis. The small but in those years politically influential group of New Dealers welcomed these scholars and intellectuals with open arms. The two sides hailed each other as brothers in spirit, and it was this milieu that gave rise to the many reported euphoric visions of "cross-fertilization." Germans and Americans had good reason to assure each other that their contact had contributed to a "deprovincialization" of their respective world views. In this "transatlantic synthesis," the immigrated scholars—the "comparative academics," as the economist Paul A. Samuelson called them—were viewed as "bridge builders" between the cultures. The emigrés for their part hoped to be able, later on, after fascism was crushed in Germany, to act as interpreters and intercessors for a "global New Deal" in Europe.[3]

It cannot be forgotten, however, that not all professions and individuals met such favorable conditions or responded as enthusiastically. Lawyers and physicians, for example, had a hard time finding acceptance because of differences in legal traditions and different qualifying requirements. And apart from these objective obstacles there were in many cases subjective factors that made adapting to the new ways of life more difficult. American literature on this period of immigration, in particular the older studies still dominated by the traditional melting-pot concept, has explored these personal problems as they were expressed in private lives, in communication with colleagues and neighbors, and in the reaction—often shock—to the less research-oriented nature of teaching in America.[4] It is debatable, however, whether some facts pointed out by Lewis Coser should be taken as signs of integration difficulties. Coser cites, for example, that Arnold Brecht and Hannah Arendt and her husband Heinrich Blücher lived for years in furnished apartments.[5] In their cases, professional integration and success speak against the assumption that these living arrangements reflected an intention to stay only for a limited time while a refuge was needed. After all, none of these intellectuals later returned to Germany. Still, these patterns of behavior may give some clues to long-lasting psychological reactions. Even among scholars—though less often than among other refugee groups—some typical symptoms of incomplete integration and consequent deculturation can be found: the retreat into a hermetic private world, laments about how different—and better—things had been in the old country, and, finally, the excessive conformity to the New World of the yes-men and new super Americans.[6]

Nor were these subjective reactions, though rare, unheard of in the small cosmos of the New School. In this final chapter we will touch on them briefly to prevent creating the impression that the Graduate Faculty as an institution automatically guaranteed its scholars an easy transition into the New World because of the public recognition and solid connection to American academe the school quite quickly won for itself. Alvin Johnson's idea of assembling an entire faculty of emigré scholars obviously facilitated the transition, making it a collective, less painful process. Here scholars could continue their work in a familiar milieu and were not forced to adjust to different conditions as they would have been at the big eastern universities or at small midwestern colleges.[7] In addition, a tolerant pluralism reigned here that grew out of John Dewey's theory of education— Dewey was a cofounder of the New School—a pluralism that was directed particularly against the white, Anglo-Saxon, Protestant pressures to conform prevalent in the eastern establishment. Johnson, as an enthusiastic promoter of the New Deal, also made sure in selecting his faculty that they brought with them the proper messages, which were then circulated through appropriate channels at the right time. But in spite of these ideal conditions, the adjustment was not unproblematic for all of the faculty members. Beneath the relatively smooth surface of entrance into the American world by way of an academic appointment there could be hidden misery typical of the fate of many immigrants. To cite some examples of this is not an indiscreet poking into private lives but is only a reminder of the personal difficulties that even successful and well-adjusted scholars faced. What matters here are not so much the individual life stories as the glimpse they give of the problems peculiar to this group.

The broad range of behavior and of reactions to emigration—reflecting age, temperament, background, and other factors—can be reduced to a few types. The first and dominant type includes the largest group of scholars, to which almost all the economists belonged, together with Hans Speier, Alfred Schütz, and, after some initial difficulties, Arnold Brecht. This was the type of dynamic and creative individual who was able to adjust to the new circumstances without apparent difficulty and to amalgamate the perspectives developed in Germany with the new experiences encountered in America. Just as most of these scholars had transcended the professional self-definition and the limits of their respective disciplines in Germany, they now became in the United States the agents of that cross-fertilization because they underwent new learning processes and developed into what might be called "citizens of the world." Their interest was focused on the future, and it was they who saw to it that the New School kept out of the squabbles among emigré circles that were so typical of the refugee metropolis of New York. Even though this group was able to become integrated quickly and without fanfare, the personal and emotional difficulties some of its members suffered cannot be overlooked. Over many years they kept having to realize, in Emil Lederer's phrase, how much "Europe stuck to their soles."

Then there were the scholars who arrived in the United States with a set and immutable world view and approach to scholarship and who refused to make any concession to the new world in which they found themselves. This was true, for instance, of Max Wertheimer, who always remained immune to new influences. This extended to his personal behavior, so that he thought nothing of walking around New York wearing a loden coat and carrying a rucksack instead of a briefcase.

A third type is represented by Eduard Heimann and Kurt Riezler. Heimann's numerous contributions to the theory of economic planning and to the analysis of fascism at first evoked considerable response in the 1930s. But his further work, in which philosophical questions came to predominate more and more, was increasingly disconnected from concrete reality and thus less and less accessible to students. Before 1945 he tried to make up for the decreasing appeal of his work with vague panegyrics to the United States. His cutting Vansittartist remarks directed against Germany—a future democratization of that country, he said, would have to be "a process of de-Germanification"[8]—and his decision to be baptized by his friend Tillich at almost sixty years of age may be seen as signs of uprootedness and search for identity. After the war he immediately started teaching as a regular guest lecturer at the Academy of Labor in Hamburg, founded by the German labor unions and directed by a former student of Heimann's, and at the University of Hamburg. Then he returned permanently to Germany, where he "found a much broader field of activity than [he] ever had in the United States."[9]

Kurt Riezler's experience was similar. He played an important role in faculty discussions at the New School, but his philosophy remained alien to Americans. He was impressed by the United States and wished he had been younger so that he could have felt more at home in this dynamic country. With ironic wit he classified himself as a kind of fossil that the Americans eyed with curiosity when he told them that he was old enough to have heard Bismarck's speeches. But he was not able to incorporate into his system of thinking and teaching the pragmatic questions related to contemporary reality that he was expected to deal with. Thus he lived relatively "isolated from the actualities and controversies of the present." The problems of communicating with the students, together with a certain resignation of age, increased as he grew older, so that he, too, returned to Europe— though not to Germany—in 1954, one year before his death. He settled in Rome.[10]

Riezler and Heimann were the only members of the Graduate Faculty to leave America, and by the time they did so intellectual and political isolation was surely not the only reason for departing. The loneliness of old age and the changes in structure and personnel at the New School probably played at least as much of a role in their decisions.

Another case, finally, is that of Karl Brandt, who was considered a critical leftist during the Weimar years but who turned into a rabid German conservative nationalist during emigration. We have discussed earlier his feelings of being out of place as an agricultural scientist in New York and the frustration he consequently felt. But beyond this there must have been latent and more deeply rooted bonds supporting a psychological predisposition that became increasingly at odds with the antifascist mentality at the New School. Thus quite a furor arose in emigré circles when it became known that Brandt had written an article about American agrarian policies for the *Frankfurter Zeitung* in 1937. It all began quite mildly with fairly restrained expressions of irritation, but Brandt's reactions then provoked a regular scandal that spread to wider circles and gives some indication of the general climate in the New York emigré milieu.

After the article appeared, Kurt Rosenfeld, formerly a lawyer in Berlin who had also been active in the Socialist Workers' party, wrote to Brandt merely to inquire whether the article had been published with Brandt's permission. Rosenfeld could not imagine a German emigré who taught at the University in Exile publishing in a German newspaper whose editorial policy went along with the regime. Brandt's answer was characteristic. Not only did he declare that the article had indeed appeared with his full knowledge, but he also rejected Rosenfeld's concern in an extremely aggressive tone. "I should hope you realize not only how offensive but also how ridiculous it must appear for you to set yourself up as censor of emigrated scholars." This tone in turn upset other emigrés. With the backing of Thomas Mann, who was known to have connections with the Graduate Faculty, and of Felix Frankfurter, a member of the Graduate Faculty's Board of Trustees, they appealed to Johnson, who himself had found Brandt's attitude and bearing embarrassing.[11]

Brandt was a guest lecturer at the Baton Rouge campus of Louisiana State University at this point, and from there emanated even stranger pronouncements. He was teaching about conditions in Europe, "the most beautiful part of the world," his intellectual nourishing ground as well as "destiny," now in danger of perishing because of the totalitarian movements that held sway there. At the same time he was fascinated with the populist movements of the American South. He saw in them a genuine political culture that showed none of the hectic and neurotic symptoms of disintegration that characterized New York life. He was particularly impressed by Louisiana's minidictator Huey Long and called the appearance of Long a stroke of good luck in the history of the South. According to Brandt, Long with his forceful decisiveness represented the ideal politician and was anyway "only half as bad as that bunch of New Dealers of Washington."[12]

Brandt had a chance to make the "feeling of perfect happiness" he had experienced in the South more permanent a few months later when he was invited to work for the Food Research Institute at Stanford, a position his New School colleagues urged him to accept. He was thus the first to leave the faculty at the beginning of the year 1938. His ambiguous political attitude changed little in the following years. On the one hand, he was one of the initiators of the Loyal Americans of German Descent, an organization formed by conservative emigrés after the outbreak of the war; on the other, he remained a German nationalist who kept trying to prove that national socialism really had very little to do with Germany.[13]

His relationship with his former colleagues continued to be strained. When, for example, the Institute of World Affairs began planning for Germany's and Europe's future, Brandt began to voice frequent criticism that became increasingly sharp in tone the more it became obvious that the planning did not aim at a quick restoration of the German status quo ante. At first the Institute members tried to discuss the issues seriously with him. But his attacks seem to have become increasingly provocative, and when he started to suspect all of postwar planning, from the Potsdam Conference on down to studies limited to the microcosm of specialized economic questions, of being motivated by the desire to put the Morgenthau plan into practice, contact with him was broken off. Johnson's assessment of Brandt was probably not much off the mark when he called him a hypertrophic Prussian egocentric who would no doubt have been an excellent scholar had he not constantly let his "guts slip into the scientific scale."[14]

Other kinds of problems and difficulties may be illustrated by the circumstances that brought Arnold Brecht to the New School. As mentioned earlier, Brecht was neither Jewish nor a socialist and faced no danger on those accounts. Instead, the National Socialists fired him because he represented the democratic elements of the legal Prussian government before the Constitutional High Court against Papen's coup d'état. It is hard to imagine what it must have felt like for a man who had worked as a civil servant for twenty-five years—most of the time in top positions within the Reich administration—to be fired simply because he had acted in accordance with the law. Apparently Brecht's long association with government bureaucracy blinded him to the new quality of the National Socialist system immediately after 1933 and contributed to his reluctance to leave Germany for good. Like many others in similar situations he did not at first give up his deeply ingrained respect for the law and asked his former employer for official permission to leave the country, declaring specifically that he would "behave abroad in every respect as a German citizen and member of the new state." His asking Johnson for a statement declaring that the name "University in Exile" was merely a name and had no political implications whatsoever grew out of this mentality. At this time, October 1933, Brecht did not yet consider himself an exile and did not wish to be regarded as such. Instead, he planned to stay in the United States only about a year because he figured national socialism would not survive for long.[15] At first Brecht stayed away from the antifascist activities of the New School, and he was the only one during the following years to return regularly to Germany for the summer vacation in order to have renewals of his teaching contract approved there.

Johnson tried with great patience to integrate Brecht into the politics of the New School. Again and again he tried to convince him that the creation of the University in Exile was not meant primarily as a propagandistic attack on Germany but was rather a call to world civilization to preserve academic freedom in all countries.[16] But apparently the rigid ethic of the German civil-servant class, the difficulties of letting go of the past, or homesickness proved stronger than all of Johnson's rational appeals. Brecht volunteered to forgo his salary during the summer months and apparently suffered more and more from bouts of profound depression in New York.[17]

When nothing changed in Brecht's attitude after two years, Johnson began to lose patience. "How is it possible for you, ethically," he asked, "to remain a member of the Faculty, when your position is antagonistic to its existence? . . . From the beginning your position with the Faculty was ambiguous because you alone of the group had not broken with Germany." He proceeded to make it very clear now to Brecht that the faculty had been set up solely as a protest against Nazi Germany. If all the members were to assume Brecht's attitude and regard criticism of German politics as a threat to their personal identity and safety, then the faculty would lose all credibility and justification.[18]

Johnson remonstrated repeatedly with Brecht in a similar vein, and every time Brecht was deeply hurt because he felt his honor and integrity had been called into question. Like all his colleagues, he said in his own defense, he had left Germany as a protest against the Nazis, and the discrimination against Jews affected him as much as if he had been Jewish himself. If he continued to return to Germany, it was because it gave him a chance to observe from close up what was happening there and to maintain contact with like-minded Germans. In addition, he argued, he had donated most of the German pension he had received to Jewish aid organizations and had contributed several hundred dollars to the solidarity fund of the New School. All this should be seen as unquestionable evidence of his allegiances. He himself, Brecht went on, perceived the external contradiction between his feelings and ideas about law and justice on the one hand and his ties to Germany on the other, but because of the objective facts he had just listed he felt that his trips to Germany, which might after all land him in a concentration camp, were not in conflict with his activities in New York. All his work was directly or indirectly "dedicated to the United States," his scholarly interests had shifted from European to American subjects, and he supported the aims of the Graduate Faculty without any reservations. He had received several inquiries as to whether he would accept an appointment at another institution but had responded negatively each time, not only because he felt an obligation toward his group but also because he considered working together at an emigré university crucial.[19]

This conflict, which went on for years, was finally laid to rest when

Brecht prepared to travel to Germany once again in the summer of 1938 and Johnson asked him point-blank to decide where he belonged: "I am sure that you yourself realize that the time comes when a man must definitely choose."[20] Somewhat shamefacedly, Brecht canceled the passage he had already booked. Although his loyalty was beyond doubt and he had become one of the faculty members most generally respected by scholars beyond the New School, the tensions of the first years continued to be felt for some time. Not until the 1940s did Johnson form the same close personal ties with Brecht that he had established much earlier with most of the other faculty members.

Brecht's problems of acculturation stand out even more clearly if they are compared to the relatively easy integration of Hans Staudinger. Staudinger, too, had belonged to the higher echelons of the Prussian government bureaucracy and had, like Brecht, been dismissed for political reasons. Hermann Göring, prime minister of Prussia at the time, asked Staudinger to return—in spite of the latter's membership in the Social Democratic party—to his former post as undersecretary in the Prussian Ministry of Trade, which he had lost in the wake of Papen's coup d'état in 1932, and to continue his previous successful work there as organizer of the public utilities (*Verbundwirtschaft*). Staudinger refused. It would never have occurred to him, after leaving Germany with official permission, to return, as Brecht did, even for a visit. The Nazi rise to power and the exodus of many like-minded Germans had destroyed all the traditions to which he felt any intellectual, political, or emotional allegiance. Although his habit and accent made him least able to hide his political background—and he had no desire to hide it—integration into American life and loyalty toward the "other Germany" presented no conflict for him. He was among the founders in the spring of 1939 of the German Labor Delegation, which represented the Social Democratic party in the United States, though he quickly left the organization during the war when it took on a more and more nationalistic stance. At the same time, it was he who transformed the Graduate Faculty into a truly American institution during the decades he served as its dean, a position he assumed in 1941. Even in later years there was never any conflict for Staudinger between his activities and commitment as an American citizen and his lasting preference for German social democracy. He not only took an intense interest up to his death in 1980 in the developments of the Social Democratic party in West Germany but also thought of himself as a member of the party in spirit.[21]

What paralyzing effects emigration could have on a promising scholarly career has already been suggested in connection with the sociologist Albert Salomon. The younger economist Alfred Kähler experienced a similar fate. The dissertation he had written on the problem of technology gained him the reputation of being one of the most fertile and innovative minds among the younger generation of economists in Germany. He had also been quite active politically and had made important contributions to workers' education as director of an adult education program near the Danish border. At the New School his articles, which continued the line of thinking begun in his dissertation, were among the most important work done there in the early years, but then he faded more and more into the background, and the impact he had on his field remained limited. Kähler was a farmer's son from Schleswig-Holstein who had learned the trade of locksmith and had acquired his education only later by going to night school. He thus lacked the upper-middle-class background that character- ized most of his colleagues and that was important for success in American society. Kähler apparently also lacked a talent for promoting himself—a necessary part of achieving academic success, especially in the United States—so that he found himself at a disadvantage in his new surroundings. Some impressions Hans Simons jotted in his journal gave a glimpse into these difficulties after Kähler invited him to his home shortly after his arrival in 1935. Simons quickly noticed the tragic aspect of the lives of "totally transplanted" emigrés. "Strange," Simons wrote,

> that such people generally lack all self-confidence and keep making futile efforts to adapt that reveal their insecurity all the more. . . . One is tempted in such cases to say to them that anything truly genuine is always appropriate and will succeed, even in New York, if it stays what it is. But this can't be said out loud; it's an insight we can jot down in a journal but that we can't share with others—at least not until we know to what extent we ourselves will be able to act according to it.[22]

It should be stressed here once more that these various problems repre- sent exceptions in the adjustment process and occurred only in some individuals. The majority of the faculty did not experience such difficulties of transition and readjustment. The common work of building up the faculty, obtaining a secure livelihood, and becoming integrated into Amer- ican academic life required all available intellectual and emotional ener- gies. These intellectuals constructed a new focus for their lives, and the absorption in it counteracted retrospective tendencies. The commitment to create a new, common future and the optimistic spirit that prevailed are perhaps best reflected in a symposium organized in celebration of the fourth anniversary of the Graduate Faculty. The topic was "Intellectual Freedom and Responsibility." In the presence of many fellow emigrés, among them Thomas Mann and Paul Tillich, the discussion digressed into a critical self-assessment of the participants' own recent experiences. It was in this context that Tillich first developed the concept of the intellectual migrant, sketching the picture of a restlessly seeking, critical spirit that transcends the finiteness of reality in a process that automatically turns the intellectual into a stranger or alien. Without this "self-alienation" no critical consciousness and consequently no culture are possible, Tillich asserted. In this way the imposed emigration was understood to be a kind of experimental dialectic that had step by step liberated him and his friends from their confined ways of thinking and their limited systems of categories.[23]

Even more optimistic was Hans Speier's vision, according to which the "ubiquitous character" of the intellectual precluded any sense of social or intellectual uprootedness. "The intellectual may change his location . . . but does not become a stranger." Speier asserted that the rise of the modern nation-states in Europe had paralyzed Western culture—which had originally been universal in nature—as different groups and promoters of nationally limited or other parochial interests claimed to represent ultimate values. Consequently, he regarded the expulsion from Europe as a liberating chance to contemplate once more the supranational values of humanity, freedom, and autonomy. In a way, Speier claimed, the intellectual who left Europe experienced a "second youth," as his life, through involvement and participation in a new world, was transformed into a renewed, permanent, and more conscious learning process.[24]

Many other contributions at the symposium contained similarly severe criticism of the speakers' own experiences of socialization, criticism especially of the German standard of education with its autochthonous cultural extremism. After the symposium this theme of the errant intellectual came up again for repeated and self-critical discussion at the Graduate Faculty.[25]

2. The Graduate Faculty and the Horkheimer Circle of the Institute of Social Research

We can get some idea of the various ways of coping with forced exile by examining the relations between members of the Graduate Faculty and those of the former Frankfurt Institute of Social Research. There are a number of similarities between the institutions themselves as well as in the biographical circumstances. The two institutions were the most significant centers of German emigré scholarship, both quantitatively—the number of scholars involved—and qualitatively—the interest the work produced. The members of both organizations shared the same background of a critical approach to the social sciences practiced in Germany during the 1920s, and there were numerous links of a professional, philosophical, and personal nature, the latter sometimes going back to youthful years spent together in the same place. In spite of this a peculiar atmosphere prevailed in the relationship between these two centers of scholarship for many years until the demise of the Institute, an atmosphere that led to strained scholarly intercommunication in spite of many personal ties between individual members. This went back much farther than 1933, although the polarization, aggravated by the different conditions under which the scholars started their new lives, did not become fully apparent until after emigration.

The core group at the New School consisted largely of veterans of political practice, a fact that strongly affected their understanding of the tasks of scholarship from the outset. This tendency received further encouragement in the United States, when under Alvin Johnson's guidance the economists in particular became a kind of think tank for New Deal strivings. After the disheartening experience of witnessing the collapse of the Weimar Republic, the members of the Graduate Faculty now found new, concrete challenges that allowed them to continue their previous work and that made for a rapid integration into the new social realities. The common effort of building up the faculty in the face of years of difficulties and uncertainty gave rise to a kind of esprit de corps in spite of the variety of temperaments and scholarly bents assembled in the faculty. There never was a common philosophy at the Graduate Faculty, even though the dominant group of economists presented a relatively unified profile to the outside world.

Though the New School people, on the basis of their political experiences, were interested in theory only to the extent to which it worked in practice, the relation between theory and practice was something the members of the Institute of Social Research reflected on only abstractly, for to them "critical thinking [was] in itself adequate practice."[26] This had been the case ever since 1931, when Horkheimer succeeded the Austrian Marxist Carl Grünberg as leader of the Frankfurt Institute. Whereas Grünberg, with his emphasis on solid, empirical, and concrete historical scholarship, had created a true connection to the tradition of the labor movement, such a connection was only an abstract consideration for Horkheimer. No doubt this situation already contained the seeds of the later reservations concerning the New School people, though on the surface relations were still quite friendly. Still, in early April 1933 Adolph Lowe declined the offer of a permanent position at the Institute in Geneva extended to him by his old friend Horkheimer.

These differences were accentuated by the external circumstances of emigration. Horkheimer was able to save his Institute as an entity, moving it first to Geneva, then to Paris, before finding a permanent home for it in facilities made available by Columbia University. The Institute's considerable endowment was saved, too, since most of it had been invested in the United States, so that the Institute was not, like the New School, dependent on financial support from third parties. Its members thus did not have to work hard and fight to establish a place for themselves in the academic world after emigration. Nor did they have to tailor their thinking to suit an American audience. The Institute did not offer a curriculum of its own until after some years, and then only sporadically as part of the Columbia course offerings. Thus an external framework was set up that further added to the hermeticism of the theoretical positions the core group of Horkheimer, Theodor Adorno, and Leo Lowenthal had brought from Europe.

Commentators have frequently pointed out that the rise and eventual victory of national socialism severely disrupted the Institute's work and led to profound intellectual self-doubt, escapism, and elitism among its members.[27] The old Marxist position of the Institute, namely, that the tasks progressive forces set themselves at certain moments of history determine the value of theory,[28] had been dealt a severe blow by fascism's easy abolishment of the labor movement. There is no need here to decide whether and how this shock caused the shift of emphasis toward a "Critical Theory of Society" after 1933 and whether this label merely camouflaged old ways of thinking. Did it stand for a new kind of object analysis—as of the modern mass culture? Or was it in fact a fundamental departure from Marxist theory, arising from deep pessimism, and a turn toward a more general approach based on anthropology and the philosophy of history? Horkheimer himself, though, did not convey the impression immediately after 1933 that the expulsion from Germany was a profound disruption for him. In the seclusion of Morningside Heights he seemed to have found the ideal place "for quiet scholarly work," especially since he had decided to turn his back on politics and to "live as a philosopher, that is, in the world of imagination and abstract ideas [because] concrete reality is too unpleasant."[29] When Theodor Adorno later spoke of the "damaged lives" of the emigrés, this condition seems to have been due less to suffering from a shattering of continuity than to a lack of interest on the part of the Institute's core group in becoming integrated. Adorno's description of himself as "European through and through" also suggests that he made no great effort to deprovincialize himself.[30] If he and his friends had been "transcendental homeless intellectuals" earlier in Germany, they now retreated into even deeper isolation in New York. This attitude is strikingly revealed by the repugnance Lowenthal expressed on visiting a Van Gogh exhibit at the Metropolitan Museum, repugnance because "these same things look different here than they do in Europe."[31]

This "Teutonic" unwillingness to compromise (H. Stuart Hughes) in turn jeopardized the ideological unity of the Institute soon after new colleagues like Franz Neumann and Otto Kirchheimer, who came from the "real" socialist movement, joined the New York group in the mid 1930s; and it was this same unwillingness that lay at the heart of the tensions between the Institute members and their colleagues at the New School. Even the "Studies in Prejudice" produced by the Institute in collaboration with the American Jewish Congress in the 1940s and edited by Horkheimer, which are more in line with American research methods, were not a negation of the group's hermeticism. This descent into the realm of empirical research was more the forced result of having exhausted the Institute's own financial resources during those years. Adorno wrote some fundamental chapters of the volume *The Authoritarian Personality*, which was published in 1950. But these essays and their philosophical approach were so far removed from the quantitative research represented in the other chapters contributed by younger American scholars that they might as well have been published separately.[32]

In his biography of the Institute, Martin Jay cites as the reason for the conflicts between the two emigré centers the fact that the "Marxist tinge" of the Institute evoked the "ire" of the New School people. In addition, he says, the latter, being influenced by Wertheimer's Gestalt psychology, were upset by the "enthusiasm for Freud" that prevailed at the Institute. Jay goes as far as to call Emil Lederer "an old Institut foe"; and of Hans Speier he says that he responded to the Institute's work with nothing but devastating criticism. Jay even blames Speier, with his "extremely hostile review," of having deprived *Studien über Autorität und Familie,* which had appeared in 1936, of a proper reception in America.[33] Apparently Jay was simply passing on, possibly in somewhat dramatic form, conjectures articulated by former Institute members he interviewed for his book. In many instances he cites, characteristically, unconfirmed reports of opinions supposedly expressed by New School members. Nowhere in the correspondence of members of the Graduate Faculty addressed to colleagues at the Institute or to third persons is there any sign that they felt irritated by the Institute's "Marxism." It may be noted in passing that Horkheimer and his friends tried to distance themselves in their concept of Critical Theory to a greater or lesser degree from their own past theoretical orientation. The accusation of anti-Freudianism is no more plausible because psychology hardly came up for discussion at the New School, and the economic studies focused on completely different problems. It is true that in his review of *Autorität und Familie* Speier expressed some doubts about the usefulness of Freudian theory in analyzing social phenomena and went on to define the desiderata of future scholarship. To see this interpreted as a devastating criticism of the book under discussion comes as all the more of a surprise if one has actually read the review, which is, on the whole, favorable.[34] The suggestion that Speier prevented this work from getting the attention it deserved does not make sense either, since the book appeared in German and would not have received much attention in the United States under any circumstances. A similar misinterpretation is evident, finally, in the attitude imputed to Emil Lederer. To be sure, Lederer had criticized the Institute for moving away, starting in the 1930s, from its earlier interest in the social sciences in favor of a more and more philosophical orientation, a change that, Lederer suspected, might have been responsible for the loss of its old political profile.[35]

Horkheimer himself had too many close ties to the New School, and in particular to Adolph Lowe, to let whatever differences of opinion existed degenerate into such polemics. When he arrived in New York he had frequent contact with various New School people, among them Gerhard Colm and Hans Staudinger. Then there was Lowe, who had acted as "liaison officer"[36] between the two institutions when he was still in Manchester and whose trip to New York in 1937 to look around in the United States Horkheimer had financed.[37]

The sharp polemic against the New School originated mostly with Leo

Lowenthal and Franz Neumann. Lowenthal was the first of the Institute's inner circle to try to block all contact with the New School and to boycott discussion even with Tillich, who was neutral between the two institutions.[38] But Lowenthal maintained his isolationist attitude only during the 1930s. After 1940 he became a regular participant in the discussion circle around Horkheimer, Lowe, and Tillich, and he gradually became so settled in the United States that he did not return to Frankfurt with the Institute after the war.

In the case of Neumann, his relatively late arrival in New York in 1936 made it harder for him to stake out his own area of work and expertise, and that may have been the reason for his perceiving the Graduate Faculty as threatening competition because it was doing research on topics he was interested in. Similar friction arose within the Institute between Neumann and the Institute's economist Friedrich Pollock. Even in Neumann's arguments against Pollock's theory of modern state capitalism it is hard to separate objective argument from personal invective, and Horkheimer had to admonish him not to attack his colleagues "in the style of anti-Dühring."[39] Neumann's opinions of the New School people were even more vitriolic. He described Max Ascoli, the school's dean at the time, as a "puffed-up idiot of unmatched vanity" and Hans Speier as a "sly, highly intelligent, and formally extremely clever scoundrel," and the work published in *Social Research* struck him as just one trite commonplace after another. The only ones to pass muster in his eyes were specialists like Marschak, whose fields of research in no way touched on areas in which he himself was interested.[40]

His attacks became even wilder when the Rockefeller Foundation failed to award a grant he and the Institute had applied for, to study national socialism and he learned that the Peace Project of the New School was going to do the necessary research. The foundation tried to work out a compromise solution. The Institute people should sit down with the scholars from the Peace Project and determine which aspects of the study the Project would not work on. The Institute could then apply for a new grant to work in those areas, and the application would have a good chance of being approved. This was the last straw for Neumann. Indignantly, he rejected the suggestion that the Institute work as a "mere handyman" for others.[41] Although Horkheimer contacted the New School to outline possible areas in which the Institute might work and asked for "constructive criticism" of the Institute's plans,[42] Neumann, the designated specialist for the project, refused not only cooperation but any communication what-soever with the Graduate Faculty. Part of the material he had already assembled he worked up later without outside financial support and incorporated it in his book *Behemoth,* which was published in 1942.[43]

Horkheimer tried repeatedly on other occasions to mend fences between the two camps. Out of a sense of intellectual isolation he begged the querulous Neumann to be a little more restrained in his attacks on others, for the Institute's circle of friends was getting smaller and smaller.[44] He sent even clearer signals to Lowe. In spite of profound differences of opinion between them, he sought out contact with Lowe because in him he found "that sense of liberality that is becoming rarer and rarer in the thinking of our own friends."[45]

The dialectic of theoretical differences and human closeness between the two men is particularly evident in the period when Lowe was working on his *Price of Liberty* and Horkheimer had finished his essay on "egoism."[46] The two works raised similar fundamental questions, one in the form of historical analysis, the other as philosophical anthropology, and resulted in an unresolved controversy during the following years. It all started with the principle of "spontaneous conformity" that Lowe's analysis found to be at the heart of the British class structure and that appeared to him at the time as the only realistic alternative to dictatorial mass rule. Horkheimer not only refused to regard conformism as an alternative to mass rule but considered Lowe's principle of spontaneous conformity an unacceptable "approval of conditions that should not exist to start with and that could be changed into something better." Even before defining the basic principle of Critical Theory in his manifesto one year later,[47] he thought he had found in Lowe's approach an example of traditional and therefore affirmative criticism. Conformity, he declared, did not preserve the *conservatio intellectus* but only swallowed it up. The opposite of mass rule should therefore be seen not in conformity—"which already is identical with it, especially today"—but in the insistence on "reason and autonomy," as they had always been postulated by the great tradition of philosophy.

Lowe's insistence on planning, by which he meant the translation of spontaneous conformity into concrete political form in the widest sense, Horkheimer greeted with even greater reservations. Here we see clearly on what different levels the discussion was being waged. For Horkheimer the concept of planning came dangerously close to that of Nazi *Volksgemein-schaft* ("national unity"), both of which implied, according to Horkheimer, an attempt to coopt whatever was still left of critical thinking. "I have always been against tacitly turning the idea of a rational society, which is the same as an association of free human beings and which critical theory is constantly defining more precisely, into the concept of a planned economy."[48]

Lowe, for his part, subscribed to Horkheimer's plea for reason and individual freedom in the face of the authoritarianism that existed in modern society; but, he asked, what ways do autonomous and reasonable human beings have to create a better society without a conscious consensus, that is, without conforming behavior and common planning for the future? The very societies that came closest to embodying Horkheimer's individualistic ideal were unthinkable without the norms of spontaneous self-restraint. In Horkheimer's reaction against the concept of planning Lowe discerned an unfortunate similarity to the "ideas of Herr Mises." Like the latter, Lowe went on, Horkheimer thoroughly misunderstood the problems of planning, planning which long since had ceased to be limited to economics but had to be defined much more broadly in order to insure the survival of any social and political order. To expect that a change in the existing capitalistic distribution of wealth or the creation of whatever structures would allow for the emergence of autonomous personalities, to expect that such initiatives would automatically resolve the conflicts between different interests in society, was to relapse into utopian harmonious thinking. Social planning had to be understood instead as a regulatory mechanism that was necessary for resolving conflicts in any society.

In his *Price of Liberty* Lowe had reflected on the magnitude and nature of the price that reasonable human beings would be willing to pay for such planning. The two extremes of autonomy and conformity were for him the starting point of any kind of "social reorganization," and it was obvious to him not only that there would always be tension between them but also that imperfect reality could be changed only gradually. In the system of concepts used in Horkheimer's Critical Theory, which used terms like "responsibility" and "reasonable intention," Lowe saw only an appeal to the autonomous individual himself, and he found in this theory no indication of how conflicts between the many individuals could be overcome or exactly what principles were to constitute a new "cohesion of society."[49] Horkheimer's new approach after 1933 seemed to Lowe only a variation of idealist philosophy, for in spite of its claims it never examined the mechanisms actually at work in real life. The central elements of Critical Theory not only were symbols of an anarchic individualism but also represented a philosophical construct of perfection that had no epistemological relation to reality. The logical consequence was necessarily a negative dialectic that rejected all of reality because the world never was or could be made to resemble what the Institute intellectuals imagined it to be. But in spite of such sharp and basic differences, Lowe, just like Horkheimer, kept up their dialogue because he too did not want "our internal differences to cause us to forget that in spite of everything we share a common front.[50]

9 / Epilogue:
The New School Scholars and the New Germany after 1945

We have already indicated at several points that the New School scholars, with a few exceptions, came to regard themselves quite quickly as immigrants rather than as exiles waiting to return to their home country. In the course of the 1940s they had all become American citizens and found a place within American academe; all the same, they continued to take a strong interest in developments in their country of origin. They continued to comment critically after 1945 on conditions there.[1] Most of them also traveled to Germany quite soon after the war—some of them, like Brecht, Colm, Simons, and Speier, in an official capacity—to get a firsthand impression of conditions and to explore what contributions they might be able to make to the revival of the social sciences and to the rebuilding of academic institutions in Germany. In the following years and decades some of the faculty members kept up their connections by going to Germany on lecture tours, as guest professors, or on private vacations. However, except for Eduard Heimann, none of them returned to stay. This was not just because they were established now in the United States. Probably just as strong reasons were the doubts and disagreements inherent in the relationship between the emigrants and the leading circles in the new Germany. The many transatlantic contacts, maintained on a purely private basis, should therefore not lead us to conclude from the perspective of today that the end of Nazi rule automatically ushered in a resumption of "normal" relations between the emigrants and their country of origin.

For the New School scholars, as for many other intellectuals, the twelve years of national socialism were not simply an intermezzo after which one could go back and continue as though nothing had changed. This was impossible not just because colleagues and compatriots had watched their expulsion in 1933 with indifference and sometimes even with satisfaction. More serious were the disappointing developments in postwar Germany that affected the emigrés' attitude for a long time to come, if not permanently.

The New School scholars took into account, of course, the situation in international politics after 1945, a situation they had not anticipated in their plans and studies, many of them produced as part of the Peace Research Project. They criticized the major role United States foreign policy played in the rise of the cold war and the way American political strategies prevented the changes that they had taken for granted would take place in Germany's social structure. But their criticism of the inconsistent, only formally imposed democratization, including the totally inadequate denazification, was not as bitter as their disappointment over how little the Germans themselves were willing to accept those formal changes and to make the real changes the formal ones were meant to implement. But what frightened them more than anything else was the degree to which those in power stayed in power, with the scandalous result that in the reconstruction old Nazis and anti-Nazis were not even on an equal footing. Whereas the careers of the National Socialists as a rule showed hardly a break after 1945, the representatives of the "other Germany"—those who had reflected for years on Germany's democratic future during their exile or emigration—were not even asked for advice by the Germans, let alone urged to return. Emil Julius Gumbel's answer in 1947 to Max Seydewitz's noncommittal question as to whether he would not like to take part in the rebuilding was surely typical. Seydewitz, a former comrade-in-arms during the days of the Paris popular front, was manager of the Berlin radio station at the time. Gumbel answered that he had been waiting for two years, hoping that university professors fired in 1933 would be asked to return. He had just become naturalized in the United States, he explained, and after working for six years as visiting professor at the New School with short-term renewals of his contract he finally had a chance to get a permanent appointment, which he had no desire to give up just to struggle for an uncertain future in Germany.[2] The few calls some of the faculty members received from German universities do not change the fact that there was no concerted effort to offer exiled university faculty their former positions, and it was for this reason that Lowe, for example, declined an invitation to Göttingen in the late 1940s.

These developments, which soon became obvious, must have seemed all the more depressing in view of the passionate appeal the New School scholars, together with other emigrated academics from all over the country, had addressed to the American public after the Potsdam Conference. The appeal spoke out against anything related to Morgenthau's ideas of deindustrializing Germany, ideas still much alive as U.S. Joint Chiefs of Staff Directive JCS 1067 showed. It also declared a comprehensive aid program for Germany and surrounding areas to be an absolutely essential condition for peace.[3] In other appeals they demanded that immediate measures be taken to relieve the most acute needs in areas devastated by the war, and they themselves organized the sending of countless food packages to colleagues in Germany.[4] But even these first personal contacts after the war were not encouraging. As an illustration we will mention the *Volkstumskundler* (a kind of Nazi sociologist) Max Hildebert Boehm, who had belonged to the "young conservative" camp during the 1920s and now called himself a "sociologist." Introducing himself by referring to the fact that they had worked together on the *Encyclopaedia of the Social Sciences* (Boehm had written the articles on national socialism and on Moeller van den Bruck), he now approached Alvin Johnson with a request for help. As he represented it—the communists had deprived him of his professorship at Jena University because of his strong Christian convictions. Johnson had some food packages sent to Boehm's family but asked in his response what Boehm had been doing for the past twelve years and what stand he, as a scholar, had taken toward the Nazis' shocking racial theories, which were bound to stain the name of Germany for generations to come. Apparently he never received a reply.[5]

Most of those asking for help showed little inclination to reflect on their past. It seemed that nobody had been a convinced National Socialist. Everybody had either opted for "inner emigration" or held merely formal membership in the party. Walther G. Hoffmann, a former student of Lowe's at Kiel who in 1933, as a passionate storm trooper, had roughed up Colm and Neisser and was later to be celebrated in the Federal Republic of Germany as a pioneer of quantitative economic history, was a case in point. He thought he could reestablish contact with his former colleagues as though nothing had happened, declaring during a visit to New York after the war that he had had no way of telling at the time where national socialism was going to "lead."[6]

The New School people were dismayed to hear from the first travelers to Germany how few people were left there with whom one could talk "the same language." With irritation they noticed—as early as 1946—how successfully the Germans repressed their past in a wave of "wild anticommunism" and how well this tactic worked with the Western occupation forces, which obviously favored the newly founded CDU party and within which, because of the word "Christian" in its name, old reactionaries and Nazis could safely gather. Only rarely, it was noted, did Germans allude to their own responsibility for the present conditions. Apparently, anticommunism was considered proof of new, democratic convictions and entitled one to put the past behind oneself.[7]

In view of all this, the Graduate Faculty's ideas for the postwar period—such as the wish to establish a school for democratic leadership—proved illusory. The school would have been set up by emigrés to reeducate young people for democracy and would initially have recruited students nominated by resistance circles, such as the White Rose and the Edelweiss Pirates.[8] Attempts to achieve similar goals with the cooperation of German academic institutions also turned out to be quite unproductive. In 1947, the first Social Democratic government to be elected in Schleswig-Holstein approached the former members of the Kiel Institute of World Economics with a request for assistance in reopening the Institute. The group promptly contacted the Rockefeller Foundation and asked if the foundation would resume its former financial commitment. But the idea was pursued no further when the Graduate Faculty stipulated that if they were to collaborate in the venture former Nazis would have to be dismissed and an international advisory council set up.[9]

There had also been hopes of establishing an international university in Heidelberg because two old allies from the past were there, namely, Alfred Weber and Alexander Rüstow, the latter having returned from his Turkish exile. But these early contacts never got beyond a student exchange.[10]

The doubts the New School scholars had about conditions in Germany also show up clearly in their reactions to Friedrich Pollock's attempt in the late 1940s to build broad support among the emigrés for the return of the Institute of Social Research to Frankfurt. For one thing, the Graduate Faculty deplored the choice of Frankfurt on principle as long as the university did not clean up its "rotten atmosphere" and get rid of some professors who had been prominent Nazis. For another, they considered it demeaning for the Institute, now a highly respected institution, to return to Frankfurt in this fashion. The Institute's work spoke for itself, they pointed out, and there was no need for it to play the role of supplicant to return.[11]

Altogether, the attitude of the New School scholars and of other emigré intellectuals remained skeptical toward political restoration in Germany. The tension in their relationship to Germany did not ease until many years later, when a new generation gradually replaced older faculty at the universities. At this point Hans Staudinger in particular became an important promoter of academic connections with Germany. It was on his initiative that in the early 1960s, on the occasion of a visit by the president of the Federal Republic of Germany to the United States, the Theodor Heuss Chair, financed by the Federal Republic, was established at the Graduate Faculty, and since that time younger German social scientists have had a chance to come to teach for a year in New York.[12] How sensitive the relationship remained became evident however in the Graduate Faculty's immediate reactions to attempts by conservative groups to discredit the Social Democratic candidate and onetime emigré Willy Brandt during the electoral campaign in the Federal Republic in the early 1970s. The disingenuous suggestion by some circles of the Christian Social Union (CSU) that Brandt should say what he had been up to when he had left the country showed how effective viciousness could still be in rousing some benighted elements of the population. When they heard of this outrageous attempt to revive the old stab-in-the-back legend, the older emigrants at the New School immediately leaped to Brandt's defense, awarding him an honorary degree and arranging a lecture tour for him in the United States to demonstrate the high repute this representative of the new Germany enjoyed in the rest of the world.[13] But by now things seemed to have changed in Germany, too. Brandt emerged the winner in 1972 from what was probably the liveliest election campaign in the Federal Republic's history, a campaign in which the young student opposition was active with numerous citizen initiatives.

Appendix:
List of European Scholars and Artists Helped by the New School for Social Research between 1933 and 1945

Name	Country of Origin	Discipline/Profession
Alt, Franz L.	Austria	economics/statistics
Arnheim, Rudolf	Germany	psychology of art
Asch, Solomon	Germany	psychology
Ascoli, Max	Italy	political science
Auger, Pierre	France	physics
Baran, Paul	Poland	economics
Barzin, Marcel	Belgium	philosophy
Benoit-Levy, Jean	France	education
Berger, Adolph	Poland	history of law
Berger, Erich	Germany	
Berghof, Herbert	Austria	acting/dramaturgy
Bienstock, Gregor	Russia	economics
Bikerman, Elie	Russia	ancient history
Birnbaum, Karl	Germany	psychiatry
Block, Herbert	Germany	economics
Borgese, G. A.	Italy	political science
Brandt, Karl	Germany	agricultural science
Brecht, Arnold	Germany	law/political science
Brentano, Felix W.	Austria	dramaturgy
Brook, Warner F.	Germany	economics
Brueckner, Camillo	Austria	food chemistry
Cahn, Theophile	France	biochemistry
Calabresi, Renata	Italy	psychology

Appendix

Name	Country of Origin	Discipline/Profession
Choucroun, Nine	Algeria	biophysics
Cohen, Gustave	France	French literature
Colm, Gerhard	Germany	economics
Contini, Paolo	Italy	political science
Czettel, Ladislas	Hungary	set designer
Döblin, Ernst	Germany	economics
Dombois-Bartenieff, Irma	Germany	dance
Dvoichenko-Markoff, Eufrosina	Russia	Russian literature
Eckardt, Gertrude von	Germany	gymnastics
Ehrmann, Henry W.	Germany	political science
Eichenberg, Fritz	Germany	graphic arts
Einaudi, Mario	Italy	political science
Eisler, Hanns	Germany	composer/theory of music
Ephrussi, Boris	Russia	genetics
Feiler, Arthur	Germany	economics
Ferand, Ernst T.	Hungary	musicology
Foerster, Friedrich Wilhelm	Germany	education/philosophy
Frank, Josef	Austria	architecture
Fried, Hans E.	Austria	comparative government
Fuchs, Victor	Austria	opera singer
Garvy, George	Russia	economics
Goth, Trude	Germany	dance
Graf, Max	Austria	musicology
Gregoire, Henri	Belgium	Byzantine studies
Gross, Leo	Poland	political science
Grunfeld, Judith	Germany	economics
Gumbel, Emil Julius	Germany	statistics
Gurvitch, Georges	Russia	sociology
Gutkind, Erich	Germany	philosophy/sociology
Hadamard, Jacques	France	mathematics
Halasi, Albert	Hungary	economics
Hamburger, Ernst	Germany	political science
Haussmann, Frederick	Germany	international law
Hegemann, Werner	Germany	city planning
Heimann, Eduard	Germany	economics
Herma, John L.	Austria	psychology
Hermberg, Paul	Germany	statistics

Appendix

Name	Country of Origin	Discipline/Profession
Herrmann, Leon	France	classics
Heythum, Antonin	Czechoslovakia	architecture
Heythum, Charlottta	Czechoslovakia	graphics
Hildebrand, Dietrich von	Germany	philosophy
Hirsch, Julius	Germany	industrial management
Hoffmann-Behrendt, Lydia	Russia	pianist
Honigmann, Ernst	Germany	historical geography
Horenstein, Jascha	Russia	conductor
Hornbostel, Erich von	Germany	sociology of music
Hula, Erich	Austria	political science/ international law
Ince, Alexander	Hungary	theater arts
Kähler, Alfred	Germany	economics
Kahler, Erich	Czechoslovakia	history
Kahn, Ernst	Germany	social policy
Kantorowicz, Hermann	Germany	law
Katona, Georg	Hungary	economics/psychology
Kaufmann, Felix	Austria	philosophy
Kelsen, Hans	Czechoslovakia	law
Koyré, Alexander	Russia	philosophy
Kraitchik, Maurice	Russia	mathematics
Kris, Ernst	Austria	psychology
Lachmann, Kurt	Germany	economics
Laskowski, Michael	Russia	agricultural chemistry
Leblond, Charles F.	France	medicine
Lederer, Emil	Germany	economics
Lehmann, Fritz	Germany	economics
Leirens, Charles	Belgium	musicology
Lenz, Friedrich W.	Germany	classics
Leser, Paul	Germany	anthropology
Leslau, Wolf	Poland	oriental languages
Levi, Nino	Italy	law
Lévi-Strauss, Claude	France	sociology/ethnology
Levy, Ernst	Germany	psychology
Ley [-Piscator], Maria	Austria	dance/theater
Littauer, Rudolf	Germany	industrial law
Loewith, Karl	Germany	philosophy
Lowe, Adolph	Germany	economics

Appendix

Name	Country of Origin	Discipline/Profession
Maes, Julian	Belgium	medicine
Magat, Michael	Russia	physical chemistry
Malinowski, Bronislaw	Poland	anthropology
Marix, Therese	France	French literature
Marschak, Jakob	Russia	economics
Mayer, Carl	Germany	sociology
Mendizabal, Alfredo	Spain	international law/ philosophy of law
Meyer, Julie	Germany	sociology
Milano, Paolo	Italy	comparative literature
Mirkine-Guetzévitch, Boris	Russia	political science
Modigliani, Franco	Italy	economics
Mosse, Robert	France	economics
Neisser, Hans	Germany	economics
Neufeld, Hans	Austria	theater arts
Nurnberg, Max	Germany	social policy
Oberling, Charles	France	medicine
Otte-Betz, Irma	Austria	dance
Ozenfant, Amedee	France	art history
Pekelis, Alexander	Russia	business law
Perrin, Francis	France	physics
Perrin, Jean	France	physics
Pese, Werner	Germany	economics
Picard, Roger	France	economics
Pinthus, Kurt	Germany	dramaturgy/literature
Piscator, Erwin	Germany	theater
Pizarro, Miguel Z.	Spain	Hispanic studies
Pless, Julius	Czechoslovakia	biochemistry
Ramos, Enrique R.	Spain	law
Reich, Wilhelm	Austria	psychology
Reiche, Fritz	Germany	physics
Reichenberger, Arnold	Germany	romance languages
Reiss, Hilde	Germany	architecture
Riezler, Kurt	Germany	philosophy
Rinner, Ernst	Germany	social policy
Rios, Fernando de los	Spain	political science
Roesch, Kurt	Germany	painting
Rolin, Henri E. A. M.	Belgium	law/sociology

Name	Country of Origin	Discipline/Profession
Rosenblum, Solomon	Poland	physics
Rougier, Louis	France	philosophy
Sagi, Eugene	Czechoslovakia	biochemistry
Salomon, Albert	Germany	sociology
Salomon, Gottfried	Germany	sociology
Salvemini, Gaetano	Italy	history
Santillana, George de	Italy	history of science
Saussure, Raymond de	Switzerland	psychiatry
Schaeffer, Rudolf	Germany	linguistics
Schrecker, Paul	Austria	philosophy
Schueck, Franz	Germany	medicine
Schueller, Richard	Austria	economics
Schütz, Alfred	Austria	sociology
Schwarz, Balduin	Germany	philosophy
Schwarz, Solomon	Russia	social policy/economics
Sereni, Angelo Piero	Italy	international law
Simons, Hans	Germany	political science
Sondheimer, Hans	Germany	theater
Speier, Hans	Germany	sociology
Spire, André	France	literature
Staudinger, Hans	Germany	economics
Stern, Catherine	Germany	psychology
Strauss, Leo	Germany	philosophy
Szell, George	Hungary	musicology
Taubenschlag, Rafael	Poland	history of law
Thomas, Alfred	Germany	engineering
Toch, Ernst	Austria	musicology
Treuenfels, Rudolf	Germany	marketing
Turyn, Alexander	Poland	classics
Vambery, Rustem	Hungary	law
Vaucher, Paul	Switzerland	social history
Venturi, Lionello	Italy	art history
Wahl, Jean	France	philosophy
Weil, André	France	mathematics
Weiller, Jean	France	economics
Wertheimer, Max	Czechoslovakia	psychology
White, John Simon	Austria	literature
Winter, Aniuta	Poland	medicine

Name	Country of Origin	Discipline/Profession
Winter, Ernst Karl	Austria	sociology/political science
Wohl, Kurt	Germany	chemistry
Wunderlich, Eva	Germany	comparative literature
Wunderlich, Frieda	Germany	social policy
Wunderlich, Georg	Germany	law
Wurmser, René	France	biophysics
Wyler, Julius	Switzerland	economics, statistics
Yahuda, A. S.	Palestine	oriental studies
Zlotowski, Ignace	Poland	chemistry
Zucker, Paul	Germany	art history
Zuckmayer, Carl	Germany	writer/dramaturgy

Abbreviations

AFL	American Federation of Labor
AfSS	*Archiv für Sozialwissenschaft und Sozialpolitik*
BoB	Bureau of the Budget
CDG Plan	Colm–Dodge–Goldsmith Plan
EC	Emergency Committee in Aid of Displaced German/Foreign Scholars
FBI	Federal Bureau of Investigation
GF	Graduate Faculty
LBI	Leo Baeck Institute
LoC	Library of Congress
NA	National Archives
NBER	National Bureau of Economic Research
NSA	New School Archive
NYPL	New York Public Library
OMGUS	Office of Military Government for Germany, U.S. Zone of Occupation
OSS	Office of Strategic Services
RFA	Rockefeller Foundation Archives
RG	Record Group
SchVfS	*Schriften des Vereins für Sozialpolitik*
SOPADE	Sozialdemokratische Partei Deutschlands
SR	*Social Research*
SUB	Stadt- und Universitätsbibliothek
SUNY	State University of New York
UCLA	University of California at Los Angeles
WA	*Weltwirtschaftliches Archiv*
WPA	Works Progress/Work Projects Administration
ZfS	*Zeitschrift für Sozialforschung*

Notes

[1]Out of print and largely unknown by the generations of social scientists trained since the beginning of the cold war, this *Encyclopaedia* remains the foremost reference work in the social sciences.

[2]The occupation of Germany by the Allied forces under the leadership of the United States provided the Americans with an opportunity to reshape the German social scientific tradition along American lines. Survey research as developed by Paul Lazarsfeld, another emigré scholar, structural functionalism as elaborated by Talcott Parsons, and American pragmatism as represented by the carriers of the work of James, Dewey, and Mead were thought by many of the next generation of German social scientists to be a part of their own legacy. The youthful generation of emigrés such as Lewis Coser and Herbert Gans who arrived in the United States in the late thirties or immediately after the war tended with few exceptions to cut themselves off from their German origins and sought to Americanize themselves. Apart from a few young emigrés such as Werner Marx, Peter Berger, Brigitte Berger, Beate Salz, and Thomas Luckmann who, by studying at the Graduate Faculty immediately after the war, were exposed to the older tradition of thought, the new generation of German students confronted a fractured intellectual culture. For them, studying American sources was difficult to resist.

[3]The ending of the cold war led to a resurgence of interest in America's emigré intellectuals and the publication of numerous books about them. Krohn cites and reviews most of them in this book. Two earlier volumes that focus on the New School and the Graduate Faculty are Lewis Coser, *Refugee Scholars in America: Their Impact and Their Experiences* (New Haven, 1984), and Peter M. Rutkoff and William B. Scott, *New School: A History of the New School for Social Research* (New

York, 1986). Both fail to grasp the long-term significance of the emigrés' ideas and erroneously assume that they have only antiquarian value. For critical reviews of Coser's work, see Wilfred M. Mcclay, "Weimar in America," *American Scholar*, winter 1985–86, pp. 119–128, who describes this book as "a form of intellectual history with the ideas left out" (p. 126), and the review symposium of Rutkoff and Scott's *New School*, "The University in Exile" by myself, Robert Jackall, Hans Speier, and Reinhard Bendix, in *Contemporary Sociology* 16, no. 3 (1987): 274–280.

Similar and even more parochial misconceptions were held by a New York State Review Board commissioned to evaluate sociology departments throughout that state. That review board, composed of William Sewell, William Gamson, E. Digby Baltzell, Ernest Campell, and Lee Rainwater, asserted that the Graduate Faculties Department of Sociology had "played a special role as an American outpost of European sociology," that the sociologists at the Graduate Faculty were "purveyors of European thought," and that what was taught was too broad and philosophically informed to be acceptable to what those reviewers called "systematic American sociology." The damage inflicted on ideas by America's cold war xenophobia has yet to be imagined, let alone calculated.

1. Introduction

[1]Franz L. Neumann et al., *The Cultural Migration: The European Scholar in America* (Philadelphia, 1953), pp. 1, 52.

[2]Donald P. Kent, *The Refugee Intellectual: The Americanization of the Immigrants, 1933–1941* (New York, 1953); see also Maurice R. Davie, *Refugees in America: Report of the Committee for the Study of Recent Immigration from Europe* (New York, 1947).

[3]Charles J. Wetzel, "The American Rescue of Refugee Scholars and Scientists from Europe, 1933–1945" (Ph.D. diss., University of Wisconsin at Madison, 1964).

[4]H. Stuart Hughes, *The Sea Change: The Migration of Social Thought, 1930–1945* (New York, 1975).

[5]John Kosa, ed., *The Home of the Learned Man: A Symposium on the Immigrant Scholar in America* (New Haven, 1968); Donald Fleming and Bernard Bailyn, eds., *The Intellectual Migration: Europe and America, 1930–1960* (Cambridge, Mass., 1969); Robert Boyers, ed., "The Legacy of the German Refugee Intellectuals," *Salmagundi* 10/11 (1969–70; reprint, New York, 1972). Some of the biographical pieces in this collection were written by Americans.

[6]Laura Fermi, *Illustrious Immigrants: The Intellectual Migration from Europe, 1930–41* (Chicago, 1968; 2nd ed., 1971).

[7]Anthony Heilbut, *Exiled in Paradise: German Refugee Artists and Intellectuals in America from the 1930s to the Present* (Boston, 1983); Lewis A. Coser, *Refugee Scholars in America: Their Impact and Their Experiences* (New Haven, 1984).

[8]Werner Röder and Herbert A. Strauss, eds., *Biographisches Handbuch der deutschsprachigen Emigration nach 1933* [*International Biographical Dictionary of Central European Emigrés 1933–1945*], vol. 1 (Munich, 1980), introduction, pp. xlix f; see also *Protokoll des II. Internationalen Symposiums zur Erforschung des deutschsprachigen Exils nach 1933 in Kopenhagen 1972* (Stockholm, 1972), pp. 489 ff.

[9]Wolfgang Frühwald and Wolfgang Schieder, eds., *Leben im Exil: Probleme der Integration deutscher Flüchtlinge im Ausland 1933–1945* (Hamburg, 1981), p. 13.

[10]Helge Pross, *Die deutsche akademische Emigration nach den Vereinigten Staaten 1933–1945* (Berlin, 1955); see also the essays by Holborn, Marcuse, Stourzh, and Wellek in *Jahrbuch für Amerikastudien* 10 (1965): 15 ff.

[11]*International Biographical Dictionary*, 3 vols. (Munich, 1980–83).

[12]Manfred Briegel, "Der Schwerpunkt Exilforschung bei der Deutschen Forschungsgemeinschaft," *Nachrichtenbrief der Gesellschaft für Exilforschung*, no. 3 (Dec. 1984): 11 ff.

[13]*Vor fünfzig Jahren: Die Emigration deutschsprachiger Wissenschaftler 1933–1939*, compiled for the Gesellschaft für Wissenschaftsgeschichte by Peter Kröner (Münster, 1983). Not included here, among others, are the names of G. Colm and A. Feiler, which appear in vol. 1 of the *Biographical Dictionary*.

[14]M. Rainer Lepsius, "Die sozialwissenschaftliche Emigration und ihre Folgen," in Lepsius, ed., "Soziologie in Deutschland und Österreich 1918–1945," in *Kölner Zeitschrift für Soziologie und Sozialpsychologie* 23 (1981, special issue): 480. See also Coser, *Refugee Scholars*, pp. 85–86.

[15]Stephen Duggan and Betty Drury, *The Rescue of Science and Learning: The Story of the Emergency Committee in Aid of Displaced Foreign Scholars* (New York, 1948); Norman Bentwich, *The Rescue and Achievement of Refugee Scholars: The Story of Displaced Scholars and Scientists, 1933–1952* (The Hague, 1953); William H. Beveridge, *A Defense of Free Learning* (London, 1959).

[16]Raymond B. Fosdick, *The Story of the Rockefeller Foundation* (New York, 1952). This account gives only some general information, such as the statement that between 1933 and 1945 approximately $1.5 million were awarded to about 300 scholars (p. 300).

[17]Monika Plessner, "Die deutsche 'University in Exile' in New York und ihr amerikanischer Gründer," *Frankfurter Hefte* 19 (1964): 181 ff.; Benita Luckmann, "Eine deutsche Universität im Exil: Die 'Graduate Faculty' der 'New School for Social Research,'" in Lepsius, "Die sozialwissenschaftliche Emigration," pp. 427 ff.; Luckmann, "Exil oder Emigration: Aspekte der Amerikanisierung an der 'New School for Social Research' in New York," in Frühwald and Schieder, *Leben im Exil*, pp. 227 ff. A recent study by Peter M. Rutkoff and William B. Scott, *New School: A History of the New School for Social Research* (New York, 1986), dealt with the whole institution and examined its emigré history only incidentally. These parts are

rather biased because the authors have only little knowledge about the historical and intellectual background of the refugees at the New School.

[18]Lepsius, "Die sozialwissenschaftliche Emigration," pp. 471, 484; Coser, *Refugee Scholars*, pp. 12, 102 ff.

[19]The author of the present work has previously examined the study of economics in Germany between 1918 and 1933 in his *Wirtschaftstheorien als politische Interessen: Die akademische Nationalökonomie in Deutschland 1918–1933* (Frankfurt and New York, 1981).

2. The Expulsion of German Scholars

[1]Figures according to the High Commissioner for Refugees (Jewish and Other) Coming from Germany, ed., *A Crisis in the University World* (London, 1935), p. 5; Emil Julius Gumbel, ed., *Freie Wissenschaft: Ein Sammelbuch aus der deutschen Emigration* (Strasbourg, 1938), p. 9; Davie, *Refugees in America*, p. 11; Bentwich, *Rescue and Achievement*, pp. 23 ff.; most recently, Jean-Philippe Mathieu, "Sur l'emigration des universitaires," in Gilbert Badia et al., *Les bannis de Hitler: Accueil et luttes des exiles allemands en France (1933–1939)* (Paris, 1984), pp. 133 ff.

[2]See, for example, High Commissioner for Refugees, *Crisis in the University World*, p. 7; Reports of the Emergency Committee in Aid of Displaced German Scholars (EC), Jan. 1, 1934, p. 6, June 1, 1940, p. 1, and Jan. 31, 1942, p. 1.

[3]Edward Y. Hartshorne, *The German Universities and National Socialism* (London, 1937), pp. 87 ff.; Pross, *Die deutsche akademische Emigration*, p. 12.

[4]Christian von Ferber, *Die Entwicklung des Lehrkörpers der deutschen Universitäten und Hochschulen 1864–1954* (Göttingen, 1956), pp. 143–144.

[5]*List of Displaced German Scholars* (London, autumn 1936). A supplement from autumn 1937 contains another 154 names.

[6]Lepsius, "Die sozialwissenschaftliche Emigration," p. 462.

[7]Adolph Lowe, "Die Hoffnung auf kleine Katastrophen," in Mathias Greffrath, ed., *Die Zerstörung einer Zukunft: Gespräche mit emigrierten Sozialwissenschaftlern* (Reinbek, 1979), p. 145; Helge Pross, in Reiner Erd, ed., *Reform und Resignation: Gespräche über Franz L. Neumann* (Frankfurt, 1985), p. 59; see also Elisabeth Young-Bruehl, *Hannah Arendt: For Love of the World* (New Haven, 1982), p. 108.

[8]Henry Pachter, *Weimar Etudes* (New York, 1982), p. 116.

[9]Davie, *Refugees in America*, pp. 314 ff.; "Refugee Scholars and the New School," mimeo (New York, ca. 1953).

[10]Coser, *Refugee Scholars*, pp. 3–4; Fermi, *Illustrious Immigrants*, p. 6.

[11]Henry Pachter, "On Being an Exile: An Old Timer's Personal and Political Memoir," in Boyers, "Legacy of German Intellectuals," p. 33; see also Martin Gumpert, *Hölle im Paradies* (Stockholm, 1939), pp. 272, 280. On the disenchantment of the immigrants with America, see also Heilbut, *Exiled in Paradise*, pp. 17 ff.

[12]Max Horkheimer to Adolf Löwe, Aug. 3 and Oct. 18, 1934, Horkheimer Archive Frankfurt, I/17.

[13]Fermi, *Illustrious Immigrants,* p. 3.

[14]Hartmut Titze, "Die zyklische Überproduktion von Akademikern im 19. und 20. Jahrhundert," *Geschichte und Gesellschaft* 10 (1984): 92 ff.

[15]As in the declaration of the Vorstand des deutschen Hochschulverbandes of Apr. 22, 1933, and the *Bekenntnis der Professoren an den deutschen Universitäten und Hochschulen zu Adolf Hitler und dem nationalsozialistischen Staat* (Dresden, 1933).

[16]Wolfgang Schlickel and Josef Glaser, "Tendenzen und Konsequenzen faschistischer Wissenschaftspolitik nach dem 30. Januar 1933," *Zeitschrift für Geschichtswissenschaft* 31 (1983): 881 ff.; see also *Die Lage der Juden in Deutschland 1933: Das Schwarzbuch—Tatsachen und Dokuments* (Paris, 1934), pp. 240 ff.

[17]Herbert E. Tutas, *Nationalsozialismus und Exil: Die Politik des Dritten Reiches gegenüber der deutschen politischen Emigration 1933–1939* (Munich and Vienna, 1975), p. 142.

[18]The theologian Paul Tillich was one of these; see Wilhelm and Marion Pauck, *Paul Tillich: Sein Leben und Denken,* vol. 1: *Leben* (Stuttgart and Frankfurt, 1976), pp. 140 ff.

3. The United States and German Intellectuals

[1]M. W. Bagster-Collins to S. P. Duggan, Institute of International Education, Oct. 6 and 20, 1933, EC, 153, NYPL.

[2]Academic Assistance Council, List of University Teachers "Placed," Nov. 22, 1933, EC, 190, NYPL.

[3]Dietrich Goldschmidt, "Transatlantic Influences: History of Mutual Interactions between American and German Education," in Max Planck Institute for Human Development and Education (Berlin West), ed., *Between Elite and Mass Education: Education in the Federal Republic of Germany* (Albany, 1983), pp. 1 ff.

[4]K. J. Arndt, Hartwick College, to S. Duggan, EC, Mar. 18, 1935, EC, 119, NYPL; see also "Tätigkeitsbericht der Notgemeinschaft deutscher Wissenschaftler im Ausland 1936/37," p. 5, EC, 146, NYPL.

[5]E. R. Murrow, Rockefeller Foundation (RF), to EC, Nov. 9, 1933, RFA RG 2, 717/92/731.

[6]According to Alvin Johnson's recollections in a letter to Clara Mayer of May 17, 1945, NSA.

[7]Memo of the Rockefeller Foundation, Oct. 19, 1938, RFA RG 2, 717/185/1324.

[8]Heilbut, *Exiled in Paradise,* p. 50. Examples of anti-Semitism at Tufts University and the University of Illinois can be found in the Felix Frankfurter Papers, film 85, LoC); Papers of C. J. Friedrich, 17.31, box 1, Harvard University; Coser, *Refugee Scholars,* p. 71.

[9]W. Beveridge, Academic Assistance Council, to E. E. Day, RF, May 25, 1933, RFA RG 2, 717/91/724; T. B. Kittredge to S. H. Walker, Nov. 22, 1933, RFA RG 1.1, 717/1/3.

[10]J. A. Schumpeter to W. C. Mitchell, Apr. 22, 1933, Schumpeter Papers, 4.7, box 6, Harvard University.

[11]R. A. Lambert, RF Paris, to A. Gregg, RF New York, Mar. 29, 1933, and J. v. Sickle, RF Paris, to E. E. Day, RF New York, Apr. 29, 1933, RFA RG 2, 717/91/725.

[12]R. B. Fosdick to S. M. Gunn, Paris, Dec. 13, 1938, RFA RG 2, 717/167/1217; Duggan and Drury, *Rescue of Science*, p. 189.

[13]Fermi, *Illustrious Immigrants*, p. 78.

[14]Wetzel, "American Rescue," p. 5; see also Kurt R. Grossmann, *Emigration: Geschichte der Hitler-Flüchtlinge 1933–1945* (Frankfurt, 1969), pp. 9 ff.

[15]High Commissioner for Refugees (Jewish and Other) Coming from Germany, Report of the Meeting of the Permanent Committee of the Governing Body, Jan. 30, 1934, EC, 153, NYPL.

[16]On the major aid organizations for scholars, see Bentwich, *Rescue and Achievement*; Duggan and Drury, *Rescue of Science*; Beveridge, *Defense of Free Learning*; Philipp Schwartz, "Notgemeinschaft: Ein Bericht zur Verteilung an die Teilnehmer des zweiten Internationalen Symposiums zur Erforschung des deutschsprachigen Exils nach 1933," MS (Copenhagen, Aug. 1972).

[17]Memo, W. M. Kotschnig, director of the High Commissariat for Refugees, "Six Thousand Eight Hundred Intellectuals in Exile from Germany," Dec. 29, 1934, EC, 153, NYPL.

[18]For a comparison of the Academic Assistance Council and the Emergency Committee, see Beveridge, *Defense of Free Learning*, pp. 6 ff., 30, 126–127.

[19]Duggan and Drury, *Rescue of Science*, p. 85, passim; Hanns Gramm, *The Oberlaender Trust, 1931–1953* (Philadelphia, 1956), pp. 64–65; Wetzel, "American Rescue," pp. 319 ff.; memo, T. B. Appleget, RF, Mar. 5, 1946, RFA RG 1.1, 200/47/545a.

[20]R. B. Fosdick to A. Johnson, Oct. 30, 1939, RFA RG 1.1, 200/339/4034.

[21]Duggan and Drury, *Rescue of Science*, pp. 72 ff.; Wetzel, "American Rescue," pp. 339–340.

[22]EC reports, Feb. 1, 1935, p. 7; Mar. 1, 1937, p. 7; Dec. 1, 1938, pp. 2–3. After the German attack on Austria the committee changed its name to Emergency Committee in Aid of Displaced Foreign Scholars.

[23]Duggan and Drury, *Rescue of Science*, p. 196.

[24]Ibid., p. 193.

[25]M. W. Bagster-Collins to S. Duggan, EC, Nov. 3, 1933, EC, 153, NYPL.

[26]J. v. Sickle, RF Paris, to RF New York, May 1, 1933, RFA RG 2, 717/91/725.

[27]Proposed budget for the Paris office, Jan. 6, 1933, RFA RG 2, 717/90/719.

[28]Fosdick, *Story of the Rockefeller Foundation*.

[29]Report on Rockefeller Foundation Activities in Germany—Social Sciences, June 20, 1933, RFA RG 1.1, 717/7/36.

[30]See, for example, the survey by Tracy B. Kittredge, RF Paris, "Social Sciences in Germany," Aug. 9, 1932, which describes in minute detail the German institutions of higher learning and research, including the quality of their staffs, RFA RG 1.1, 717/20/186.

[31]Ibid.

[32]John van Sickle, "Suggestions for a German Trip," May 31, 1932, RFA RG 2, 717/77/617.

[33]Report on Activities in Germany—Social Sciences, June 20, 1933, RFA RG 1.1, 717/7/36.

[34]Memo, Program and Politics in the Social Sciences, Jan. 3, 1929, RFA RG 3, 910/1/1.

[35]See the reports from Germany of the American consulates and the attitude of the State Department after 1933, cited in Arthur D. Morse, *While Six Million Died: A Chronicle of American Apathy* (New York, 1968), pp. 105 ff.

[36]D. O'Brien to A. Gregg, Apr. 11, 1933, RFA RG 2, 717/91/725.

[37]J. v. Sickle to E. E. Day, director of the Social Science Program, Apr. 29 and May 8, 1933, RFA RG 2, 717/91/725.

[38]M. W. Bagster-Collins to E. R. Murrow, EC, Oct. 6, 1933, and Jan. 29, 1934, EC, 153, NYPL.

[39]J. v. Sickle to E. E. Day, Feb. 24/25, 1933, RFA RG 2, 717/91/725.

[40]J. v. Sickle to E. E. Day, May 5, 1933, RFA RG 1.1, 717/20/181; Myrdal report of July 20, 1933, ibid.; also S. Walker, RF New York, to J. v. Sickle, RF Paris, Sept. 23, 1933, RFA RG 2, 717/91/721.

[41]R. B. Fosdick to S. Walker, Sept. 25, 1936, RFA RG 2, 717/141/1050.

[42]List of Appointments Made, Sept. 7, 1933, RFA RG 2, 717/91/724; memos, T. B. Kittredge, Aug. 2 and Sept. 23, 1933, ibid., 92/728.

[43]*List of Displaced German Scholars;* also memo of the RF, Oct. 20, 1939, RFA RG 1.1, 717/1/2.

4. What the Exiled Social Scientists Brought to the United States

[1]Coser, *Refugee Scholars*, pp. 137 ff.

[2]Frank A. Fetter, "Amerika," in Hans Mayer, ed., *Die Wirtschaftstheorie der Gegenwart,* vol. 1: *Gesamtbild der Forschung in den einzelnen Ländern* (Vienna, 1927), p. 46. There is also an extensive account in Ben B. Seligmann, *Main Currents in Modern Economics: Economic Thought since 1870* (Glencoe, Ill., 1962), pp. 614 ff.

[3]Adolf A. Berle and Gardiner C. Means, *The Modern Corporation and Private Property* (New York, 1932); Wesley C. Mitchell, *Business Cycles: The Problem and Its Setting* (New York, 1927); William T. Foster and Waddill Catchings, *Business without a Buyer* (Boston, 1927) and *The Road to Plenty* (Boston, 1928).

[4]W. Leontief to J. A. Schumpeter, May 31, 1930, Schumpeter Papers, 4.7, box 5,

Harvard University; Eugen Altschul to Hans Neisser, Jan. 25, 1927, Neisser Papers, SUNY, Albany.

⁵John Dewey, *Human Nature and Conduct* (New York, 1922), pp. 107 ff., and *Individualism Old and New* (New York, 1929), p. 18, passim; Charles A. Beard, ed., *Whither Mankind?* (New York, 1928), pp. 406 ff., and *Toward Civilization* (New York, 1930), pp. 299 ff.

⁶This is the essence of his views as expressed in a report on the reform of economics prepared in Oct. 1932 for the Rockefeller Foundation, RFA RG 3, 910/1/2; see also Rexford G. Tugwell, *The Industrial Discipline and the Governmental Arts* (New York, 1933).

⁷For more detail, see Daniel F. Fusfeld, *The Economic Thought of Franklin D. Roosevelt and the Origins of the New Deal* (New York, 1956), pp. 207 ff.

⁸ *America and the Intellectuals: A Symposium*, Partisan Review Series 4 (New York, 1953), p. 101; William E. Leuchtenburg, *Franklin D. Roosevelt and the New Deal* (New York, 1963; 2nd ed., 1983), pp. 326 ff.; Arthur M. Schlesinger, *The Age of Roosevelt: The Crisis of the Old Order, 1919–1933* (Boston, 1957), pp. 161 ff.; the Coolidge-quotation p. 177. New approaches to economic policy were also discussed by other economists. Cf. J. Ronnie Davis, *The New Economics and Old Economists* (Ames, Iowa, 1971). However, Davis tries to show only that, compared to the stir created by Keynes's revolutionary theories in England, the idea of combating the depression by resorting to public spending instead of wage reductions was relatively widely accepted among American economists from about 1931 on.

⁹For a recent account of the various reforms, cf. Katie Louchheim, ed., *The Making of the New Deal: The Insiders Speak* (Cambridge, Mass., 1983).

¹⁰Schlesinger, *Age of Roosevelt*, pp. 402–403; Fusfeld, *Economic Thought*, pp. 227 ff.; Louchheim, *Making of the New Deal*, pp. 196 ff., 267.

¹¹Heilbut, *Exiled in Paradise*, pp. 115, 193, 196.

¹²For example, see the anxious inquiries Max Ascoli at the New School addressed to Felix Frankfurter, professor at the Harvard Law School and trusted friend of Roosevelt, Oct. 30, 1933, and Mar. 2, 1934, Frankfurter Papers, box 115, LoC.

¹³Schlesinger, *Age of Roosevelt*, pp. 437–438; Leuchtenburg, *Roosevelt and the New Deal*, pp. 275 ff.

¹⁴Schlesinger, *Age of Roosevelt*, p. 204.

¹⁵Schumpeter's former student Herbert Zassenhaus related this incident to me in a conversation in Washington in June 1984.

¹⁶For a more detailed account, see Krohn, *Wirtschaftstheorien als politische Interessen*, pp. 33 ff.

¹⁷Ludwig Mises, *Liberalismus* (Jena, 1927), p. 45.

¹⁸Yale University Press to L. Mises, May 10, 1943, Mises Papers, Grove City College, Pa. The Yale University Press recommended that Mises revise the manu-

script and adopt a more moderate tone. The revised version was published as *Omnipotent Government* (New Haven, 1944).

[19]Laurence S. Moss, ed., *The Economics of Ludwig von Mises: Toward a Critical Reappraisal* (Kansas City, 1976). The series Studies in Economic Theory, also edited by Moss, is devoted exclusively to spreading Mises's and Hayek's ideas in the United States. Recently, a so-called Laissez Faire Book-Shop, in the style of the political bookshops of the time of the student movement and offering mostly political pamphlets by Mises and Hayek, opened in New York.

[20]Martha S. Browne "Erinnerungen an das Mises-Privatseminar," *Wirtschaftspolitische Blätter* 4 (1981): 110 ff.

[21]Gerhard Winterberger, "Generationen der österreichischen Schule der Nationalökonomie," *Schweizer Monatshefte* 64 (1984): 1 ff.

[22]Seymour E. Harris, ed., *Schumpeter: Social Scientist* (Cambridge, Mass., 1951); Fritz Karl Mann, "Bemerkungen über Schumpeters Einfluss auf die amerikanische Wirtschaftstheorie," *Weltwirtschaftliches Archiv* (*WA*) 81 (1958): 149 ff.

[23]Joseph A. Schumpeter, "Die Wirtschaftstheorie der Gegenwart in Deutschland" (1927), reprinted in his *Dogmenhistorische und biographische Aufsätze* (Tübingen, 1954), p. 271.

[24]For biographical information on Leontief, see L. Silk, "Wassily Leontief: Apostle of Planning," in *The Economists* (New York, 1978), pp. 139 ff.

[25]Gerhard Colm, *Beitrag zur Geschichte und Soziologie des Ruhraufstandes vom März–April 1920* (Essen, 1921); his "Der finanzwirtschaftliche Gesichtspunkt des Abrüstungsproblems," in *Handbuch des Abrüstungsproblems* (Kiel, 1927); and his article "Masse," in A. Vierkandt, ed., *Handwörterbuch der Soziologie* (Stuttgart, 1931), pp. 353 ff.

[26]Mises and Haberler were working in the Vienna Chamber of Commerce, Hayek and Morgenstern in the Austrian Institute for Business Cycles Research founded by the Vienna Chamber of Commerce; Machlup was an active partner of a firm in the cardboard industry; and Fürth was a practicing lawyer.

[27]For more detail, see Krohn, *Wirtschaftstheorien als politische Interessen*, pp. 123 ff.; also his "Gegen den Dogmatismus in den Wirtschafts- und Sozialwissenschaften: Zur wissenschaftlichen und politischen Biographie Adolph Lowes," in Harald Hagemann and Heinz D. Kurz, eds., *Beschäftigung, Verteilung und Konjunktur: Zur Politischen Ökonomik der modernen Gesellschaft: Festschrift für Adolph Lowe* (Bremen, 1984), p. 37.

[28]Memo, J. v. Sickle, May 10, 1933, RFA RG 1.1, 717/20/181.

[29]Gerhard Colm and Hans Neisser, *Der deutsche Aussenhandel unter der Einwirkung der weltwirtschaftlichen Strukturwandlungen*, 2 vols. ("Enquete-Ausschuss, 1. Unterausschuss, 5. Arbeitsgruppe," vol. 20) (Berlin, 1932). On Lowe's and Marschak's activities, see same series, vols. 1–19. Gerhard Colm and Hans Neisser, *Kapitalbildung und Steuersystem*, 2 vols. (Berlin, 1930).

[30]According to this theory, the workers only had to wait until the progressive concentration of capital resulted in a small, all-powerful "general cartel," at which point only a small functional elite would have to be replaced to realize socialism.

[31]Mannheim dedicated his *Die Gegenwartsaufgaben der Soziologie* (Tübingen, 1932) to this cooperation with Adolph Lowe. After Mannheim's death in 1947, Lowe was initially to edit his posthumous writings for publication.

5. The New School for Social Research

[1]A. Johnson to J. A. Schumpeter, May 6, 1933, Schumpeter Papers, 4.7, box 6, Harvard University.

[2]*To Alvin Johnson: Great American—Citizen of the World: Festschrift zum 75. Geburtstag* (New York, [1943]); Alvin Johnson, *Pioneer's Progress: An Autobiography* (New York, 1952), pp. 290 ff. Interview with A. Johnson, 1960, Columbia University, Oral History Collection.

[3]On the origins of the *Encyclopaedia of the Social Sciences*, see the correspondence between E. R. A. Seligman and A. Johnson, 1927 and later, Seligman Papers, boxes 104–105, Columbia University. The German reform economists of the New School contributed the following entries: Gerhard Colm—Production (Statistics), Unearned Increment, War Finance, Adolph Wagner; Emil Lederer—Socialist Economics, Labor, National Economic Councils, National Economic Planning, Technology, Walther Rathenau, and others; Fritz Lehmann—Knut Wicksell; Jakob Marschak—Consumption (Problems of Measurement), Wages (Theory and Policy); Hans Speier—Max Weber, Karl von Vogelsang.

[4]Johnson, *Pioneer's Progress*, p. 347.

[5]A. Johnson to his secretary, Agnes de Lima, May 30, 1934, to Else Staudinger, May 8, 1955, and to Robt. MacIver, Apr. 10, 1957, Johnson Papers, 2/28 and 5/83, Yale University, and Staudinger Papers, 4/28, SUNY, Albany.

[6]Alvin Johnson, "Economic Security and Political Insecurity," *SR* 6 (1939): 135 ff.

[7]A. Johnson to E. R. A. Seligman, Apr. 24, 1933, Seligman Papers, 54/142, Columbia University.

[8]Alvin Hansen, Univ. of Minnesota, to RF, Apr. 26, 1933; H. J. Schlesinger, Dept. of Chemistry, to President Hutchins, Univ. of Chicago, RFA RG 2, 717/91/725; J. A. Schumpeter to W. C. Mitchell and Abraham Flexner, May 26, 1933, and May 8, 1934, Schumpeter Papers, 4.7, box 4, and 4.8, box 1, Harvard University.

[9]A. Johnson to A. de Lima, Apr. 14 to June 9, 1933, Johnson Papers, 2/27, Yale University; Johnson to E. R. A. Seligman, Apr. 24, 1933, Seligman Papers, 54/142, Columbia University. This is the crucial "Letter that Created a Faculty." It was sent with a cover letter by Seligman to over 200 university faculty, all but four of whom approved of the project. Cf. *New York Times*, May 13, 1933, "Faculty of Exiles Is Projected Here."

[10]E. Lederer to J. A. Schumpeter and Koppel S. Pinson, Apr. to July, 1933, Lederer Papers, SUNY, Albany; see also Hans Speier, "Emil Lederer: Leben und Werk," in Jürgen Kocka, ed., *Emil Lederer: Kapitalismus, Klassenstruktur und Probleme der Demokratie in Deutschland 1910–1940* (Göttingen, 1979), pp. 253 ff.; J. Marschak to J. A. Schumpeter, Apr. 27, 1933, and later, Schumpeter Papers, 4.7, box 7, Harvard University; memo, J. v. Sickle, RF, May 2, 1933, RFA RG 2, 717/91/725. On Karl Mannheim, see "Gespräch mit Kurt H. Wolff," in Lepsius, "Die sozialwissenschaftliche Emigration," pp. 325 ff.

[11]E. Lederer, J. Marschak, A. Löwe, Otto Nathan, F. Wunderlich, and others to J. A. Schumpeter, Apr. 27, 1933, and later, Schumpeter Papers, 3.7, boxes 6–7, Harvard University.

[12]Colm's father, an appeals court justice in Düsseldorf, had his name changed from Cohn to Colm in 1902. Neisser had left the Protestant church as early as 1928. Biographical information is from the Colm Papers at LoC and the Neisser Papers at SUNY, Albany. The FBI also has voluminous records on Colm. As an employee of the American government, he was subject to security checks, and during the McCarthy era the FBI compiled comprehensive dossiers on him, including copies of his birth certificate and his report cards from school.

[13]Hans Staudinger, *Wirtschaftspolitik im Weimarer Staat: Lebenserinnerungen eines politischen Beamten im Reich und in Preussen 1889 bis 1934*, ed. H. Schulze (Bonn, 1982), cf. esp. pp. 108 ff.; Arnold Brecht, *Mit der Kraft des Geistes: Lebenserinnerungen, Zweite Hälfte 1927–1967* (Stuttgart, 1967), pp. 326 ff. The details of Brecht's reluctant arrangements with Johnson are not discussed there; on this, see correspondence between Brecht and Johnson, beginning Sept. 24, 1933, Brecht Papers, 2/37, SUNY, Albany.

[14]Personal papers of Hans Simons, SUNY, Albany.

[15]The *New York Times* reported on the arrival of the first two scholars, Colm and Feiler, in a major article on Aug. 19, 1933, after having devoted a full page to the University in Exile on Aug. 8.

[16]Ascoli's curriculum vitae of Sept. 29, 1942, Ascoli Papers, 196/6, Boston University; correspondence of A. Johnson with the RF concerning the financing of Ascoli's salary, RFA RG 1.1, 200/339/4031.

[17]Johnson's negotiations with the RF, Dec. 29, 1933, and Mar. 23, 1934; A. Löwe to RF, Feb. 1, 1934; grant announcements, Apr. 20, 1934, RFA RG 1.1, 200/388/4029.

[18]Rudolf M. Littauer to W. K. Thomas, Carl Schurz Foundation, Oct. 27, 1938, EC, 146, NYPL.

[19]Constitution of the Graduate Faculty of Political and Social Science, Jan. 30, 1935, minutes of the Graduate Faculty, NSA.

[20]Dept. of Social Economy, Bryn Mawr College, to EC, July 5, 1934, EC, 63, NYPL.

[21]Horace M. Kallen to Harry Friedenwald, Apr. 13, 1934, Kallen Papers, YIVO Institute, New York.

[22]Speech given by Max Ascoli, dean of the Graduate Faculty, Apr. 24, 1941, on the occasion of the school's being granted the "permanent charter," NSA.

[23]Figures of the RF, June 3, 1947, RFA RG 1.1, 200/338/4030; Rosenwald records of payments in Ascoli Papers, 205/1, Boston University; New York Foundation, *Forty Year Report, 1909–1949* (New York, 1950), pp. 36, 46; New School for Social Research, Report of the Director, 1942–43, p. 5, NSA.

[24]A. Johnson to E. E. Day, RF, Mar. 25, 1935, RFA RG 1.1, 200/338/4029.

[25]"Graduate Faculty, Budget for First Two Years," ibid.

[26]E. E. Day to A. Johnson, Apr. 17, 1935, ibid.

[27]For more detail, see Coser, *Refugee Scholars*, pp. 202 ff.; see also M. F. Burnyeat, "Sphynx without a Secret," *New York Review of Books* 32, no. 9 (May 30, 1985): 30 ff.

[28]For biographical information on Riezler, see Karl Dietrich Erdmann, ed., *Kurt Riezler: Tagebücher, Aufsätze, Dokumente* (Göttingen, 1972), pp. 19 ff.

[29]J. A. Schumpeter to W. C. Mitchell, May 8, 1934: "Harvard has not done anything," Mitchell Papers, Columbia University.

[30]J. A. Schumpeter, correspondence with A. Johnson, May 2, 1933, and later; Schumpeter to Gottfried Haberler, Mar. 20, 1933; Schumpeter to Carl Landauer, Dec. 21, 1940, Schumpeter Papers, 4.7, box 1, and 4.8, box 1/3, Harvard University; Carl J. Friedrich to Heinz Beckmann, Oct. 6, 1938, Friedrich Papers, 17.31, box 1, Harvard University; cf. also Joseph A. Schumpeter, *History of Economic Analysis*, ed. (from the MS) E. B. Schumpeter (London, 1954; 8th ed., 1972), p. 1155.

[31]"The University in Exile," speech by I. Bowman at the Waldorf Astoria dinner, Jan. 15, 1935, Johnson Papers, 9/154, Yale University.

[32]Correspondence between E. Heimann and the Society for the Protection of Science and Learning (Academic Assistance Council), July/Aug. 1938, American Council for Emigrés in the Professions, SUNY, Albany.

[33]See esp. the reports by E. Heimann, G. Colm, and E. Lederer in the files of the EC, NYPL.

[34]Notgemeinschaft deutscher Wissenschaftler im Ausland, Landesgruppe Vereinigte Staaten, Jahresbericht 1936/37, RFA RG 1.1, 717/2/13.

[35]Summaries of contributions in the appeal of the Notgemeinschaft of Apr. 1, 1935, ibid.

[36]Ibid.; see also G. Colm to Felix Kaufmann, June 23, 1938, Kaufmann Papers, roll 5, no. 8307, Social Science Archive, University of Constance.

[37] Protocol of the founding committee for Selfhelp, Nov. 24, 1936, Landauer Papers, LBI; 1st annual report, Oct. 1937, Staudinger Papers, 7/15, SUNY, Albany; annual report, 1938, Tillich Papers, G 12/2, Harvard University.

[38]Originally, Johnson had hoped that Bert Brecht might head the project, but when Brecht declined he hired Piscator; see correspondence between Johnson and Brecht, starting May 3, 1940, Johnson Papers, 1/17, Yale University; Heilbut, *Exiled in Paradise*, pp. 225 ff.; see also Thea Kirfel-Lenk, *Erwin Piscator im Exil in den USA*

1939–1951: Eine Darstellung seiner antifaschistischen Theaterarbeit am Dramatic Workshop der New School for Social Research (Berlin, GDR, 1984).

[39]Cf. Table 3, program 2, p. 30.

[40]Memo of the RF, Oct. 10, 1939; J. H. Willits, RF, "If Hitler Wins," June 3, 1940, and "Arrangements for European Refugees in This Country," July 9, 1940, RFA RG 1.1, 700/15/115 and 1.1, 200/46/530.

[41]A. Johnson to T. B. Appleget, RF, July 11, 1940, Staudinger Papers, 6/1, SUNY, Albany.

[42]Alvin Johnson, "The Refugee Scholar in America," *Survey Graphic*, Apr. 1941, pp. 226 ff.

[43]Memo, J. H. Willits, RF, Aug. 19, 1940, RFA RG 1.1, 200/52/621; R. B. Fosdick to A. Johnson, July 22, 1940, and T. B. Appleget to Johnson, Aug. 21, 1940, Staudinger Papers, 6/1, SUNY, Albany.

[44]Memo, J. H. Willits, Aug. 14, 1940, RFA RG 1.1, 200/46/531.

[45]Memo, J. H. Willits, Aug. 19, 1940, RFA RG 1.1, 200/52/621. On this subject, see also correspondence between RF and A. Johnson, Aug. 1940 to June 1942, Staudinger Papers, 6/1, SUNY, Albany, and memoranda by the RF in this same period, RFA RG 1.1, 200/53/625 ff.

[46]See, for example, "Note on the New School Plan for Bringing in Refugee Scholars," Mar. 31, 1934, Staudinger Papers, 6/1, SUNY, Albany.

[47]Report by the RF, "Refugee Scholars at the New School," June 16, 1944, RFA RG 1.1, 200/53/629; T. B. Appleget to A. Johnson, June 1, 1945, Staudinger Papers, 6/2, SUNY, Albany.

[48]Varian Fry to U.S. Consul General Fullerton, Marseille, July 1, 1941, NA, State Dept. RG 48, box 151, vol. 33, NA. See also Varian Fry, *Surrender on Demand* (New York, 1945).

[49]Press release of the New School, June 13, 1941; correspondence between Frieda Wunderlich and Ruth Fischer, starting Feb. 19, 1942, R. Fischer Papers, bMS Ger 204, no. 1001, Harvard University. This study later culminated in Fischer's *Stalin and German Communism* (Cambridge, Mass., 1948).

[50]Cf. Appendix, herein.

[51]As late as 1944, the sociologist Georges Gurvitch still considered the Graduate Faculty a "breeding ground of Pan-Germanism" and the professors there "Pan-Germans," who had barely made room for their poor French relatives.

[52]Memos, RF, Oct. 6, 1941, and later, RFA RG 1.1, 200/53/625; Peter M. Ruttkoff and William B. Scott, "The French in New York: Resistance and Structure," *SR* 50 (1983): 185 ff.

[53]A. Johnson to State Dept., July 25, 1940, and reply of the Visa Division, Aug. 31, 1940, Staudinger Papers, 5/28, SUNY, Albany.

[54]Long diary, Feb. 6, 1938, Long Papers, 5, LoC.

[55]Long memo, Oct. 21, 1940, Long Papers, 212, LoC. The recommendation to the

consuls reads literally: "to put every obstacle in the way and to resort to various administrative advices which would postpone and postpone the granting of the visas." On the refugee policy of the United States in general, see, among others, Henry L. Feingold, *The Politics of Rescue: The Roosevelt Administration and the Holocaust, 1938–1945* (New Brunswick, N.J., 1970), Long quotation, p. 142; Saul S. Friedman, *No Haven for the Oppressed: United States Policy toward Jewish Refugees, 1938–1945* (Detroit, 1973); David S. Wyman, *Paper Walls: America and the Refugee Crisis, 1938–1941* (New York, 1985).

[56]A. Johnson to B. Long, Dec. 20, 1940, and Long's reply, Dec. 23, 1940, Staudinger Papers, 5/28, SUNY, Albany; telegram from U.S. Consulate, Marseille, to Long, Nov. 25, 1940, State Dept. RG 84, box 148, vol. 43, NA.

[57]Note by B. Long, Oct. 4, 1940, Long Papers, 212, LoC; A. Johnson to Felix Frankfurter, Feb. 9, 1942, Frankfurter Papers, box 70, LoC.

[58]A. Makinsky, RF Lisbon, to T. B. Appleget, RF New York, Mar. 12 and 14, 1941, RFA RG 1.1, 200/53/624.

[59]A. Johnson to A. Berle, Mar. 28, 1941; Johnson to B. Long, Mar. 20, 1943; Grenville Clark, New School Board of Trustees, to Fred Keppel, Carnegie Foundation, Feb. 17, 1942, Staudinger Papers, 5/28, SUNY, Albany.

[60]Max Ascoli to the Emergency Rescue Committee, SUNY, Albany.

[61]Grant announcement of the RF for a two-year fellowship for Hedwig Hintze, Oct. 4, 1940, RFA RG 2, 717/192/1368; A. Johnson to A. Berle, Mar. 28, 1942, concerning Hintze's difficulties, Staudinger Papers, 5/28, SUNY, Albany; cf. also Hans Schleier, *Die bürgerliche deutsche Geschichtsschreibung der Weimarer Republik* (Berlin, GDR, 1975), p. 302.

[62]Marc Bloch to A. Johnson, July 31, 1941, NSA; Ruttkoff and Scott, "French in New York," p. 187.

[63]Details of Gumbel's and his family's flight from Lyon to the United States in his anonymously published essay "The Professor from Heidelberg," in William A. Neilson, ed., *We Escaped: Twelve Personal Narratives of the Flight to America* (New York, 1941), pp. 28 ff.; Marie Louise Gumbel, "Report on My Activities in Order to Immigrate to the United States," MS, Aug. 1941, RFA RG 1.1, 200/50/583.

[64]A. Johnson to Fred Keppel, Mar. 20, 1942, Staudinger Papers, 5/28, SUNY, Albany.

6. Contributions of the Emigré Scholars at the New School

[1]For more detail, see J. M. and G. Mandler, "The Diaspora of Experimental Psychology: The Gestaltists and Others," in Fleming and Bailyn, *Intellectual Migration*, pp. 371 ff.; Coser, *Refugee Scholars*, pp. 28 ff.

[2]Complete bibliography of Brecht's writings in Morris D. Forkosch, ed., *The Political Philosophy of Arnold Brecht* (New York, 1954), pp. 161 ff.

[3]Arnold Brecht, *Political Theory: The Foundation of Twentieth-Century Political*

Thought (Princeton, N.J., 1959; also published in German, Spanish, and Portuguese); cf. also Brecht, *Mit der Kraft des Geistes,* pp. 333 ff.

[4]Albert Salomon articles: "Max Weber's Methodology," *SR* 1 (1934): 147 ff.; "Max Weber's Sociology," *SR* 2 (1935): 60 ff.; "Max Weber's Political Ideas," *SR* 2 (1935): 131 ff.; see also his "Max Weber," *Die Gesellschaft* (Berlin) 3 (1926): 131 ff.; Carl Mayer, "In Memoriam: Albert Salomon, 1891–1966," *SR* 34 (1967): 213 ff.

[5]For more detail, see Ulf Matthiesen, " 'Im Schatten einer endlosen grossen Zeit': Etappen der intellektuellen Biographie Albert Salomons," in Ilja Srubar, ed., *Exil, Wissenschaft, Identität: Die Emigration deutscher Sozialwissenschaftler 1933–1945* (Frankfurt, 1988), pp. 299–300.

[6]For further bibliographical information, see Coser, *Refugee Scholars,* pp. 121 ff.; Helmut R. Wagner, "Die Soziologie der Lebenswelt: Umriss einer intellektuellen Biographie von Alfred Schütz," in Lepsius, "Die sozialwissenschaftliche Emigration," pp. 379 ff.; Jürgen Habermas, "Alfred Schütz," in *Philosophisch-politische Profile* (Frankfurt, 1981), pp. 402–403.

[7]Symposia on Dec. 3, 1933, and Jan. 7, 1934, *New School Bulletin,* no. 3 (Nov. 20, 1933), and no. 5 (Jan. 3, 1934).

[8]Alvin Johnson, "Foreword," *SR* 1 (1934): 1–2; on the origin of the periodical, see also Hans Speier to J. A. Schumpeter, Dec. 29, 1933, Schumpeter Papers, 4.7, box 8, Harvard University.

[9]On this topic, see Allan G. Gruchy, *Contemporary Economic Thought: The Contribution of Neo-institutional Economics* (Clifton, N.J., 1972), pp. 19 ff.

[10]Adolf Löwe, "Wie ist Konjunkturtheorie überhaupt möglich?" *WA* 24 (1926): 165 ff.

[11]Friedrich August Hayek, *Geldtheorie und Konjunkturtheorie* (Vienna and Leipzig, 1929), p. 111.

[12]*Schriften des Vereins für Sozialpolitik* (*SchVfS*), vol. 175 (Munich and Leipzig, 1929), p. 287, passim; the relevant papers are contained in *SchVfS,* vol. 173 (Munich and Leipzig, 1928).

[13]Eugen von Böhm-Bawerk, *Positive Theorie des Kapitales,* vol. 1 (Jena, 4th ed., 1921), p. 130, passim; this approach also appears in Hayek, *Geldtheorie,* pp. 114 ff., and in his *Preise und Produktion* (Vienna, 1931), pp. 68 ff. Cf. Harald Hagemann, "The Structural Theory of Economic Growth," in Mauro Baranzini and Roberto Scazzieri, eds., *The Economic Theory of Structure and Change* (Cambridge, 1991), pp. 144 ff.

[14]Emil Lederer, "Social versus Economic Law," *SR* 1 (1934): 3 ff.

[15]Peter Kalmbach and Heinz D. Kurz, "Klassik, Neoklassik und Neuklassik," in Peter de Gijsel et al., eds., *Jahrbuch Ökonomie und Gesellschaft,* vol. 1 (Frankfurt and New York, 1983), pp. 57 ff.

[16]Prime examples of this are Ludwig Mises, *Die Ursachen der Wirtschaftskrise* (Tübingen, 1931), and John R. Hicks, *The Theory of Wages* (London, 1932).

[17]Löwe, in *SchVfS,* vol. 175, pp. 342 ff.

[18]Jakob Marschak, "Das Kaufkraft-Argument in der Lohnpolitik," *Magazin der Wirtschaft* 2 (1930): 1443 ff.; Adolf Löwe, "Lohnabbau als Mittel der Krisenbekämpfung," *Neue Blätter für den Sozialismus* 1 (1930): 289 ff.; Emil Lederer, *Wirkungen des Lohnabbaus* (Tübingen, 1931), p. 32.

[19]Hans Neisser, "'Permanent' Technological Unemployment: Demand for Commodities Is Not Demand for Labor," *American Economic Review* 32 (1942): 70.

[20]Emil Lederer, *Technischer Fortschritt und Arbeitslosigkeit* (Tübingen, 1931), p. 72, and "Die Lähmung der Weltwirtschaft," *Archiv für Sozialwissenschaft und Sozialpolitik* (*AfSS*) 67 (1932): 1 ff.

[21]Fritz Burchardt, "Die Schemata des stationären Kreislaufs bei Böhm-Bawerk und Marx," *WA* 35 (1932): 525 ff.; Alfred Kähler, *Die Theorie der Arbeiterfreisetzung durch die Maschine: Eine gesamtwirtschaftliche Abhandlung des modernen Technisierungsprozesses* (Greifswald, 1933), p. 7, passim.

[22]This model consists of a matrix, where the individual sectors of the economy are entered along horizontal and vertical lines and where the input and output flows from one sector to another are quantitatively recorded. From these data equilibrium relations can be calculated in numerical terms. Cf. Bernd Mettelsiefen, "Der Beitrag der 'Kieler Schule' zur Freisetzungs- und Kompensationstheorie," in Harald Hagemann and Peter Kalmbach, eds., *Technischer Fortschritt und Arbeitslosigkeit* (Frankfurt and New York, 1983), pp. 204 ff.

[23]Hans Neisser, "Zur Theorie des wirtschaftlichen Gleichgewichts," *Kölner sozialpolitische Vierteljahresschrift* 6 (1927): 105 ff.; reader's letter by Fritz Sternberg and Neisser's response in the next issue, 7 (1928): 33 ff.; Neisser, "Lohnhöhe und Beschäftigungsgrad im Marktgleichgewicht, *WA* 36 (1932): 415 ff.; Neisser, "Öffentliche Kapitalanlagen in ihrer Wirkung auf den Beschäftigungsgrad," in *Economic Essays: In Honour of Gustav Cassel, Oct. 20th, 1933* (London, 1933), pp. 459 ff.

[24]Hans Neisser, *Der Tauschwert des Geldes* (Jena, 1928), pp. 12 ff., 154 ff., and "Der Kreislauf des Geldes," *WA* 33 (1931): 365 ff.

[25]On this debate, see Wilhelm Grotkopp, *Die grosse Krise: Lehren aus der Überwindung der Wirtschaftskrise 1929/32* (Düsseldorf, 1954); Gerhard Kroll, *Von der Wirtschaftskrise zur Staatskonjunktur* (Berlin, 1958). Grotkopp acknowledges the contributions by the Kiel school; Kroll does not mention them at all. For a comparative assessment from an international perspective, see the essay by the fellow emigré George Garvy, "Keynes and the Economic Activities of Pre-Hitler Germany," *Journal of Political Economy* 83 (1975): 391 ff.

[26]A. Löwe to H. Neisser, Nov. 18, 1932, Neisser Papers, SUNY, Albany.

[27]Neisser, "'Permanent' Technological Unemployment," p. 50.

[28]Alvin Hansen, "Institutional Frictions and Technological Unemployment," *Quarterly Journal of Economics* 45 (1931): 684 ff.; David Weintraub, "Displacement of Workers by Increase in Efficiency and Their Absorption by Industry, 1920–1932," *Journal of the American Statistical Association* 27 (1932): 394 ff.

[29]Nicholas Kaldor, "A Case against Technological Progress," *Economica* 12 (1932): 180 ff.

[30]Emil Lederer, "The Problem of Development and Growth in the Economic System," *SR* 2 (1935): 20 ff., and *Technischer Fortschritt und Arbeitslosigkeit: Eine Untersuchung der Hindernisse des ökonomischen Wachstums,* Internationales Arbeitsamt: Studien und Berichte, series C, vol. 22 (Geneva, 1938), newly edited and with an afterword by Robert A. Dickler (Frankfurt, 1981), my reference is to this edition, esp. p. 28, passim.

[31]Alfred Kähler, "The Problem of Verifying the Theory of Technological Unemployment," *SR* 2 (1935): 439 ff.; Kähler and Ernst Hamburger, *Education for an Industrial Age* (Ithaca and New York, 1948).

[32]Hagemann and Kalmbach, *Technischer Fortschritt und Arbeitslosigkeit;* Hagemann and Kurz, *Beschäftigung, Verteilung und Konjunktur;* Bernd Mettelsiefen, *Technischer Wandel und Beschäftigung: Rekonstruktion der Freisetzungs- und Kompensationsdebatten* (Frankfurt and New York, 1981). For discussions of the Kiel school's work by American scholars, see esp. the essays in *Eastern Economic Journal: Special Issue in Honor of Adolph Lowe* 10, no. 2 (1984); also David L. Clark, "Studies in the Origins and Development of Growth Theory, 1925–1950" (Ph.D. diss., Sidney, 1974); Vivian Walsh and Harvey Gram, *Classical and Neoclassical Theories of General Equilibrium: Historical Origins and Mathematical Structure* (New York and Oxford, 1980).

[33]Lederer, *Wirkungen des Lohnabbaus,* pp. 17 ff.

[34]Adolf Löwe, "Lohn, Zins—Arbeitslosigkeit," *Die Arbeit* 7 (1930): 425 ff.

[35]A. Löwe to Alexander Rüstow, Oct. 25, 1932, Rüstow Papers 6, Bundesarchiv Koblenz; Löwe, in *Der Stand und die nächste Zukunft der Konjunkturforschung: Festschrift für Arthur Spiethoff* (Munich, 1933), pp. 154 ff.

[36]Hans Neisser and Emil Lederer, "Commentary on Keynes I/II," *SR* 3 (1936): 459 ff., quotation p. 485; Alfred Kähler, "Business Stabilization in Theory and Practice," *SR* 5 (1938): 1 ff.; Neisser, "Öffentliche Kapitalanlagen," pp. 459 ff., "Investment Fluctuations as Cause of the Business Cycle," *SR* 4 (1937): 440 ff., and "Keynes as an Economist," *SR* 13 (1946): 225 ff.

[37]Gerhard Colm, "Is Economic Security Worth the Cost?" *SR* 6 (1939): 297.

[38]John Maynard Keynes, "Am I a Liberal?" (1925), in *Essays in Persuasion* (New York, 1932), pp. 323 ff., quotes from p. 335; cf. also Keynes, "The End of Laissez Faire" (1926), in the same collection, pp. 312 ff.

[39]John Maynard Keynes, *The General Theory of Employment, Interest, and Money* (London, 1936), pp. 320, 378.

[40]Adolph Lowe, *On Economic Knowledge: Toward a Science of Political Economics* (New York and Evanston, 1965), p. 217.

[41]Adolf Löwe, *The Price of Liberty: A German on Contemporary Britain* (London, 1937).

[42]Alfred Kähler, "The Trade Union Approach to Economic Democracy," in Max Ascoli and Fritz Lehmann, eds., *Political and Economic Democracy* (New York, 1937), p. 56; Kähler, "Business Stabilization," p. 18.

[43]Gerhard Colm, "Is Economic Planning Compatible with Democracy?" in Ascoli and Lehmann, *Political and Economic Democracy*, p. 26.

[44]Eduard Heimann, *Soziale Theorie des Kapitalismus: Theorie der Sozialpolitik* (Tübingen, 1929) and *Sozialistische Wirtschafts- und Arbeitsordnung* (Potsdam, 1932).

[45]Eduard Heimann, "Socialism and Democracy," *SR* 1 (1934): 301 ff.; "Planning and the Market System," ibid., pp. 486 ff; "Types and Potentialities of Economic Planning," *SR* 2 (1935): 176 ff.; "Building Our Democracy," *SR* 6 (1939): 445 ff.

[46]Ascoli and Lehmann, *Political and Economic Democracy;* Hans Speier and Alfred Kähler, eds., *War in Our Time* (New York, 1939). On the symposium on "Struggle for Economic Security in Democracy," see the essays in *SR* 6 (1939): 133 ff.

[47]For example, Lepsius, "Die sozialwissenschaftliche Emigration," pp. 470–471, 484.

[48]Findlay Mackenzie, ed., *Planned Society: Yesterday, Today, Tomorrow: A Symposium by Thirty-five Economists, Sociologists, and Statesmen* (New York, 1937).

[49]Wesley C. Mitchell, "The Social Sciences and National Planning," ibid., p. 124.

[50]E. Heimann to A. Löwe, Dec. 30, 1935, Tillich Papers, F 5/21, Harvard University.

[51]"Report of the Appraisal Committee," Dec. 11, 1934, RFA RG 3, 910/2/13.

[52]Gerhard Colm, *Volkswirtschaftliche Theorie der Staatsausgaben: Ein Beitrag zur Finanztheorie* (Tübingen, 1927).

[53]According to Ernst Döblin, a former colleague of Colm in the Reich statistical department who was at this time working for the Brookings Institution in Washington, in a letter to Jakob Marschak, Dec. 8, 1936, Marschak Papers, UCLA.

[54]Gerhard Colm, "The Ideal Tax System," *SR* 1 (1934): 319 ff. This and a number of his many other essays published in the United States are collected in his *Essays in Public Finance and Fiscal Policy* (New York, 1955).

[55]Argument cited by the Rockefeller Foundation as a reason for setting up a large research program on "Public Finance and Taxation," Apr. 10, 1935, RFA RG 3, 910/2/13.

[56]Cf. bibliography of Colm's writings in his *Essays in Public Finance*, pp. 359 ff.

[57]Memo, J. v. Sickle, RF, Mar. 29, 1938, RFA RG 1.1, 200/338/4029. See also Gerhard Colm and Fritz Lehmann, "Economic Consequences of Recent American Tax Policy," *SR*, supp. 1 (New York, 1938).

[58]Colm, *Volkswirtschaftliche Theorie*, p. 1, passim.

[59]Ray E. Untereiner, *The Tax Racket* (Philadelphia and London, 1933), p. 42: "We have 25 per cent socialism in the United States today."

[60]Gerhard Colm, "Theory of Public Expenditures," *Annals of the American Academy of Political and Social Science* 183 (Jan. 1936): 2–3.

[61]Colm, "Ideal Tax System," pp. 319 ff.

[62]As Colm did later in his essay "Zur Frage einer konjunktur- und wachstumsadäquaten Finanzpolitik," *Konjunkturpolitik* 2 (1956): 112.

[63]Gerhard Colm, "The Revenue Act of 1938," *SR* 5 (1938): 255 ff., and "The Basis of Federal Fiscal Policy," *Taxes—The Tax Magazine* 17 (1939): 338 ff.; Colm and Fritz Lehmann, "Public Spending and Recovery in the United States," *SR* 3 (1936): 129 ff.

[64]Colm, "Theory of Public Expenditures," p. 6.

[65]Gerhard Colm, "Comment on Extraordinary Budgets," *SR* 5 (1938): 168 ff.

[66]Arnold Brecht, *Internationaler Vergleich der öffentlichen Ausgaben* (Leipzig and Berlin, 1932), p. 6.

[67]Solomon Fabricant, *The Trend of Government Activity in the United States since 1900*, NBER, no. 56 (New York, 1952), esp. pp. 122 ff.

[68]Arnold Brecht, "Three Topics in Comparative Administration: Organization of Government Departments, Government Corporations, Expenditures in Relation to Population," in Carl Jakob Friedrich and E. S. Mason, eds., *Public Policy* (Cambridge, Mass., 1941), pp. 289 ff., esp. pp. 305 ff. For a recent view, see J. Kaehler, "Agglomeration und Staatsausgaben: Brechtsches und Wagnersches Gesetz im Vergleich," *Finanzarchiv*, n.s. 40 (1982): 445 ff.

[69]Colm, "Theory of Public Expenditures," pp. 6–7. See also L. Edelberg et al., "Public Expenditures and Economic Structure in the United States," *SR* 3 (1936): 57 ff., which grew out of a Colm seminar; cf. also Gerhard Colm and Theodore Geiger, *The Economy of the American People* (Washington, D.C., 1958), pp. 106 ff.

[70]G. Colm to A. Brecht, Aug. 14, 1939, Brecht Papers, SUNY, Albany.

[71]Gerhard Colm, *The Federal Budget and the National Economy* (Washington, D.C., 1954), p. 20.

[72]Colm, "Comment on Extraordinary Budgets," pp. 168 ff.: correspondence between Colm and Brecht, starting Oct. 5, 1940, Brecht Papers, SUNY, Albany.

[73]Memo, Gerhard Colm, Mar. 27, 1941, Bureau of the Budget (BoB), series 39.3, box 1, NA; Marriner Eccles, *Beckoning Frontiers: Public and Personal Recollections* (New York, 1951), pp. 367 ff.

[74]Gerhard Colm, "From Estimates of National Income to Projections of the Nation's Budget," *SR* 12 (1945): 350 ff.

[75]Memos on the planning studies by L. H. Bean, G. Colm, J. W. Jones, and others, Sept. 9, 1943, May 31, 1944, and later, BoB, series 39.3, box 71, NA; on England, see William Beveridge, *Full Employment in a Free Society* (New York, 1945).

[76]Alvin Hansen, *The American Economy* (New York, 1957), pp. 81 ff. Oral history interview with Walter C. Salant, Mar. 30, 1970, Truman Library, Independence, Mo.

[77]The act speaks of "maximum employment" rather than full employment.

[78]Gerhard Colm, "Economic Planning in the United States," *WA* 92 (1964): 31 ff.; see also his *Entwicklungen in Konjunkturforschung und Konjunkturpolitik in den Vereinigten Staaten von Amerika* (Kiel, 1954), pp. 14–15.

[79]Colm, *Entwicklungen in Konjunkturforschung*, pp. 18 ff.; Gerhard Colm, "Notes for a 'Depression Issue,' " Jan. 2, 1952, Colm Papers, box 26, LoC; see also "Gerhard Colm's Economics of National Programming," chap. 4 in Gruchy, *Contemporary Economic Thought*, pp. 237 ff.

[80]In the following discussion the terms "national socialism" and "fascism" are used interchangeably.

[81]Giuseppe A. Borgese, "The Intellectual Origins of Fascism," *SR* 1 (1934): 475 ff.

[82]Paul Tillich, "The Totalitarian State and the Claims of the Church," *SR* 1 (1934): 405 ff.

[83]Jakob Marschak, "Kerensky und von Papen," MS for the unpublished "Festschrift für Emil Lederer zum 50. Geburtstag, Juli 1932," Lederer Papers, SUNY, Albany.

[84]In the biographical information requested by the Emergency Committee in Aid of Displaced German Scholars, both had answered the question of whether they would accept employment in the Soviet Union in the affirmative.

[85]Max Ascoli and Arthur Feiler, *Fascism for Whom?* (New York, 1938).

[86]Eduard Heimann, *Communism, Fascism, or Democracy?* (New York, 1938), "What Marx Means Today," *SR* 4 (1937): 33 ff., and "The 'Revolutionary Situation' and the Middle Classes," *SR* 5 (1938): 227 ff.; Heimann to Karl Mannheim, Jan. 18, 1936, Tillich Papers, F 5/21, Harvard University. See also Ernst Bloch, *Erbschaft dieser Zeit* (1935; Frankfurt, 1962), pp. 67 ff.

[87]E. Heimann to A. Löwe, Dec. 30, 1935, Tillich Papers, F 5/21, Harvard University.

[88]Emil Lederer, *Einige Gedanken zur Soziologie der Revolutionen* (Leipzig, 1918), p. 5, passim.

[89]Emil Lederer, *State of the Masses: The Threat of the Classless Society* (New York, 1940), pp. 17 ff.; see also his "On Revolution," *SR* 3 (1936): 1 ff.

[90]Lederer, *State of the Masses*, p. 18.

[91]Franz Neumann, *Behemoth: The Structure and Practice of National Socialism* (New York, 1942), pp. 365 ff.; cf. also Goetz Briefs, "Intellectual Tragedy," *Commonweal*, Oct. 25, 1940.

[92]Löwe, *Price of Liberty;* a 2nd and 3rd ed. appeared in 1937 and 1948, and an extract was published in German by the Allied Information Service in its periodical *Neue Auslese* 2, no. 4 (1947): 1 ff.

[93]Albert Einstein, *Mein Weltbild* (Amsterdam, 1934), pp. 57–58; Young-Bruehl, *Hannah Arendt*, pp. 166, 210.

[94]Löwe, *Price of Liberty* (3rd ed., New York 1948), p. 6; Löwe, "The Task of

Democratic Education: Pre-Hitler Germany and England," *SR* 4 (1937): 381 ff.; Lowe, *The Universities in Transition* (London, 1940); Lowe, "Is Present-Day Higher Learning 'Relevant'?" *SR* 38 (1971): 563 ff.

[95]Neumann et al., *Cultural Migration*, p. 18.

[96]Speier and Kähler, *War in Our Time*.

[97]Adolf Hitler, *Mein Kampf: Complete and Unabridged, Fully Annotated* (New York, 1939). For a detailed discussion, see James J. and Patience P. Barnes, *Hitler's "Mein Kampf" in Britain and America: A Publishing History, 1930–39* (Cambridge, 1980).

[98]Office of Strategic Services, Research and Analysis Branch, Report no. 948: "Psychological Warfare Literature," Aug. 1948, p. 17.

[99]The manuscript was not published until after Staudinger's death; Hans Staudinger, *The Inner Nazi: A Critical Analysis of Mein Kampf*, ed. Peter M. Ruttkoff and William B. Scott (Baton Rouge and London, 1981). The editors apparently did not know about the origin of the manuscript and dated it 1943–44, but it was actually finished by early 1941. Cf. M. Ascoli to Prof. E. M. Earle, Princeton, Feb. 3, 1941, Ascoli Papers, 206/4, Boston University.

[100]Ernst Kris and Hans Speier, *German Radio Propaganda: Report on Home Broadcasting during the War* (London and New York, 1944); Heinz Paechter, *Nazi Deutsch: A Glossary of Contemporary German Usage* (New York, 1944).

[101]*The City of Man: A Declaration of World Democracy* (New York, 1941). On the origin of the book, see Paul Michael Lützeler, "*The City of Man* (1940): Ein Demokratiebuch amerikanischer und emigrierter europäischer Intellektueller," in Thomas Koebner et al., eds., *Exilforschung: Ein internationales Jahrbuch* 2 (1984): 299 ff. In a similar spirit Alvin Johnson participated in a protest meeting of American intellectuals held on the tenth anniversary of national socialism's rise to power; cf. Stephen S. Wise, ed., *Never Again: Ten Years of Hitler: A Symposium* (New York, 1943).

[102]Leuchtenburg, *Roosevelt and the New Deal*, pp. 299 ff.

[103]A. Johnson to T. B. Appleget, Apr. 1, 1942, RFA RG 1.1, 200/53/626.

[104]First RF grant approval of over $10,000 for the research project "On the Organization of Peace," Feb. 16, 1940, RFA RG 1.1, 200/383/4528.

[105]Memo of the RF, Feb. 12, 1942, RFA RG 1.1, 200/383/4529.

[106]See the many articles on these topics in *SR* from May 1940 on.

[107]Graduate Faculty, Minutes, Oct. 1, 1941, NSA.

[108]Memos of the acting dean, Max Ascoli, Nov. 6, 1940, Ascoli Papers, 205/4, Boston University.

[109]Alvin Johnson, "War and the Scholar," *SR* 9 (1942): 1 ff. At this same time Colm had written in a different context: "People fight today not only to win the war but to win the peace"; Gerhard Colm, "Washington Fiscal Policy: Its War and Postwar Aims," *Fortune* 26, no. 4 (1942).

[110]The Brookings Institution and other offices like the National Bureau of Economic Research were dealing only with "domestic affairs."

[111]A. Johnson to J. H. Willits, June 6, 1940, RFA RG 1.1, 200/383/4525.

[112]Memo, J. H. Willits, Aug. 8, 1940, RFA RG 1.1, 200/46/531.

[113]Memo, J. H. Willits, Aug. 19, 1940, RFA RG 1.1, 200/52/621; H. Staudinger to M. Ascoli, Oct. 31, 1940, Ascoli Papers, 207/1, Boston University.

[114]*The Study of World Affairs: The Aims and Organization of the Institute of World Affairs. Two Addresses Delivered [by Alvin Johnson and Adolph Lowe] at the Inaugural Meeting on November 17th, 1943* (New York, 1943); see also A. Johnson to W. C. Mitchell, June 3, 1943, NSA.

[115]This is shown, for instance, in the correspondence of the Harvard sociologist Talcott Parsons and Adolph Lowe, Mar. 9, 1942, and later, Parsons Papers, 15.2, box 3, Harvard University; also in a letter of the Committee on International Relations to Lowe, Dec. 14, 1949, Lowe's private papers.

[116]*The Study of World Affairs*, p. 14.

[117]Hannah Arendt, "German Emigres," MS (ca. 1943), pp. 5–6, Arendt Papers, 63, LoC.

[118]A. Löwe to Joe Oldham, chairman of the research committee of the World Council of Churches for Practical Christianity, July 31, 1934, Staudinger Papers, 3/27, SUNY, Albany.

[119]Hans Staudinger, "The United States and World Reconstruction," *SR* 8 (1941): 283 ff.

[120]Outline of a project, "Germany's Position in Postwar Reconstruction," Nov. 1943, NSA; Hans Neisser, *The Problem of Reparations* (New York, 1944) (mimeo, "American Labor Conference on International Affairs: Studies in Postwar Reconstruction," no. 4); statement by A. Lowe for Eleanor Roosevelt, June 15, 1943, containing the summary of an oral report for the U.S. president.

[121]Ernst Fraenkel, *Military Occupation and the Rule of Law: Occupation Government in the Rhineland, 1918–1923* (New York and London, 1944).

[122] Arnold Brecht, "European Federation: The Democratic Alternative," *Harvard Law Review* 55 (1942): 561 ff. and *Federalism and Regionalism in Germany: The Division of Prussia* (New York and London, 1945); Josef Berolzheimer, "Evolution of Political Opinion in Germany," mimeo (New York, 1944); Joseph Schechtmann, "European Population Transfers during World War II," mimeo (New York, 1944).

[123]Reports, "Economic Controls in Britain and Germany" and "Social and Economic Controls in Germany and Russia," mimeos (New York, 1944); see also Frieda Wunderlich, *Labor under German Democracy: Arbitration, 1918–1933*, SR, supp. 2 (New York, 1940); Gregory Bienstock, Salomon M. Schwarz, and Aaron Yugow, *Management in Russian Industry and Agriculture*, ed. Arthur Feiler and Jakob Marschak (New York, 1944; 3rd ed., 1948).

[124]A. Lowe to J. Marschak, Nov. 16, 1943, Marschak Papers, UCLA.

[125]"Final Report on the Research Project on Germany's Position in European Postwar Reconstruction," Feb. 13, 1945, RFA RG 1.1, 200/383/4533.

[126]Hans Neisser, "Industrialization and the Pattern of World Trade," mimeo (New York, 1944), and "International Trade in Raw Materials at Various Levels of Employment," mimeo (New York, 1944); Neisser and Franco Modigliani, *National Incomes and International Trade* (Urbana, Ill., 1953); see also A. Lowe to J. Marschak, July 6, 1943, on the hiring of Modigliani as a research assistant, Marschak Papers, UCLA.

[127]Kähler and Hamburger, *Education for an Industrial Age.*

[128]Wilbert E. Moore, *Industrialization and Labor: Social Aspects of Economic Development* (Ithaca and New York, 1951).

[129]A. Brecht to A. Lowe, Mar. 27, 1949, Brecht Papers, SUNY, Albany.

[130]A. Lowe to H. Simons, president of the New School, June 1951, NSA.

[131]Lowe, *On Economic Knowledge* (2nd enlarged ed., White Plains, N.Y., 1977); German editions: *Politische Ökonomik* (Frankfurt, 1968); 2nd ed., Königstein, 1984); Lowe, *The Path of Economic Growth* (Cambridge and London, 1976).

[132]The Rockefeller Foundation had awarded the Graduate Faculty a grant for editing Mannheim's writings; the project director was Adolph Lowe. See Lowe's preface to the first volume, Karl Mannheim, *Freedom, Power, and Democratic Planning*, ed. Hans Gerth and Ernest K. Bramstedt (London, 1951). Lowe also wrote the chapter "Control of the Economy," pp. 119 ff., on the basis of Mannheim's notes.

[133]Adolph Lowe, "A Structural Model of Production," *SR* 19 (1952): 135 ff., and "The Classical Theory of Economic Growth," *SR* 21 (1954): 127 ff.; Lowe, "Technological Unemployment Reexamined," in Gottfried Eisermann, ed., *Wirtschaft und Kultursystem: Festschrift für Alexander Rüstow* (Stuttgart and Zürich, 1955), pp. 229 ff. For a collection of his articles, cf. Adolph Lowe, *Essays in Political Economics: Public Control in a Democratic Society*, ed. Allen Oakley (Brighton, 1987).

[134]Adolf Löwe, *Economics and Sociology: A Plea for Co-operation in the Social Sciences* (London, 1935).

[135]Ibid., pp. 11 ff.

[136]Ibid., esp. pp. 25–26, 44 ff., 88 ff., 131 ff.

[137]Ibid., pp. 89–90.

[138]In the first edition of his *On Economic Knowledge*, Lowe cited economic growth as a goal on which a political and social consensus could be reached relatively quickly and without polarization. In the following years he became more skeptical in view of the ecological problems involved, and in the postscript of the second edition he therefore questioned whether growth could be a universally supported goal. For many decades it had been the safety valve that had defused the conflict between classes in the West. But growth had been pursued at the expense

of the underdeveloped countries and of the environment. Cf. Lowe, *On Economic Knowledge* (2nd ed.), p. 339.

[139]Ibid., (2nd ed.), pp. 32 ff., 95 ff., 130 ff., 249 ff.; Lowe, "What Is Evolutionary Economics? Remarks upon Receipt of the Veblen–Commons Award," *Journal of Economic Issues* 14 (1980): 247 ff.; see also Lowe, "Die Hoffnung auf kleine Katastrophen," pp. 167 ff. A concise summary of *On Economic Knowledge* is given in Richard X. Chase, "Adolph Lowe's Paradigm Shift for a Scientific Economics: An Interpretative Perspective," *American Journal of Economics and Sociology* 42 (1983): 167 ff.

[140]Alvin Johnson to Eduard Heimann, Dec. 19, 1949, Johnson Papers, 3/54, Yale University.

[141]See Adolph Lowe to Friedrich Pollock, July 9, 1964, Pollock Papers, in Max Horkheimer Papers, 23, 16/289, SUB, Frankfurt am Main.

[142]The papers presented are collected in Robert L. Heilbroner, ed., *Economic Means and Social Ends: Essays in Political Economics* (Englewood Cliffs, N.J., 1969). In a broader historical and political context Lowe discussed his model in a recent book; cf. Adolph Lowe, *Has Freedom a Future?* (New York, 1988). On the reception of Lowe's work, cf. the comprehensive bibliography in the Lowe *Festschrift*, Hagemann and Kurz, *Beschäftigung*, p. 269 ff.

[143]On this point, see the review by Kenneth Boulding in *Scientific American*, 1965, pp. 139 ff.; also Eberhard K. Seifert's review of the Lowe *Festschrift* in *Europäische Zeitschrift für Politische Ökonomie* 1 (1985): 187 ff.

[144]Gerhard Colm, "The Dismal Science and the Good Life," *The Reporter*, July 15, 1965, pp. 46 ff.; in German: "Die heillose Wissenschaft und das 'Summum Bonum': Bemerkungen zu Adolph Lowes *Politische Ökonomik*," *Hamburger Jahrbuch für Wirtschafts- und Gesellschaftspolitik* 14 (1969): 221 ff.

[145]John R. Hicks, *Capital and Time: A Neo-Austrian Theory* (Oxford, 1973).

7. The Influence of the New School Scholars in the United States

[1]Carl Landauer to J. A. Schumpeter, Mar. 7, 1934, Schumpeter Papers, 4.7, box 6, Harvard University.

[2]Cf. Chapter 5, section 3, herein.

[3]Johann L. Schmidt, "Die deutschen Wissenschaftler in Amerika," *Freies Deutschland* (Mexico) 1, no. 1 (1941): 23.

[4]Conversations with Herbert Zassenhaus, June 4, 1984, in Washington, and with Edith Hirsch, Apr. 26, 1984, in New York.

[5]On Zassenhaus's and Julius Hirsch's connections with Adolph Lowe prior to 1933, see Zassenhaus's letters to Schumpeter, Nov. 25, 1932, and later, Schumpeter Papers, 4.7, box 9, Harvard University; Julius Hirsch's diary, (unpublished MS, 1921–22), pp. 92 ff.

[6]K. J. Arndt, Hartwick College, New York, to EC, Mar. 18, 1935, EC, 119, NYPL.

[7]G. Clark to RF, Mar. 25, 1938, also R. Donner, Aug. 27, 1941, RFA RG 1.1, 200/338/4029 and 200/383/4528.

[8]FBI, Washington, memo, Mar. 15, 1943, and FBI, Cincinnati, Aug. 3 and 7, 1951, FBI files, Washington, D.C.

[9]FBI reports, New York, to central office in Washington, June 11, 1941, and Mar. 16, 1942, FBI files, Washington, D.C.

[10]E. Adamson, Report for Congress, Dec. 23, 1946. The report had not been authorized by HUAC; cf. FBI memo of Jan. 9, 1947, FBI files, Washington, D.C.

[11]Alvin Johnson to Reinhold Niebuhr, Apr. 2, 1951, Niebuhr Papers, box 2, LoC.

[12]Cf. speech by Gerhard Colm as dean on occasion of the Graduate Faculty's sixth anniversary, RFA RG 1.1, 200/338/4029.

[13]Dorothy Thompson, *Refugees: Anarchy or Organization?* (New York, 1938), p. 49; Louis Wirth, "The Intellectual Exile" (contribution to the discussion), *SR* 4 (1937): 330; Oscar Jaszi, "Political Refugees," *Annals of the American Academy of Political and Social Sciences* 203 (May 1939): 91.

[14]Thomas Mann, Foreword to Alvin Johnson, *Great American: Citizen of the World* (New York, 1943), p. 1.

[15]Office of Strategic Services (OSS), Research and Analysis Branch, Report no. 1568, "The German Political Emigration," Dec. 3, 1943, p. 21.

[16]On this subject, see John H. Herz, a former staff member of the OSS, *Vom Überleben: Wie ein Weltbild entstand. Autobiographie* (Düsseldorf, 1984), pp. 135 ff.; Alfons Söllner, ed., *Zur Archäologie der Demokratie in Deutschland: Analysen politischer Emigranten im amerikanischen Geheimdienst*, vol. 1: *1943–1945* (Frankfurt, 1982). On the staff of the Central European Branch of the OSS, cf. the personnel lists in OSS RG 226, ser. 38, box 5, NA.

[17]Coser, *Refugee Scholars*, pp. xi ff.

[18]For criticism of economic forecasting in the United States, see Wassily Leontief, "What Hope for the Economy?" *New York Review of Books* 29, no. 13 (Aug. 12, 1982): 31 ff.

[19]Rolf Krengel, "Die Anfänge der Input-Output-Rechnung des DIW für die Bundesrepublik Deutschland," *Kyklos* 32 (1979): 392 ff.

[20]See the protocols in Benjamin F. Lippincott, ed., *Government Control of the Economic Order: A Symposium* (Minneapolis, 1935).

[21]Gerhard Colm to Arnold Brecht, Mar. 28, 1939, Brecht Papers, SUNY, Albany.

[22]Emil Lederer to J. A. Schumpeter, Jan. 8, 1935, Schumpeter Papers, 4.8, box 1, Harvard University.

[23]Joint Program for the Meetings of the American Economic Association, American Marketing Association . . . , American Sociological Society . . . , Econometric Society, Detroit, Dec. 27–30, 1938.

[24]Alvin Johnson to Agnes de Lima, Dec. 28, 1935, Johnson Papers, 2/28, Yale University.

[25]Gerhard Colm, "Public Revenue and Public Expenditure in National Income," in National Bureau of Economic Research, ed., *Studies in Income and Wealth*, vol. 1 (New York, 1937), pp. 175 ff.; contributions to the discussion by J. M. Clark, S. Kuznets, and M. Newcomer, pp. 228–229.

[26]Program of the Universities—National Bureau Conference on Business Cycle Research, Nov. 25–27, 1949, New York.

[27]Reports of the dean of the Graduate Faculty of Political and Social Science in the New School for Social Research, Sept. 1936 and Sept. 1939. In the reports there are summaries in the form of tables on faculty engagements at other institutions. From 1936 to 1939 faculty members held lectures or gave courses at eleven conferences and at fifty-eight universities or colleges.

[28]Ibid. In 1939 *Social Research* had about 800 subscribers, and 125 copies were sold separately.

[29]A. Johnson to G. Bacon, Nov. 9, 1945, Johnson Papers, 1/4, Yale University.

[30]A. de Lima, press release, June 15, 1945, Johnson Papers, 9/150, Yale University.

[31]"Translation into English of Foreign Social Science Monographs by U.S. Works Progress Administration," mimeos—for example, no. 3, Emil Lederer and Jakob Marschak, "The New Middle Class" (New York, 1937) (from the German "Der neue Mittelstand," in *Grundriss der Sozialökonomik*, sec. 9/1 [Tübingen, 1926]), and no. 5, Emil Lederer, "The Problem of the Modern Salaried Employee: Its Theoretical and Statistical Basis" (New York, 1937) (the German original formed chaps. 2 and 3 of *Die Privatangestellten in der modernen Wirtschaftsentwicklung* [Tübingen, 1912]).

[32]No. 25 in the same translation series is Hans Speier, "The Salaried Employee in Germany," vol. 1 (New York, 1939). This sociological study, which is very important for an understanding of the rise of national socialism, was not published in Germany until a German historian happened to come across the text in the Columbia University library. It appeared in German as Hans Speier, *Die Angestellten vor dem Nationalsozialismus: Ein Beitrag zum Verständnis der deutschen Sozialstruktur 1918–1933* (Göttingen, 1977).

[33]Proposal (for the founding of the Institute of World Affairs) in a letter, May 1943, RFA RG 1.1, 200/382/4516; memorandum of the RF: "The New School and the War," Mar. 1, 1943, RFA RG 1.1, 200/53/628.

[34]Correspondence between A. Brecht and A. Johnson, May 21, 1942, and later, Brecht Papers, SUNY, Albany; Hans Neisser to Jakob Marschak, Mar. 26, 1943, Marschak Papers, UCLA.

[35]William Green, president of AFL to Horace M. Kallen, Nov. 25, 1942; Varian Fry to Kallen, Apr. 13, 1943, Kallen Papers, 27, YIVO Institute, New York.

[36]Friedrich Stampfer to SOPADE, Feb. 10, 1943, in Erich Matthias, ed., *Mit dem Gesicht nach Deutschland: Eine Dokumentation über die sozialdemokratische Emigration* (Düsseldorf, 1962), p. 582.

[37]*International Postwar Problems: A Quarterly Review of the American Labor Conference on International Affairs* 1, no. 1 (Dec. 1943) to no. 4 (Sept. 1944). Essays by Albert Halasi, Alfred Braunthal, Georg Denicke, Paul Vignaux, Wladimir Woytinski, Hans Neisser, and others.

[38]Neisser, *The Problem of Reparations* (mimeo, "The American Labor Conference on International Affairs: Studies in Postwar Reconstruction," no. 4).

[39]Adolph Lowe, "Project on the Introduction of the Social Sciences into the Program of Instruction and Research at the Hebrew University" (1939); Salo Baron, Hebrew University, to dean of the Graduate Faculty, May 25, 1945, Ascoli Papers, 171/4, Boston University.

[40]National Economic and Social Planning Association to Hans Staudinger, Oct. 4, 1940, Ascoli Papers, 206/4, Boston University.

[41]"Opinions on the Work of the Graduate Faculty" (1940), collection of excerpts from ca. 100 letters the Graduate Faculty had received during the last few years, Ascoli Papers, 207/1, Boston University.

[42]Max Ascoli to B. Hovde, president of the New School, Apr. 10, 1946, Ascoli Papers, 204/4, Boston University.

[43]Board of Economic Warfare to RF, June 24, 1942, RFA RG 1.1, 200/383/4531.

[44]See the numerous letters in the Rockefeller Foundation files of 1942 and later, RFA RG 1.1, 200/383/4520 ff.; Wartime Information Board, Ottawa, to Institute of World Affairs, Mar. 26, 1944, NSA.

[45]After Lowe rejected Chicago's offer, Johnson wrote to him on Dec. 12, 1945: "Your letter greatly increases my happiness. I should have felt desolate if you had decided to go to Chicago. . . . You are the kind of economist I would have liked to be"; Johnson Papers, 4/81 Yale University.

[46]G. Colm to A. Johnson, Jan. 9, 1946, Colm Papers, box 28, LoC; Johnson's answers, Jan. 11 and Feb. 19, 1946, Johnson Papers, 1/22, Yale University.

[47]G. Colm to Leon Keyserling, Council of Economic Advisers, Jan. 29, 1948, Colm Papers, box 29, LoC. The plan is reprinted in Hans Möller, *Zur Vorgeschichte der Deutschen Mark: Die Währungsreformpläne 1945–1948* (Basel and Tübingen, 1961), pp. 214 ff.

[48]Eckhard Wandel, *Die Entstehung der Bank deutscher Länder und die deutsche Währungsreform 1948: Die Rekonstruktion des westdeutschen Geld- und Währungssystems 1945–1949 unter Berücksichtigung der amerikanischen Besatzungspolitik* (Frankfurt, 1980), pp. 95 ff.

[49]Lecture given at George Washington University, Sept. 5, 1949, Colm Papers, box 28, LoC.

[50]Memo, Weldon Jones, BoB, June 7, 1946, on inquiry by Dept. of the Navy; Colm Papers, box 29, LoC; report by H. Feis for the War Dept., June 19, 1946, ibid.

[51]John Kenneth Galbraith, *A Life in Our Time: Memoirs* (Boston, 1981), p. 252.

[52]FBI office memorandum, Jan. 9, 1947, FBI files, Washington, D.C.

[53]Correspondence between G. Colm and J. Dodge, July 3, 1946, and later, Colm Papers, box 29, LoC.

[54]Jack Bennett (Clay's financial adviser), OMGUS, to G. Colm, Jan. 13, 1947, and Colm's answer, May 9, 1947, Colm Papers, box 29, LoC.

[55]G. Colm to J. Bennett, Feb. 5, 1948, Colm Papers, box 16, LoC.

[56]G. Colm to Lucius D. Clay, Oct. 26, 1948, and Clay's answer, Nov. 27, 1948, Colm Papers, box 28, LoC.

[57]Cf. Feiler and Marschak, eds., *Management in Russian Industry and Agriculture*, pp. xiii ff.

[58]Tjalling Koopmans, in his obituary for Jacob Marschak, *American Economic Review* 68, no. 2 (May 1978): ix.

[59]J. A. Schumpeter to Abraham Flexner, Princeton, May 8, 1934, Schumpeter Papers, 4.7, box 4, Harvard University.

[60]On Marschak's influence on Franco Modigliani, see Arjo Klamer, *The New Classical Macroeconomics: Conversations with New Classical Economists and Their Opponents* (Brighton, 1984), pp. 114 ff.

[61]See, for example, Jacob Marschak, "Statistical Inference in Economics: An Introduction," in Tjalling Koopmans, ed., *Statistical Inference in Dynamic Economic Models*, Cowles Commission Monograph no. 10 (New York, 1950).

[62]See, for example, Lawrence Klein, *Economic Fluctuations in the United States, 1921–1941*, Cowles Commission Monograph no. 11 (New York, 1950); also Koopmans, Marschak obituary, p. x.

[63]Kenneth Arrow, "Jacob Marschak's Contributions to the Economics of Decision and Information," *American Economic Review* 68, no. 2 (May 1978): xii ff. On Marschak's life during this period, see Roy Radner, "Jacob Marschak," *Behavioral Science* 23 (1978): 63 ff.; Coser, *Refugee Scholars*, pp. 154 ff. The most important of Marschak's works are reprinted with a comprehensive bibliography in C. B. McGuire and Roy Radner, eds., *Decision and Organization: A Volume in Honour of Jacob Marschak* (Amsterdam and London, 1972).

[64]Hans Speier, "'Reeducation'—the U.S. Policy" (1947) and "The Future of German Nationalism" (1947), reprinted in Speier, *Social Order and the Risks of War: Papers in Political Sociology* (Cambridge, Mass., 1969), pp. 397 ff.; see also Speier, *From the Ashes of Disgrace: A Journal from Germany, 1945–1955* (Amherst, Mass., 1981).

[65]Brecht, *Mit der Kraft des Geistes*, pp. 357 ff.

[66]A. Johnson to H. M. Kallen, Dec. 21, 1945, Johnson Papers, 4/69, Yale University; H. Speier to Johnson, Nov. 30, 1947, Johnson Papers, 6/109, Yale University.

[67]On the history, see Bruce L. A. Smith, *The Rand Corporation: Case Study of a Nonprofit Advisory Corporation* (Cambridge, Mass., 1966), pp. 30 ff.

[68]Conversation with Hans Speier, Sept. 16, 1983, Hartsdale, N.Y.

[69]For example: Abram Bergson and Hans Heymann, *Soviet National Income and*

Product, 1940–1948 (New York, 1954); Margaret Mead, *Soviet Attitudes toward Authority* (New York, 1951); Nathan Leites, *The Operational Code of the Politburo* (New York, 1951); also J. C. C. McKinsey, *Introduction to the Theory of Games* (New York, 1952); Cecil Hastings, *Approximations for Digital Computers* (New York, 1955).

[70]Hans Speier and W. Phillips Davison, eds., *West German Leadership and Foreign Policy* (Glencoe, Ill., 1957); also Herz, *Vom Überleben*, pp. 150 ff.

[71]Hans Speier, *German Rearmament and Atomic War: The Views of German Military and Political Leaders* (Evanston and New York, 1957); Speier, *Divided Berlin: The Anatomy of Soviet Blackmail* (New York, 1961); H. J. C. Grimmelshausen, *Courage: The Adventures and the False Messiah*, trans. and introduction by H. Speier (Princeton, 1964).

[72]Max Ascoli, personal papers, Ascoli Papers, Boston University.

[73]R. A. Young, NBER, to J. H. Willits, RF, Sept. 23, 1943, RFA RG 1.1, 200/382/4516.

8. Problems of Integration

[1]Lowe, "Die Hoffnung auf kleine Katastrophen," p. 145; Paul Tillich, "Mind and Migration," *SR* 4 (1937): 305.

[2]Tillich, "Mind and Migration," pp. 328–329.

[3]On this, see activities report of the Notgemeinschaft deutscher Wissenschaftler im Ausland, sec. USA, winter 1934–35, p. 2, EC, 146, NYPL; Hughes, *The Sea Change*, pp. 30 ff.; Herbert A. Strauss, "The Immigration and Acculturation of the German Jew in the United States of America," *Yearbook of the LBI* 16 (1971): 82; Paul A. Samuelson, "American Economics," in Ralph E. Freeman, ed., *Postwar Economic Trends in the United States* (New York, 1960), p. 41; Pachter, "On Being an Exile," p. 31.

[4]Davie, *Refugees in America*, p. 47, passim; Duggan and Drury, *Rescue of Science*, pp. 146 ff.; Kent, *Refugee Intellectual*, pp. 111 ff.

[5]Coser, *Refugee Scholars*, p. 11.

[6]Herbert A. Strauss, "Changing Images of the Immigrant in the U.S.A.," *Jahrbuch für Amerikastudien* 21 (1976): 132.

[7]See Fritz Redlich's complaints about working in a small southern college; F. Redlich to Frieda Wunderlich, Oct. 9, 1937, Redlich Papers, box 4, Harvard University.

[8]Eduard Heimann, "The Refugee Speaks," *Annals of the American Academy of Political and Social Sciences* 203 (1939): 106 ff.

[9]Eduard Heimann to Arnold Brecht, Oct. 29, 1963, Brecht Papers, SUNY, Albany.

[10]Erdmann, *Kurt Riezler*, pp. 155 ff.

Notes to Pages 184–191

[11]Kurt Rosenfeld to Karl Brandt, Apr. 22, 1937, and Brandt's reply, Apr. 27, 1937, and the correspondence between Felix Frankfurter and Alvin Johnson that followed on this, Frankfurter Papers, film 102, LoC. Cf. also Alfons Goldschmidt's account, "Der Fall Dr. Karl Brandt," *Die neue Weltbühne*, no. 20 (May 13, 1937): 635–636.

[12]Karl Brandt, Baton Rouge, to Max Ascoli, June 12 and July 11, 1937, Ascoli Papers, 168/8, Boston University.

[13]Memo, FBI, Washington, Mar. 28, 1942, FBI files, Washington, D.C.

[14]Correspondence between Adolph Lowe and Karl Brandt, Jan. 1947 and later; A. Johnson to Lowe, Feb. 10, 1947, Johnson Papers, 4/81, Yale University.

[15]Arnold Brecht to the Prussian Ministry of the Interior, Sept. 24, 1933, correspondence between Brecht and A. Johnson, Oct. 4, 1933, and later, Brecht Papers, 2/37, SUNY, Albany.

[16]A. Johnson to A. Brecht, Apr. 6 and July 26, 1934, Nov. 30, 1935, Brecht Papers, 2/38, SUNY, Albany.

[17]A. Brecht to Julie Braun-Vogelstein, Dec. 17, 1938, Braun-Vogelstein Papers, 4, box 36/5, LBI.

[18]A. Johnson to A. Brecht, Jan. 3, 1936, Brecht Papers, 2/38, SUNY, Albany.

[19]A. Brecht to A. Johnson, Jan. 5, 1936, and May 16, 1938, Brecht Papers, 2/38, SUNY, Albany.

[20]A. Johnson to A. Brecht, May 20, 1938, and Brecht's reply, May 29, 1938, Brecht Papers, 2/38, SUNY, Albany.

[21]Conversation with Hans Staudinger, Oct. 3, 1979. See also Matthias, *Mit dem Gesicht nach Deutschland*, pp. 149 ff.

[22]Hans Simons diaries, entry of Feb. 8, 1935, p. 41, Simons Papers, SUNY, Albany.

[23]Tillich, "Mind and Migration," pp. 195 ff.

[24]Hans Speier, "The Social Conditions of the Intellectual Exile," *SR* 4 (1937): 316 ff.

[25]See, for example, Alfred Schütz's lecture, "The Stranger," given when he first started teaching at the New School, published in *American Journal of Sociology* 49 (1944): 499 ff.

[26]On this, see Leo Löwenthal, "Adorno und seine Kritiker," in his *Schriften*, vol. 4 (Frankfurt, 1984), p. 69.

[27]Martin Jay, *The Dialectical Imagination: A History of the Frankfurt School and the Institute of Social Research, 1923–1950* (London, 1973), pp. 253 ff.; Phil Slater, *Origin and Significance of the Frankfurt School: A Marxist Perspective* (London, 1977), pp. 26 ff.; H. Stuart Hughes, "Social Theory in a New Context," in Jarrell C. Jackman and C. M. Borden, *The Muses Flee Hitler: Cultural Transfer and Adaptation, 1930–1945* (Washington, D.C., 1983), pp. 111 ff.; Coser, *Refugee Scholars*, pp. 88 ff.

[28]Max Horkheimer, "Zum Rationalismusstreit in der gegenwärtigen Philosophie," *ZfS* 3 (1934): 26–27.

[29]Max Horkheimer to Friedrich Pollock, May 27, 1934, and Horkheimer to Adolf Löwe, Jan. 28, 1935, Horkheimer Papers, 6, 31/93, and 1, 17/109, SUB, Frankfurt.

[30]Theodor W. Adorno, "Scientific Experiences of a European Scholar in America," in Fleming and Bailyn, *Intellectual Migration*, p. 338.

[31]Leo Löwenthal to Max Horkheimer, Dec. 11, 1936, in Löwenthal, *Schriften*, vol. 4, p. 193.

[32]Theodor W. Adorno, Else Frenkel-Brunswik, et al., *The Authoritarian Personality* (New York, 1950), esp. chaps. 21 ff.

[33]Jay, *Dialectical Imagination*, pp. 133, 164.

[34]Hans Speier, in *SR* 3 (1936): 501 ff.

[35]Emil Lederer to Wesley C. Mitchell, Apr. 20, 1934, Mitchell Papers C, Columbia University.

[36]Max Ascoli to Adolph Lowe, Jan. 9, 1941, Ascoli Papers, 205/2, Boston University.

[37]On the contacts with the New School, see Adolf Löwe to Max Horkheimer, Aug. 25, 1934, and later; Horkheimer to Gerhard Colm, Nov. 21, 1938, Horkheimer Papers, 1, 4/411, 1, 17/99 ff., SUB, Frankfurt.

[38]Leo Löwenthal to M. Horkheimer, Nov. 22, 1935, in Löwenthal, *Schriften*, vol. 4, pp. 19 ff.

[39]On this, see Franz Neumann to Max Horkheimer, July 23, 1941, and Horkheimer's reply, Aug. 2, 1941, Horkheimer Papers, 6, 30/49 ff., SUB, Frankfurt.

[40]Franz Neumann to M. Horkheimer and Leo Löwenthal, July 20 and 26, 1940, and Sept. 29, 1941, Horkheimer Papers, 6, 30/15 and 111, SUB, Frankfurt.

[41]Franz Neumann, report on the negotiations with T. B. Kittredge, RF, May 6, 1941, Horkheimer Papers, 6, 30/81, SUB, Frankfurt.

[42]Max Horkheimer to Max Ascoli, dean of the Graduate Faculty, Jan. 2 and Mar. 7, 1941, and Ascoli's reply, Mar. 12, 1941, Ascoli Papers, 205/6, Boston University.

[43]The New School circle was responsible for a highly negative review (written by Eduard Heimann [*SR* 13 [1946]: 113 ff.]). The criticism focusing on the book's weakness in the area of economics and in the depiction of the Nazi mass movement is unjustified because Neumann had not set out to write a comprehensive analysis of national socialism.

[44]Max Horkheimer to Franz Neumann, Aug. 2, 1941, Horkheimer Papers, 6, 30/52, SUB, Frankfurt.

[45]Max Horkheimer to Adolph Lowe, Aug. 14, 1944, Horkheimer Papers, 1, 17/32, SUB, Frankfurt.

[46]Max Horkheimer, "Egoismus und Freiheitsbewegung (Zur Anthropologie des bürgerlichen Zeitalters)," *ZfS* 5 (1936): 161 ff.

[47]See Max Horkheimer, "Traditionelle und kritische Theorie," *ZfS* 6 (1937): 245 ff.

[48]M. Horkheimer to A. Löwe, Oct. 23, 1936, and later, esp. Jan. 4, and May 4, 1938, Horkheimer Papers, 1, 17/86 ff., SUB, Frankfurt.

[49]A. Löwe to M. Horkheimer, Oct. 8, 1936, and later, esp. Nov. 21, 1936, and Dec. 15, 1937, Horkheimer Papers, 1, 17/43 ff., SUB, Frankfurt.

[50]A. Löwe to M. Horkheimer, Feb. 9, 1938, Horkheimer Papers, 1, 17/88, SUB, Frankfurt.

9. Epilogue: The New School Scholars and the New Germany after 1945

[1]For example, Ernest Hamburger, "The Economic Problem of Germany," *SR* 13 (1946): 135 ff.; the unsigned "Denazification," *SR* 14 (1947): 59 ff.; or the reprint of the speech given by Professor Ebbinghaus at the reopening of the University of Marburg, *SR* 13 (1946): 236 ff.

[2]Emil J. Gumbel to Max Seydewitz, May 28, 1947, Gumbel Papers, 2/7, University of Chicago.

[3]"An Appeal," Dec. 1945, signed by ca. 100 scholars and intellectuals, Schumpeter Papers, 4.7, box 1, Harvard University.

[4]Appeal in *Aufbau* (New York) 11, no. 43 (Oct. 26, 1945).

[5]Max H. Boehm to Alvin Johnson, Mar. 9, 1946, and Johnson's reply, Apr. 30, 1946, Johnson Papers, 1/7, Yale University.

[6]Conversations with Adolph Lowe, July 5, 1983, and Apr. 2, 1986. See also Gerd Hardach's tribute to Hoffmann, "Walther G. Hoffmann: Pionier der quantitativen Wirtschaftsgeschichte," *Geschichte und Gesellschaft* 11 (1985): 541 ff.

[7]Fritz Burchardt to A. Lowe, Oct. 3, 1946, and Lowe to Paul Tillich, Dec. 13, 1949, Lowe's private papers; report of the Rockefeller Foundation on the situation in Germany, Nov. 8, 1947, RFA RG 2, 389/2623.

[8]"School for Democratic Leadership" (draft, n.d.), ca. 1945, Kallen Papers, 26428 ff., YIVO Institute, New York.

[9]A. Lowe to J. H. Willits, RF, July 15, 1947, NSA; Lowe to Alexander Rüstow, May 24, 1949, Lowe's private papers. The attitude toward the work of the Institute of World Economics remained skeptical; cf. Hans Neisser's letter to Arnold Brecht after hearing a lecture in Kiel, Aug. 22, 1952, Brecht Papers, 1/1, SUNY, Albany.

[10]A. Lowe to Alfred Weber, Jan. 30, 1950, Lowe's private papers.

[11]A. Lowe to Friedrich Pollock, June 10, 1949, ibid. See also Michael Neumann, "Lektionen ohne Widerhall: Bemerkungen zum Einfluss von Remigranten auf die Entwicklung der westdeutschen Nachkriegssoziologie," *Exil-Forschung: Ein internationales Jahrbuch* 1 (Munich, 1984): 339 ff.

[12]On the initiative of Richard von Weizsäcker, president of the Federal Republic of Germany and former mayor of Berlin, a second chair, financed by the Berlin Senate, was established at the Graduate Faculty in late 1984. By this time very few of the emigré generation were still alive.

[13]Arnold Brecht to Hans Staudinger, Sept. 3, 1973, Staudinger Papers, 1/23, SUNY, Albany.

Index

Index

Berger, Adolph, 205
Berger, Erich, 205
Berghof, Herbert, 205
Bergson, Henri, 96
Berle, Adolf, 41, 42, 43, 89, 160
Bernhard, Georg, 77
Beveridge, William, 32
Bienstock, Gregor, 205
Bikerman, Elie, 205
Birnbaum, Karl, 205
Bloch, Ernst, 131
Bloch, Marc, 90
Block, Herbert, 205
Blücher, Heinrich, 180
Boas, Franz, 60
Boehm, Max Hildebert, 201
Böhm-Bawerk, Eugen von, 49, 102, 105
Bolshevism, 130, 131. *See also* Marxism
Borgese, Giuseppe Antonio, 130, 138, 205
Bortkievicz, Ladislaus von, 172
Boulding, Kenneth, 156
Bowman, Isaiah, 77
Brando, Marlon, 79
Brandt, Karl, 65, 66, 69, 82, 168, 183–185, 205
Brandt, Willy, 203
Brecht, Arnold, 73, 158, 205; emigré experience of, 180, 181, 185–187; foreign policy and, 146–147, 148; founding of University in Exile and, 66–67; Germany after 1945 and, 199; individual influence of, 94–95; influence of New School and, 166, 175; *Political Theory*, 94; work on public finance and, 124–125, 126
Brentano, Felix W., 205
Broch, Hermann, 138
Brod, Max, 77
Brook, Warner F., 205
Brueckner, Camillo, 205
Brüning, Heinrich, 169
Burchardt, Fritz, 82, 101, 105
Burns, Arthur F., 164

Business cycles, research on, 53, 101–120, 165
Butler, Nicholas M., 45

Cahn, Theophile, 205
Calabresi, Renata, 205
Carnap, Rudolf, 96
Carnegie Foundation, 28, 90
Cassirer, Ernst, 66
Catchings, Waddill, 41
Chamberlain, Neville, 136
Choucroun, Nine, 206
Circular flow theory, 54, 105–106, 107
City of Man manifesto, 138–139, 176
Clark, John B., 40, 99
Clark, John M., 164
Clay, Lucius D., 169, 171–172
Cohen, Gustave, 206
Colm, Gerhard, 77, 201, 206; economic theory and, 53–54, 112, 113, 120–129; founding of University in Exile and, 61, 65, 69; Germany after 1945 and, 199; Horkheimer and, 193; influence of, 157, 169–172, 175; influence of New School and, 163, 164, 165; Kiel Institute and, 55, 56–57; Lowe and, 156; national socialism and, 129, 130, 137; *Volkswirtschaftliche Theorie der Staatsausgaben*, 120
Colm–Dodge–Goldsmith (CDG) Plan, 169–171
Columbia University, 5. *See also* Institute of Social Research
Commons, John R., 99
Contini, Paolo, 206
Coolidge, Calvin, 43
Coser, Lewis, 3, 6, 39, 157, 162, 180, 213 n.3
Cowles, Alfred, 173
Cowles Commission for Research in Economics, 173–174
Credit, 107–108
Croce, Benedetto, 130
Czettel, Ladislas, 206

246

Index

Index

Index

Hadamard, Jacques, 206
Hagen, Paul, 84
Halasi, Albert, 206
Halle, Hiram, 63, 73
Halm, Georg, 39
Hamburger, Ernst, 84, 206
Hansen, Alvin, 62, 108, 160, 164
Harms, Bernhard, 56, 57
Harvard University, 76–77
Haussmann, Frederick, 206
Hayek, Friedrich August, 48–49, 53, 102
Hebrew University (Jerusalem), 167
Hegemann, Werner, 206
Heilbut, Anthony, 3
Heimann, Eduard, 57, 206; background of, 55, 56; *Communism, Fascism, or Democracy?* 131–132; economic planning and, 117–118, 119; emigré experience and, 182, 183; founding of University in Exile and, 65–66, 69, 70; Germany after 1945 and, 199; national socialism and, 131–132, 137; *Soziale Theorie des Kapitalismus,* 54, 117–118
Heimann, Hugo, 56
Heller, Hermann, 66
Henle, Mary, 94
Herma, John L., 206
Hermberg, Paul, 206
Herrmann, Leon, 207
Herz, John, 75, 176
Heuss, Theodor, 203
Heythum, Antonin, 207
Heythum, Charlotta, 207
Hicks, John, 156
Hildebrand, Dietrich von, 207
Hilferding, Rudolf, 55, 58, 95
Hintze, Hedwig, 89
Hintze, Otto, 89
Hirsch, Julius, 159, 207
Historical economics, 45–47
Hitler, Adolf, 37, 137–138, 139
Hoffmann, Walther G., 201
Hoffmann-Behrendt, Lydia, 207
Honigmann, Ernst, 207

Hoover, Herbert, 45
Horenstein, Jascha, 207
Horkheimer, Max, 4, 17; Institute of Social Research and, 58, 143, 158, 190–191, 193–197; relations with Graduate Faculty and, 191, 194–197. *See also* Institute of Social Research
Hornbostel, Erich von, 66, 69, 207
House Committee on Un-American Activities, 86–87
Hughes, H. Stuart, 3, 192
Hula, Erich, 35, 75, 93, 158, 207
Husserl, Edmund, 75, 96
Hutchins, Robert M., 70, 165

Immigration history, scholarship on, 1–4
Ince, Alexander, 207
Input-output analysis, 54, 106, 156, 163
Institute of Social Research, 4, 5, 58, 143, 158, 189–197, 202–203. *See also* Horkheimer, Max
Institute of World Affairs, 82, 83, 141–149, 184
Institutionalism, 40–41, 52, 98–101
Instrumental analysis, 152–154
Intellectual migrant, 179, 189
Internationalization, 70, 139–149
International Postwar Problems (publication), 167
Interventionism, 46–47, 52. *See also* Economic planning; Fiscal policy
Isolationism: influence of leftist intellectuals and, 176; New School for Social Research and, 161–162; peace research and, 139–140; views of German scholars and, 22, 25, 27, 179

Jaeckh, Ernst, 37
Jay, Martin, 192–193
Jewish intellectuals, 14. *See also* German academics
Jewkes, John, 149
Johnson, Alvin: American social science and, 155; *City of Man* manifesto and,

249

Index

138; emigré transition process and, 97, 181, 184, 185–187; founding of New School and, 6, 22–23, 59–60, 64, 69, 71; impact of New School scholars and, 164, 166, 168, 190; McCarthyism and, 160; peace research and, 140–141; postwar requests for help and, 201; refugee aid programs and, 76, 79, 81, 82–83, 86, 90; *Social Research* and, 98

Kähler, Alfred, 79, 207; economic theory and, 53, 54, 101, 105, 108, 109–110, 117; emigré experience of, 188; founding of University in Exile and, 68, 73; influence of, 162–163; national socialism and, 137
Kahler, Erich, 207
Kahn, Ernst, 207
Kaldor, Nicholas, 108
Kallen, Horace M., 68
Kantorowicz, Hermann, 66, 207
Katona, Georg, 94, 207
Kaufmann, Felix, 75, 207
Kelsen, Hans, 35, 38, 75, 96, 207
Keynes, John Maynard, 54, 145, 151; New School economists and, 107, 108, 110, 111–117, 123, 152
Kiel Institute of World Economics, 15, 34, 53–54, 202. *See also* Colm, Gerhard; Kähler, Alfred; Lowe, Adolph; Neisser, Hans
Kirchheimer, Otto, 177, 192
Klein, Lawrence, 174
Knapp, Georg Friedrich, 107
Knies, Karl, 60
Knowledge, sociology of, 10
Köhler, Wolfgang, 93
Koffka, Kurt, 93, 94
Koopmans, Tjalling, 165, 173, 174
Koyré, Alexander, 85, 207
Kraitchik, Maurice, 207
Kris, Ernst, 138, 207
Kuhn, Thomas, 10
Kuznets, Simon, 127

Labor, and technological change, 103–111
Labor unions, 166
Lachmann, Kurt, 207
Landauer, Carl, 158
Lange, Oscar, 174
Laski, Harold, 60, 64
Laskowski, Michael, 207
"Law to Restore the Professional Civil Service" (Germany, 1933), 12, 64
Lazarsfeld, Paul, 213 n.2
League of Nations, 25–26, 27
Leblond, Charles F., 207
Lederer, Emil, 77, 95, 164, 182, 207; background of, 55, 56; death of, 110; economic theory and, 54, 101, 102, 106, 108–109, 111; founding of University in Exile and, 61, 62, 63, 64, 65, 67, 69, 73, 158; Horkheimer circle and, 192, 193; national socialism and, 129, 132–134, 137; "The Problem of the Modern Salaried Employee," 166; Rockefeller Foundation and, 34; *Social Research* and, 112; *State of the Masses*, 132–134; *Technischer Fortschritt und Arbeitslosigkeit [Technical progress and unemployment]*, 105, 108–109
Lehmann, Fritz, 61, 68, 122, 207
Leirens, Charles, 207
Lenz, Friedrich W., 207
Leontief, Wassily, 41, 54, 106, 156, 163, 165, 173
Lepsius, Rainer, 4, 6, 157
Lerner, Abba, 173, 177
Leser, Paul, 207
Leslau, Wolf, 207
Levi, Nino, 68, 75, 207
Lévi-Strauss, Claude, 85, 207
Levy, Ernst, 207
Ley [-Piscator], Maria, 207
List of Displaced German Scholars (Emergency Association of German Scholars Abroad), 12, 15, 28
Littauer, Lucius D., 72

Index

Littauer, Rudolf, 69, 207
Loewith, Karl, 207
Logical positivism, 96–97
Long, Breckinridge, 87–88
Long, Huey, 184
Lowe, Adolph [Adolf Löwe], 15, 159, 201, 207; economic theory and, 101–102, 111, 115, 142, 149–156; emigré experience and, 179; founding of University in Exile and, 62, 63, 64, 66, 68, 82, 83; Frankfurt Institute and, 58, 191; Germany after 1945 and, 201; Horkheimer circle and, 193, 194, 195–197; influence of, 157, 162–163, 165, 168; influence of New School and, 166, 167; Kiel group and, 53, 55, 56–57, 58; national socialism and, 130; *On Economic Knowledge*, 149, 151–156, 235 n.138; *The Path of Economic Growth*, 149, 156; peace research and, 142, 143–144, 145, 148, 149; *The Price of Liberty*, 134–136, 195, 196; Rockefeller Foundation and, 35, 38
Lowenthal, Leo, 191, 192, 193–194
Lucius D. Littauer Fund, 72
Lutz, Friedrich A., 39, 49

McCarthy era, 160, 223 n.12
Machlup, Fritz, 49, 50
Maes, Julian, 208
Magat, Michael, 208
Malinowski, Bronislaw, 208
Mann, Heinrich, 64
Mann, Thomas, 77, 130, 138, 160, 184, 189
Mannheim, Karl, 10, 95; founding of University in Exile and, 62, 63, 64, 66; Lowe and, 58, 150; Rockefeller Foundation and, 35, 38
Marginal utility, 46
Marix, Therese, 208
Marschak, Jakob, 95, 148, 208; economic theory and, 104; founding of University in Exile and, 61, 62, 63, 64, 66; Horkheimer circle and, 194; influence of, 165, 166, 172–175; Kiel group and,

54, 55, 57; national socialism and, 130; Rockefeller Foundation and, 38
Marshall, Alfred, 52
Marshall Plan, 145
Marxism, 151; emigré critique of, 131–133, 134; Institute of Social Research and, 191, 192–193; institutionalists and, 99–100; reform economists and, 52, 102–103, 105
Mayer, Carl, 68, 208
Means, Gardiner, 41, 42, 43
Mein Kampf (Hitler; New School translation), 137–138
Melting pot theory, 1–2, 162, 180
Mendizabal, Alfredo, 208
Menger, Carl, 49
Merton, Robert K., 97
Meyer, Julie, 208
Milano, Paolo, 208
Mill, John Stuart, 103
Miller, Arthur, 79
Millis, H. A., 167
Mirkine-Guetzévitch, Boris, 85, 208
Mises, Ludwig, 36, 46, 47–48, 53, 96
Mitchell, Wesley C., 41, 60, 99, 119
Modigliani, Franco, 148, 173, 174, 208
Moeller van den Bruck, Arthur, 201
Money, theory of, 54
Monopolies, 111–112
Morgenstern, Oskar, 48, 49, 174
Morgenthau, Hans, 35, 75, 201
Morgenthau plan, 144, 169, 185
Moss, Laurence S., 221
Mosse, Robert, 208
Münzenberg, Willi, 79
Mumford, Lewis, 138
Myrdal, Gunnar, 36, 37, 164

Nansen, Fridtjof, 25
National budget: extraordinary budget and, 126; fiscal policy and, 121–124; public spending and, 124–125. *See also* Economic planning; Fiscal policy

Index

Index

Index